HEBREWS

Jesus: Our Perfect Sacrifice

Written by Bob Warren

ISBN: 978-1-62727-010-6

All scripture, unless otherwise noted, is from the New American Standard Bible.

Cover design by Dan Carter

Table of Contents

Hebrews 11

Hebrews 12

Hebrews 13

Reference Section

Introduction

About the Course

We are encouraged that you are taking this journey through the book of Hebrews. The course is easy to follow. Six days of each week you will read Scripture and answer a set of corresponding questions. Also included in the study are lessons that should answer all of the questions and tie everything together covered during the week. If you find you cannot answer a question dealing with a particular verse (after you have exhausted all resources), feel free to read the portion of the lesson that deals with the verse in question. (Verse addresses are provided throughout the lessons for easy reference.) You will observe how this works once you begin the study.

Ideally, you should have someone take the course with you (Ecclesiastes 4:9-12), either one person or a group; the choice is yours. Accountability with others is, in most cases, a necessity. Discussing what you learn with your group members can also be a wonderful tool to stimulate growth. Even so, if your only alternative is to go it alone, that will be fine. Just make sure that you hold yourself accountable to finish what you have started.

Be sure to set your own pace. If, in your opinion, insufficient material is covered on a daily basis, you may complete the study in fewer weeks. On the other hand, if the assignments are too lengthy to accommodate your schedule, you can cover less material than is prescribed. I would suggest, however, that you complete as much of the daily assignments as possible. You don't want the course to drag on.

Take time to look up all Scripture references. You will be glad you did. Scripture text is taken from the New American Standard Bible unless otherwise noted. If you do not have a copy of the NASB, it might be a good idea to purchase one. I have used it for years and have found it to be a reliable resource for biblical study. If this is not possible, use the version you have—you will be fine.

The audio teaching associated with this series can be ordered online at www.lifeonthehill.org. You can also call 270-437-4172.

If you need copies of the course, we would appreciate your contacting us. We can send them to you no more than a week after placing your order. Because the proceeds from the study are used to meet the ministry's needs as well as our own personal needs, we would ask you not to make copies. Thank you for honoring our request. You will also note that the *Romans 1-8* study distributed by this ministry is mentioned on a variety of occasions. If you should desire a copy, just get in touch.

To proceed, go to page 1 (at the end of the **Introduction**) and begin answering the questions under First Day of Week 1. Tomorrow you will answer the questions under Second Day of Week 1 and continue from there.

Have fun! Don't forget to pray each day before starting your assignments.

About the Book

The epistle to the Hebrews is truly fascinating and, in my opinion, one of the most important books in the entire Word of God. In fact, outside of the first eight chapters of the book of Romans, I have found no portion of Scripture more informative or enlightening. Hebrews is basically a book about Jesus: Who He is and what He has done, and is presently doing, for those who have accepted Him as Savior. Thus, Hebrews is a "must" book if you are seeking to comprehend the depths of the Person of Christ.

This epistle will assist you in many ways, for it confirms the supremacy of Christ over all created things—be they angels, Moses, or even the Levitical priesthood. Not only will this letter allow you to know Christ more intimately, and grant new insights relating to the cross, but it will also deepen your understanding of the Old Testament. It will explain, therefore, the purpose of the Old Testament sacrificial system as well as the regulations associated with worship in both the tabernacle and the temple. The book also addresses faith and its importance. All in all, Hebrews is a powerful treatise on the fundamental truths of the gospel of Christ.

Authorship

Although the writer's identity is uncertain, those who first received the epistle knew who he was (Hebrews 13:19 and 23). He had such a vast knowledge of the Law and the Levitical priesthood that it is almost unquestionable that he was of Jewish descent. Since he heard the gospel from those who had walked with Christ (Hebrews 2:3), he probably lived outside Jerusalem. Had he lived inside the city, he more than likely would have heard the message from Jesus Himself, since almost all the church at Jerusalem had heard Christ's teachings.

Audience

This book was written to Hebrew Christians of Judea living outside the city of Jerusalem (Hebrews 3:1 and additional passages confirm that the readers were believers). Because of persecution from non-Christian Jews (Hebrews 12:3-4), they were tempted to return to the temple sacrifices to avoid such maltreatment. This "circumstance" is why the writer spends much time in Hebrews 5-10 proving that Jesus is greater than both the sacrificial system and the Levitical priesthood.

The readers' temptation to recommit to the temple sacrifices indicates that they lived near Jerusalem, the location of the temple. Also, according to Hebrews 12:4, no one in their group had suffered death due to persecution. The church at Jerusalem, on the other hand, had lost Steven (Acts 7:59-60) and James (Acts 12:2) by this time. Hebrews 6:10 and 10:34 also indicate that the recipients of this epistle had assisted the needy. By contrast, the church in Jerusalem was poor, lacking even the means to support its own ministry (Acts 11:29; Romans 15:25-27; 1Corinthians 16:1-3). These facts seem to indicate that the author wrote to Hebrew Christians of Judea living outside the city of Jerusalem.

Date

Timothy, who became a believer around A.D. 50, is mentioned in Hebrews 13:23 as having been *"released"* from prison. Thus, this epistle had to be written sometime after A.D. 50 and prior to Timothy's death. In Hebrews 7:8, the writer uses the present tense when referring to the sacrificial system (*"mortal men receive tithes"*—emphasis added), indicating that the temple in Jerusalem was still intact. The author confirms this fact in Hebrews 8:4, 10:1-2, 11, and 13:10-11. Since the temple and sacrificial system were destroyed in A.D. 70, this work had to be written between A.D. 50 and A.D. 70. But consider Hebrews 2:3. These readers had heard the gospel through the first generation of believers, meaning they were second-generation believers. Also, Hebrews 5:11-12 shows that they had been believers long enough to have become *"teachers."* Ponder this next thought as well. The author twice mentions Israel's 40-year rebellion *"in the wilderness"* (Hebrews 3:9 and 17). Could he be saying that these Hebrew Christians were approaching the 40-year anniversary of the church, and that they should beware lest they lose their physical lives as did many in Israel during the 40 years of wilderness wanderings (Hebrews 3:17)? Because the church began in A.D. 30, 40 years from that date would be A.D. 70—the year Jerusalem was destroyed.

A good percentage of the statements in the remainder of this section, plus the next section ("Historical Background"), can be confirmed by historians who lived and wrote during the first through the fourth centuries A.D. Three such historians are: (1) Josephus, an unsaved Jew of the first century A.D. who witnessed the destruction of Jerusalem in A.D. 70 (2) Hegesippus, a Jewish believer who lived during the second century A.D. and whose parents fled from Jerusalem before the destruction of A.D. 70 (3) Eusebius, a Gentile believer of the fourth century A.D.

The first Jewish revolt against Rome began brewing in A.D. 64 and grew into a full-fledged uprising by A.D. 66. In October of A.D. 66, Cestius Gallus, the Roman governor of Syria, took Roman troops to Jerusalem to suppress the unrest. He surrounded Jerusalem and was close to overthrowing the city, when for some reason—probably a lack of supplies—he recalled his troops and withdrew. The recipients of this epistle fled from Jerusalem after observing this withdrawal, and not one of them died when the Romans returned and eventually destroyed the temple and city. This letter, plus Jesus' words of Luke 21:20-24, were the motivating factors that caused them to leave. When they saw Cestius' troops surrounding Jerusalem, they viewed this as a fulfillment of Luke 21:20 and fled according to the instruction given in Luke 21:21. Note the passages:

> *"But when you see Jerusalem surrounded by armies, then recognize that her desolation is at hand. "Then let those who are in Judea flee to the mountains, and let those who are in the midst of the city depart, and let not those who are in the country enter the city;* (Luke 21:20-21)

Their departure was timely. Soon afterwards the Romans, under the leadership of Vespasian, first came against Galilee to the north of Jerusalem (A.D. 67) and progressed toward the city in A.D. 68. Eventually, led by Vespasian's son Titus, the Romans destroyed Jerusalem and King Herod's temple in A.D. 70, fulfilling Luke 21:22-24:

> because these are days of vengeance, in order that all things which are written may be fulfilled. "Woe to those who are with child and to those who nurse babes in those days; for there will be great distress upon the land, and wrath to this people, and they will fall by the edge of the sword, and will be led captive into all the nations; and Jerusalem will be trampled under foot by the Gentiles until the times of the Gentiles be fulfilled. (Luke 21:22-24)

Josephus recorded that the total number of prisoners taken during the war was 97,000, and that those who died during the siege numbered 1.1 million—most of whom were Jews. Again, the epistle to the Hebrews greatly influenced the believing Jews to abandon Jerusalem. Not one Hebrew Christian died in the conflict.

In light of these facts, I date the writing of this book between A.D. 64 and A.D. 66, before Cestius Gallus surrounded Jerusalem in A.D. 66. Certainly, it could not have been written after A.D. 70, since the temple was standing when God inspired the writer to record this fascinating work.

Historical Background

This book was written at a unique time in history. As was stated earlier, almost 40 years had passed since Acts 2—when Jesus sent the Holy Spirit and established the church. Yes, the church was almost 40 years old. Remember this!

Many years earlier the Roman Empire had overthrown Judea, Samaria, Galilee, and other

Jewish territories. In fact, Pompey, a Roman general, had seized Jerusalem in B.C. 63. Thus, Roman rule prevailed in the land of Canaan. But a group of non-Christian Jews (Zealots as well as Pharisees) began to rebel against Rome between A.D. 64 and 66. These Jews succeeded initially, gaining control not only of Jerusalem but also the surrounding areas—meaning that they regulated what occurred in and around Jerusalem, even in the regions some distance from the city. As a result, the non-Christian Jews pressured the Jewish Christians living in these areas to offer sacrifices in the temple and live according to the Law.

Only two solutions to these Hebrew Christians' dilemma <u>seemed</u> to exist. They could disassociate themselves from the temple sacrifices, accept persecution from the non-Christian Jews, and go on to spiritual maturity. This option most definitely was the wiser choice. Or they could, as they incorrectly assumed, place themselves under the sacrificial system in Jerusalem, forfeit their salvation, and later, when the persecution ceased, recommit themselves to Christ. This second "option" contained two flaws. First, if believers could denounce Christ and lose their salvation, they could never gain it back. Why? Jesus would need to be re-crucified—a total impossibility. (This statement will be confirmed when we study Hebrews 6:4-6). Second, the Romans would soon destroy the temple, the city of Jerusalem, and its inhabitants. For these Hebrew Christians to join themselves to the temple sacrifices would mean certain physical death.

That which unfolded is extremely interesting. In A.D. 67, Vespasian, a Roman general, overpowered the revolting Jews in Galilee, returning the rule of Galilee to Roman hands. Vespasian also overthrew Samaria. Then, in A.D. 68 and continuing into the spring of A.D. 69, he systematically overthrew district after district in Judea until only a small portion of the land remained under Jewish control. However, when Vespasian became Emperor of Rome in the summer of A.D. 69, his son Titus conquered the remaining Jewish territories. Titus destroyed Jerusalem and the temple in A.D. 70, and many non-Christian Jews lost their lives. (This fulfilled what Jesus had promised in Matthew 24:2 and Luke 21:6, 20-24—promises that resulted from the Jews rejecting His Messiahship.) But as a result of reading this epistle, none of the Hebrew Christians died in the takeover. They had all disavowed temple worship and fled from Jerusalem and its surrounding areas by the time Titus arrived. In fact, they fled (with other Jewish believers throughout Judea—about 100,000 in all) beyond the Jordan River and remained there until the war ceased.

This historical background will serve us well as we continue. Be sure to remember where it is located for future reference.

By failing to examine this book from its historical setting, many have misinterpreted its content. For that reason, I would ask you to approach this study with an open mind, viewing these verses as though you are reading them for the first time. If you will do so, amazing things can occur. Welcome aboard!

Hebrews 1 Questions

First Day

1. Read Hebrews 1 just for pleasure. We will answer questions on the chapter tomorrow. Read the section of the **Introduction** to the course titled *"About the Book."* From what is stated there, what excites you most about studying the book of Hebrews?

2. Read the sections of the **Introduction** titled *"Authorship"* and *"Audience"* and answer the following questions. What verses confirm that the readers knew the author? Can we assume that the author was a Jew? If so, why? What problems did the readers face, and what were they contemplating as a remedy to their difficulties? How can we know that the readers did not live in Jerusalem?

3. Read the section of the **Introduction** titled *"Date."* A word of warning: The following questions are necessary to answer, but don't be concerned if you don't understand everything you write down. Understanding will come later. How can we know that this epistle was written sometime after A.D. 50? How can we know that it was written before A.D. 70? Are there historians who relate information about this time period? Name three of them. In what year did the Jews begin to revolt against Roman? When did their actions turn into a full-scale uprising? What was the Roman's name who initially brought Roman troops to suppress the revolt, and in what year did he arrive in Jerusalem? Did he overthrow Jerusalem? Jerusalem was next attacked by a different Roman general. What was his name? What was the name of his son who eventually overthrew Jerusalem, and in what year did the city fall?

4. Read the section of the **Introduction** titled "Historical Background" and answer the following questions. Who, at this time, was pressuring the Christian Jews in and around Jerusalem to return to the sacrificial system? What two options did these Christian Jews *"seem"* to have? Which was the wise option and why? Why was the unwise option so unwise? What was their final decision? Where did they stay during the war of A.D. 70, and how many Jews were in their group?

Second Day

Note: Remember to consider the material you studied yesterday as you answer each question in the course. Believe me, you will need to refer back to this resource from time to time. In writing the course I continually reviewed the introductory information.

1. Read Hebrews 1. Verse 1 mentions a particular means through which God *"spoke"* in Old Testament times. What was that means? Read Deuteronomy 18:15 and Psalm 110:4 to see how Moses and King David fit into what is expressed in Hebrews 1:1. What does the writer mean by the statement *"in many portions"*? What does he mean by the statement *"and in many ways"*?

2. *"In these last days"* (v.2) God *"has spoken"* through another source. Who is that source? What does the Samaritan woman's statement in John 4:25 reveal regarding the importance of Christ's message? Did His message reveal more truth than the messages proclaimed by the Old Testament prophets? Considering the background of this epistle, why would the writer want his readers to view Christ's message as "carrying more weight" than the messages of the Old Testament prophets (such as Moses)?

3. Jesus is *"heir of"* what (v.2)? How do Revelation 20:4, Ephesians 1:10, and 1Corinthians 15:25-28 relate to this wonderful truth? How do we fit into this picture (see Romans 8:17)? Now that you realize the magnitude of your inheritance, how does this affect your walk with Christ?

4. Who *"made the world"* (v.2), and how does this tie in with John 1:1, 14, and Colossians 1:16? Challenge question: Who created the order that keeps the creation operating smoothly?

Third Day

1.   Read Hebrews 1. Don't forget to pray. Verse 3 states that Jesus is *"the radiance of"* God's *"glory."* How does this truth tie in with John 1:14? Challenge question: What comes to mind when you think of the *"glory"* of God?

2.   Jesus is also *"the exact representation of His"* Father's *"nature"* (v.3), which means that He is an *"exact"* expression of the Father. How does this truth relate to John 14:9? Press on. You are doing great!

3.   Jesus also *"upholds all things by the word of His power"* (v.3). The word *"upholds"* actually means *"upholding."* If so, is Jesus in heaven doing nothing, or is He actively involved in all facets of our lives? How does this encourage you?

4.   After Jesus *"made purification of sins"* (v.3), what did He do? Does this encouraging news confirm that Jesus' sacrifice was the perfect and final sacrifice for sin, the sacrifice that forever satisfied the Father? If so, why? According to Romans 8:34, what is Jesus doing now? What other encouragement should we draw from the fact that Jesus is *"at the right hand of the Majesty on high"* (read Luke 22:69)?

Fourth Day

1.   Read Hebrews 1. Moses received the *"Law...through angels"* (Galatians 3:19; Acts 7:38), but angels are not to be worshipped. Many of the Jews, however, chose to worship angels instead of God. Consequently, the writer spends the remainder of this chapter and part of the next proving that Jesus is greater than angels. In so doing he confirms that the old covenant, the *"Law...ordained through angels"* (Galatians 3:19, Acts 7:38), was inferior to the new covenant instituted through Christ. Why? Christ is greater than angels. The writer will verify that Jesus alone is worthy of worship. Before we go further, record what Hebrews 13:2, Matthew 4:11, Matthew 18:10, Matthew 22:30, Matthew 28:2-3, and Revelation 5:11 say about angels. Do any of these passages mention a need to worship angels?

2.   In verse 4 we find that Jesus *"has inherited a more excellent name than"* the angels. A name is a title or rank; it also signifies character. If Jesus *"inherited a more excellent name than"* the angels, who has the greater rank—angels or Jesus? In verse 5, what does the writer say about Jesus that cannot be said about angels? According to verse 6, is Jesus to worship the angels, or are the angels to worship Jesus?

Fifth Day

1.   Read Hebrews 1. According to verse 7, are angels Christ's ministers, or is Christ the angels' minister? Who then is the greater, Jesus or angels? Now observe verse 8. Did you notice that God the Father refers to the Son as *"God"*? How can this assist you the next time someone questions Jesus' deity? How long will Christ's *"throne"* endure (v.8)? What type of *"scepter"* does He possess (v.8)? How does this encourage you?

2.   What is stated about Jesus in the first phrase of verse 9? With what has the Father *"anointed"* Jesus as a result of His obedience, and how is it described (v.9)? If the Father *"anointed"* Jesus but does not anoint angels, what does this say about Jesus' superiority over angels?

3. What does verse 9 communicate concerning the manner in which the Father rewards obedience? Can you experience true *"gladness"* without loving *"righteousness"* and hating *"lawlessness"*? If not, why not? How does this relate to Paul's words in Galatians 5:22 and Ephesians 5:18?

Sixth Day

1. Read Hebrews 1. The writer quotes Psalm 102:25-27 in Hebrews 1:10-12. What phrase in Hebrews 1:10-12 confirms that Jesus is Lord? What phrases verify that Jesus created the heavens and the earth? How does the fact that the Son created all things, and will never die, verify that He is greater than angels?

2. What is stated about Jesus in the last two phrases of verse 12? What encouragement do you draw from these words?

3. According to verse 13, what instructions did Jesus receive from the Father? Has the Father made such a statement to any *"of the angels"* (v.13)? How does the fact that Jesus is seated, not running about, relate to what we learned in verse 3? From what is recorded in verse 14, would you say that angels are seated, or do they have responsibilities that keep them on the move? What responsibilities do angels have today (v.14)? Has there been a situation when you sensed that angels were *"ministering"* to you? If so, when did it occur?

4. Make sure to read all of this week's lesson before continuing in the course. Isn't this fun!?!

Hebrews 1 Lesson

Hebrews is about the Person of Jesus. In this lesson we will see that, among everything else, He was a prophet at His First Coming.

This epistle was addressed to Hebrew Christians living near Jerusalem who were contemplating returning to Judaism due to severe persecution from the unbelieving Jews. Because unsaved Jews were making it extremely difficult, the Jews who had accepted Christ were tempted to say, *"Enough of this! I will denounce Christ, go back under the sacrificial system in the temple, and reunite myself with Christ when this wave of persecution ceases."* The author of this letter wrote to Hebrew Christians contemplating such action, warning that if they did so they would encounter the excruciating circumstances that the unbelieving Jews would face when God judged Jerusalem. God brought this judgment through Titus, a Roman general, who in A.D. 70 destroyed Jerusalem and burned King Herod's temple to the ground.

In Hebrews 1:1, we find that God *"spoke long ago"* through His *"prophets"*:

> *God, after He spoke long ago to the fathers in the prophets in many portions and in many ways,* (Hebrews 1:1)

The word used here for *"prophets"* includes all through whom God *"spoke"* in Old Testament times. For instance, Moses, as a prophet (Deuteronomy 18:15), wrote Genesis through Deuteronomy. David, as a prophet, wrote many of the Psalms (for example, read Psalm 110:4 to see that David *"spoke"* of Jesus' priesthood). And, of course, all of the prophets from Isaiah through Malachi served as the writing prophets. The fact that God *"spoke"* through these individuals (Hebrews 1:1) verifies that the Old Testament is absolute truth and literally God's words.

According to verse 1, God also *"spoke...in many portions."* Compare the book of Obadiah (one chapter) to the book of Jeremiah (55 chapters) and the book of Isaiah (66 chapters). God also *"spoke...in many ways"* (v.1)—to Ezekiel through *"visions"* (Ezekiel 1:1), but to Daniel through *"a dream and visions"* (Daniel 7:1), etc.

From Hebrews 1:2, it is clear that *"in these last days"* God *"has spoken"* through Jesus Christ:

> *in these last days has spoken to us in His Son, whom He appointed heir of all things, through whom also He made the world.* (Hebrews 1:2)

The Rabbis perceived the *"last days"* as that time when the Messiah would come because the Messiah was the goal of all Old Testament revelation. John 4:25 confirms this view, for even the Samaritan woman realized the importance of the Messiah's message—that He would *"declare all things to"* man. Stated another way, Jesus would bring a fuller revelation of what God had originally spoken through the Old Testament writers (prophets). Thus, Jesus' message was greater than that of any Old Testament prophet. Consequently, Jesus is greater than Moses, the prophet who initially received God's Law and communicated it to the Hebrew nation. The new covenant, established by Jesus, therefore supersedes the old covenant, mediated by Moses. These Hebrew readers needed to take heed, abandon the Law, and live the Spirit-filled life promised by Christ.

The word *"His"* in Hebrews 1:2, not being in the original text (notice that it is in italics), means the verse can be read, *"in these last days has spoken to us in Son."* This detail verifies that when Jesus spoke, God's very nature spoke (also verified later in verse 3). God had previously used prophets (mere men) to

When Jesus spoke, God's very nature spoke.

communicate messages to His people, but at Christ's First Coming He communicated through His only begotten Son. This method was radically different. Here the emphasis is not on what was said but the nature of the Source through Whom the words were spoken.

Jesus is also *"heir of all things"* (v.2). Consider as well that you and I (along with all church saints) are co-heirs with Christ (Romans 8:17). Note: From Revelation 20:4, Jesus will rule over the earth *"for a thousand years"* during the Millennium. Then, when *"the last enemy," "death"* (1Corinthians 15:26), is conquered, and *"all things"* are summed *"up"* in Him (Ephesians 1:10), Jesus will present all that He owns to the Father, *"that God may be all in all"* (1Corinthians 15:25-28).

Notice too that Jesus *"made the world"* (Hebrews 1:2). The word *"world"* here actually means "ages." So the writer is speaking of more than what we see, hear, taste, touch, or smell. He is also referring to the order that Jesus created along with everything else. Since Jesus is the *"Word"* of God (John 1:1, 14), and since God spoke all things into existence, then Jesus *"created" "all things"* (read Colossians 1:16). Therefore, God has been in control throughout the different dispensations of time through His Son.

God has been in control throughout the different dispensations of time through His Son.

Jesus is also *"the radiance of"* God's *"glory"*:

> And He is the radiance of His glory and the exact representation of His nature, and upholds all things by the word of His power. When He had made purification of sins, He sat down at the right hand of the Majesty on high; (Hebrews 1:3)

John 1:14 also confirms that Jesus is the *"glory"* of God:

> And the Word became flesh, and dwelt among us, and we beheld His glory, glory as of the only begotten from the Father, full of grace and truth. (John 1:14)

God's character is so holy that when He shows up glory is manifested. No doubt, Jesus was and is the shining forth of His Father's character to a world in desperate need of a Savior (read John 14:9).

In addition, Jesus is *"the exact representation of"* His Father's *"nature"* (Hebrews 1:3). In the Greek, the words *"exact representation"* can be interpreted *"an exact expression."* Have you used the services of a notary? If so, your paper received an imprint (an exact expression) of the notary's seal. Like the notary's seal, Jesus is an exact imprint of His Father. Therefore, Philip had *"seen the Father"* as a result of seeing the Son (John 14:9).

According to Hebrews 1:3, Jesus also *"upholds all things by the word of His power."* Since the word *"upholds"* means "upholding" in the Greek, Jesus is not just sitting in heaven doing nothing, twiddling His thumbs until the time of the Rapture and His Second Coming. (By the way, I used to believe this error.) He is, today, actively and intimately involved in our lives. For instance, when we eat, Jesus changes the food into energy so our bodies can function properly. He also changes the gas we buy for our cars into mechanical energy by allowing a spark plug to ignite the fuel. You see, He is very much involved in the common things of life, for He not only created all things, but preserves and sustains them as well.

We must understand something else regarding Jesus' present position. After *"He had made purification of sins"* (v.3) by dying on the cross, He was resurrected and *"sat down at the right hand of the Majesty on high"* (v.3). Why shouldn't He sit down if His sacrifice was the perfect and final sacrifice for sin? Since *"the right hand of"* the Father contains limitless *"power"* (Luke 22:69), Jesus *"upholds all things by the word of His power"* (Hebrews 1:3). And guess what else He is doing while seated at the Father's right hand? He is interceding for us who believe (Romans 8:34). We will study later that Jesus is a faithful high priest *"who has been tempted in all things as we are, yet without sin"* (Hebrews 4:15). Isn't it wonderful knowing that He is interceding on our behalf, all the while understanding the magnitude of our daily temptations?

The writer now begins speaking of *"angels"*:

> *having become as much better than the angels, as He has inherited a more excellent name than they.* (Hebrews 1:4)

God gave the Law to the Jews through Moses, a *"mediator,"* and Moses received the Law through *"angels"* (Galatians 3:19; Acts 7:38). Consequently, the average Jew believed that Moses had received the Law through angels. No problem. But some Jews went a step further and began worshiping the angels, the agency through which God had communicated the Law to Moses. Many strange ideas resulted from this warped manner of thinking. The Jews actually began viewing God as surrounded by a council of angels, needing their approval before possessing the freedom to act. They believed that angels were everywhere, and that one brought the dew, another the rain, another the wind, and so on. Plainly put, they thought angels controlled the universe.

The heresy known as Gnosticism, which included angel worship, was prevalent in the early church. Is it any wonder that Paul warned against *"the worship of…angels"* in Colossians 2:18? We may think that we are beyond such things, but many in the body of Christ do much the same. God established the church and ordained that she carry the gospel to the world. Many, however, worship the church instead of the Christ who established it.

What do we know about angels? They can appear as men (Hebrews 13:2), and they continually *"behold the face of the Father"* on behalf of every child (Matthew 18:10). Angels don't *"marry"* (Matthew 22:30) and can appear in different forms (such as *"lightning"* in Matthew 28:2-3). They ministered to Jesus (Matthew 4:11), and we also know that their numbers are *"myriads of myriads, and thousands of thousands"* (Revelation 5:11). Even so, they are not worthy of worship, for they are created beings. Only God is to be worshipped, for that which is created is exceedingly inferior to the Creator.

With this truth in mind, refer back to Hebrews 1:4. Here we read that Jesus is *"better than the angels."* The writer is saying that the old covenant (the Law), *"ordained through angels"* (Galatians 3:19; Acts 7:38), was inferior to the new covenant instituted through Christ. Why? Christ is greater than angels. But those who read this letter needed more convincing proof, so the writer spends the remainder of this chapter and part of the next making his point.

If you have a King James Version of the Bible, observe the first phrase of verse 4. It says, *"Being made so much better than the angels."* The cults have taken the words, *"Being made,"* which apply to Jesus, and taught that Jesus is a created being. With this mistake, they erroneously conclude: "Since I am created, and Jesus is created, then Jesus is like me." The epistle to the Hebrews proves such thinking nonsense.

Because the Gnostics refused to believe that Deity could inhabit humanity, they would take the above mentioned falsehood and erroneously conclude: "Since God cannot inhabit humanity, it is impossible for Jesus to have been God in the flesh." We must make certain, therefore, to properly answer the following question: Was Jesus God in the flesh, or was He a great prophet who lost His mind and thought He was God? Shortly, we will study Hebrews 1:8 which provides the solution.

Notice too that Jesus *"has inherited a more excellent name than"* the *"angels"* (Hebrews 1:4). What is in a name? A name is a title, or rank, which also signifies character. If Jesus *"inherited"* a greater *"name"* than *"the angels,"* who has the greater rank, angels or Jesus? Jesus, of course!! This greater rank is confirmed in verse 5 where God refers to Jesus as His *"Son"*:

For to which of the angels did He ever say, "THOU ART MY SON, TODAY I HAVE BEGOTTEN THEE"? And again, "I WILL BE A FATHER TO HIM AND HE SHALL BE A SON TO ME"? (Hebrews 1:5)

Scripture never refers to angels as God's offspring, because God has never begotten an angel. If you read Colossians 1:16 you will observe again that Jesus *"created" "all things."* Thus, if Jesus created the angels, He is clearly greater than angels.

We need to closely examine Hebrews 1:6:

And when He again brings the first-born into the world, He says, "AND LET ALL THE ANGELS OF GOD WORSHIP HIM." (Hebrews 1:6)

The writer speaks of a time when the Father will *"again"* bring Christ *"into the world."* This verse does not reference Jesus' First Coming, but His Second. Notice too that He is *"the first-born."* This phrase has nothing to do with time, but deals with position only. Since He is *"the first-born,"* He holds the highest position of any man, for He is God-man. Also notice the word *"world"* in verse 6. This word points to the inhabited earth rather than the universe. Combining these truths, we find that when the Father *"brings the first-born"* (Who has all rule and authority) into the inhabited earth for a second time, *"all the angels of God"* will *"worship Him"* (v.6). But you might ask, "Don't the angels already worship Him to the fullest degree possible? Don't the angels already comprehend what Jesus has done for mankind?" Not according to 1Peter 1:10-12 and Ephesians 3:5-10 which verify that *"the church"* is presently explaining to the angels the significance of Christ's work on the cross. Have you considered that you, as a member of the body of Christ, are making known to the angels *"the manifold wisdom of God"* (Ephesians 3:10; 1Peter 1:12)? Ponder this next truth as well. The church will continue to function as instructor to the angels until she is raptured prior to the Tribulation—a reality that makes Revelation 5:11-12 exceptionally inspiring. Here we see angels worshiping *"the Lamb"* shortly before the Tribulation begins. Why? As a result of the ministry of the church, they finally comprehend the depths of *"the manifold wisdom of God"*!

> *The church is presently explaining to the angels the significance of Christ's work on the cross.*

Notice the phrase, *"Who makes His angels winds, and His ministers a flame of fire"* (Hebrews 1:7). The angels are under the authority of the Son, for they are *"His ministers."* Who then is the greater? Jesus, of course!!

How would you respond should someone ask, "This Jesus whom you serve, did He ever say, 'I am God'? If not, how can we know that He is God?" The first time I was confronted with these questions I went directly to the four Gospels. I found instances where Jesus stated that He *"and the Father are one"* (John 10:30), but no place where He said "I am God." Then I ran across Hebrews 1:8 which states:

But of the Son He says, "Thy throne, O God, is forever and ever, and the righteous scepter is the scepter of His kingdom." (Hebrews 1:8)

Here the Father refers to *"the Son"* as *"God."* What further proof do we need? Also notice that the Son's *"throne...is forever and ever"* (v.8). He rules eternally on the *"throne"* of David, thus fulfilling Nathan's words to King David in 1Chronicles 17:11-14.

Notice too that the Son possesses *"the righteous scepter"* which is *"the scepter of His kingdom"* (Hebrews 1:8). Since this *"scepter"* is *"righteous,"* He never engages it unwisely. As a result, Jesus is not in heaven waiting to pounce on us at the first sign of disobedience. He loves us and is for us!! He will *"discipline"* us when we sin and refuse to repent (Hebrews 12:5-11), but He takes no pleasure in such activity.

Because Jesus *"loved righteousness and hated lawlessness,"* God *"anointed"* Him *"with the oil of gladness"* (Hebrews 1:9). Have you found any place in Scripture where God anointed an angel? Lucifer was *"anointed"* (Ezekiel 28:14), but he was a *"cherub,"* not an angel. (Three orders of angelic beings exist—the cherubim, seraphim, and angels; angels being the lowest order.) Thus, if Jesus is *"anointed,"* and angels are not, then Jesus must be greater than angels (Jesus is greater than the cherubim and seraphim as well, since they, along with angels, are created beings). Think on this as well. If we love righteousness and hate sin, God will fill us with His *"Spirit"* (Ephesians 5:18). *"The fruit of the Spirit"* (Galatians 5:22) will then be manifested in our lives, and *"the anointing"* that *"abides in"* us (1John 2:27) will be evident to all.

Since the writer is speaking of Christ in Hebrews 1:10-12, a quote from Psalm 102:25-27, Christ is *"Lord"* (Hebrews 1:10). He laid *"the foundation of the earth,"* made *"the heavens,"* and will never change (Hebrews 1:10-12). Therefore, if the Son created all things—will never change and will never die—He must be greater than angels whom He created. Isn't it comforting to know that Jesus never changes? He is always consistent, a truth we need to apply every second of every day—especially when things look to be totally out of control.

Much food for thought is associated with Hebrews 1:13:

> But to which of the angels has He ever said, *"SIT AT MY RIGHT HAND, UNTIL I MAKE THINE ENEMIES A FOOTSTOOL FOR THY FEET"?* (Hebrews 1:13)

The Father did something for Jesus that He has never done for angels. He told Christ to *"sit at"* His *"right hand until"* He made His *"enemies a footstool for"* His *"feet."* Consequently, Jesus is at rest at the *"right hand"* of the Father, even though He remains in charge of the universe (review Hebrews 1:3). In contrast, no angel has been told to be seated at the Father's right hand. That position is reserved for the Son alone. Also, angels are up and about, moving around as *"ministering spirits":*

Jesus is at rest at the right hand of the Father, even though He is still in charge of the universe.

> Are they not all ministering spirits, sent out to render service for the sake of those who will inherit salvation? (Hebrews 1:14)

Angels are not seated, for they are *"sent out to render service for the sake of those who will inherit salvation"* (v.14). No doubt, Jesus is greater than angels in every respect.

Don't misunderstand. The writer doesn't prove that Jesus is greater than angels to degrade angels or the work to which they are called. They serve a very special purpose in God's economy. I am thankful to know that believers have angels who minister to their needs (v.14). But great as they are, they must never be worshipped. Only the Father, Son, and Spirit are worthy of our worship and praise.

In Hebrews 2, the writer will continue to build upon what we have discussed here. It should be interesting!

Hebrews 2 Questions

First Day

1. Read Hebrews 2. Don't forget to pray. Considering the input included in the **Introduction** to the course, what were these Hebrew Christians contemplating doing to avoid the persecution from the unbelieving Jews? What were they encouraged to do with the truth they had *"heard"* (v.1)? The phrase, *"drift away from it,"* does not refer to these believers losing their salvation but to their drifting back under the sacrificial system in the temple to temporarily avoid persecution. When was the last time you caught yourself drifting away from truth? What did you do to get back on course?

2. Drawing on last week's lesson, how can we know that the statement, *"For if the word spoken through angels proved unalterable,"* refers to the Law (v.2)? What does the writer mean by the phrase, *"and every transgression and disobedience received a just recompense"*? Read Leviticus 10:1-2, Numbers 16:1-50, and Joshua 7:24-26 to see how God frequently punished sins committed under the Law. What consequences did these individuals reap from their sin?

3. We next want to examine the phrase, *"how shall we escape if we neglect so great a salvation"* (v.3). First we must define what the writer means when he uses the word *"escape."* In light of the historical background of the book, would you say that he means escaping from hell or escaping from the judgment of A.D. 70? Now look at the word *"neglect"* (v.3). We find the same word in 1 Timothy 4:14. What if Timothy had neglected his spiritual gift? Would his spiritual gift have been taken away? Read Romans 11:29 to find your answer. If a believer, therefore, neglects his salvation for a period of time, does this mean he loses it? What happened to you the last time you neglected your salvation? What do you think the writer means by the phrase, *"so great a salvation"* (Hebrews 2:3)?

4. According to verse 3, through what source did the writer and his readers hear the gospel? Based on this input, could the writer have been one of the original eleven disciples, or even Paul? If not, why not? Try not to make these questions harder than they actually are.

Second Day

1. Read Hebrews 2. Tying verse 3 in with verse 4, who is the *"them"* in the phrase, *"God also bearing witness with them"* (v.4)? From verse 4, what did God do through the original eleven apostles, plus Paul, that confirmed their apostleship and validated their message as truth? In our day, should you automatically believe a man's message just because he possesses the power to perform miracles—or has large numbers of people listening to his message? Read 2Thessalonians 2:8-10 before answering. What do you look for in a man before deciding to believe his message?

2. The phrase, *"the world to come"* (v.5), makes reference to the Millennium, the one thousand years when we (the church) will reign with Christ. Will the angels rule during this time period? Read Zechariah 14:4-11, Isaiah 30:23-26, 35:1-2, 55:12-13, 65:17-25, Joel 2:21-27, and 3:18 to find out more about the topographical changes that will occur in association with the Millennium. What stood out the most as you read these passages?

Third Day

1. Read Hebrews 2. In verses 6-8, the writer quotes Psalm 8:4-6. However, before quoting these verses he says, *"But one has testified somewhere, saying"* (v.6). Do you think the writer didn't know (or had maybe forgotten) the address of the Scriptures he was quoting? Could it be that he chose his words for another reason? If so, what was the reason?

2. The word *"man"* in verse 6 definitely refers to mankind. Does the phrase, *"the son of man,"* refer to Jesus, or could it point to mankind as well? Read Ezekiel 2:1 for input. Have you considered that God made mankind *"lower than the angels"* (Hebrews 2:7)? Remembering what we discussed in verse 5, will this condition always exist, or during the Millennium will mankind rule over the angels?

3. According to verses 7 and 8, what did God do for man? When did this action occur (read Genesis 1:28)? When did man lose his dominion over the earth (read Genesis 3:6)? Because man lost his dominion, the writer of Hebrews states, *"But now we do not yet see all things subjected to him"* (Hebrews 2:8). From what we learned earlier, when will man once again rule over God's creation? For additional help, read Revelation 20:4. Isn't the book of Hebrews exciting?!

Fourth Day

1. Read Hebrews 2. According to verse 9, who else was *"made…a little while lower than the angels"*? During what stage of Christ's existence did this occasion come about? When Jesus died on the cross, He tasted *"death"* for whom (v.9)? Does this mean that all of mankind's sins were placed on Christ or just the sins of those who would accept Him as Savior? For help, read 1John 2:2. After Christ had suffered, with what was He *"crowned"* (Hebrews 2:9)? What will you receive for the suffering you encounter as a believer (2Corinthians 4:17)? How will this truth affect the way you respond to your next trial or difficulty?

2. In verse 10 we see the phrase, *"for whom are all things,"* which refers to God the Father. According to Ephesians 1:10 and 1Corinthians 15:24-28, when and through what means will the Father eventually receive *"all things"*? Explain how the writer can state, *"through whom are all things,"* in referring to God the Father (Hebrews 2:10), if Jesus *"created"* *"all things"* (Colossians 1:16). For help, consider that the Father had to speak (Genesis 1:3) before Jesus, the *"Word"* of God (John 1:1-2), could go to work.

3. The cross allowed God the Father to bring *"many sons to glory"* (v.10). What does Colossians 1:27, tied in with Hebrews 1:3, say about the means through which a person becomes a possessor of God's *"glory"*? If you are a three-part being—*"spirit…soul and body"* (1Thessalonians 5:23)—and a believer, which part of you is not yet glorified? When will this part be glorified (for help, read 1Thessalonians 4:14-17)?

4. According to verse 10, along with Hebrews 5:8, what did the Father use to *"perfect"* the Son? If Jesus was sinless, in what way did He need to be perfected? For what purpose does God use suffering in your life? The writer describes Jesus as *"the author of"* our *"salvation"* (Hebrews 2:10)? What does he mean by this statement?

Fifth Day

1. Read Hebrews 2. If the *"He"* in the phrase, *"For both He who sanctifies,"* points to Jesus, then who are *"those who are sanctified"* (v.11)? The word *"sanctified"* in the phrase *"those who are sanctified"* actually means *"being sanctified."* What is continually *"being sanctified"* in the New Testament believer's experience? What is completely sanctified (made holy) the moment we accept Christ? (The preceding question might be difficult if you have not yet worked through *Romans 1-8,* a course distributed by this ministry. This week's lesson will provide the answer, but the previously mentioned study addresses the subject matter in much greater depth.)

2. Is Jesus *"ashamed to call"* you His brother (v.11)? Do you sometimes face situations where you are ashamed to call Jesus your brother? If so, when, and how can you remedy this problem?

3. According to verse 12, what was Jesus' mission while on earth? Had you been Christ, what would you have said about the Father when relating truth regarding His *"name"*? What does verse 13 say about the Son's confidence, as well as His brethren's confidence, in the Father? Is your confidence in the Father flourishing at this present time? If so, why? If not, why not?

4. Why did Jesus take on *"flesh and blood"* (v.14)? What did Christ accomplish through His *"death"* and resurrection (v.14)? Must a New Testament believer, therefore, be controlled by Satan's lies and schemes? How can this truth assist you while facing spiritual battles? Why should our relationship with Christ *"deliver"* us from the *"fear of death"* (v.15)?

Sixth Day

1. Read Hebrews 2. Don't forget to pray. Is redemption offered to fallen *"angels"* (v.16)? Are the redeemed, dealing with redemption only, greater than those to whom no redemption is offered? Is Jesus greater than the redeemed? Then, is Jesus greater than angels? Considering what we learned earlier in the course, why is the writer so determined to prove that Jesus is greater than angels?

2. The second phrase of verse 16 reads, *"but He gives help to the descendant of Abraham."* This phrase can actually be interpreted, "but of the seed of Abraham He took on." Why did Jesus become a Jew, and how does this tie in with Leviticus 25:25—a passage relating to the *"kinsman"* redeemer? If you need assistance after exhausting all resources, read the section of the lesson that pertains to this question.

3. Verse 17 addresses the reason Jesus took on humanity. Why did He do so? The last phrase of this verse states, *"to make propitiation for the sins of the people."* *"Propitiation"* means "to appease—to satisfy—to pardon." What does this tell you about the degree to which the Father was pleased with Jesus' offering?

4. What comfort do you draw from verse 18?

5. Be sure to read all of this week's lesson before going further into the course. Record any new insights below. In two more weeks we will be out of the storm and into some smoother sailing. Carry on, in His strength of course!

Hebrews 2 Lesson

The first phrase in verse 1 states, *"For this reason"*:

> *For this reason we must pay much closer attention to what we have heard, lest we drift away from it.* (Hebrews 2:1)

For what *"reason"*? The *"reason"* is the new covenant established by Jesus is greater than the old covenant of Law that Moses received through angels. The *"reason"* for what? The *"reason"* to *"pay much closer attention to"* the new covenant and not *"drift away from it"* (v.1). Keep in mind that this statement is directed toward believing Jews living outside Jerusalem who were contemplating resubmitting to the old covenant

> *None of the verses in the book of Hebrews teach that a believer can lose his/her salvation.*

of Law. The phrase, *"drift away from it,"* does not refer to their losing salvation, but to their drifting back under the sacrificial system in the temple to temporarily avoid persecution from the unbelieving Jews. In fact, none of the verses in the book of Hebrews (or anywhere else in Scripture) teach that a believer can lose his/her salvation.

In verse 2 we find:

> *For if the word spoken through angels proved unalterable, and every transgression and disobedience received a just recompense,* (Hebrews 2:2)

Before we can properly interpret this passage, we must first define some terms. The word *"unalterable"* means "firm, stable, and steadfast." Thus, the Law Moses received through angels is firm, stable, and steadfast—never changing, always pointing out man's mistakes but incapable of empowering him to perform righteously. But functioning as such it fulfills its purpose (Romans 3:19-20; Galatians 3:24)! The word *"transgression"* means "the breaking of a law." Consequently, if man has no law to break, no *"transgression"* results (Romans 4:15). Also, the word *"disobedience"* means "refusing to hear." When do transgressions, therefore, occur? If a man refuses to "hear"—that is, if he is disobedient to the Law to which he has been exposed and breaks the Law—a *"transgression"* results. So every *"transgression"* is a by-product of *"disobedience."* If a man disobeys and says, *'So what if God gave the Law; I don't need it,"* he will transgress the Law and suffer the consequence. He will, in fact, *"receive a just recompense"* (v.2). *"Recompense"* means punishment. As a result, whoever transgresses the Law will receive *"a just recompense"*—a fair punishment.

In summary, the writer is saying: *"the word spoken through angels"* is *"unalterable"* (firm and steadfast), and *"every transgression"* (every violation of the Law) *"and disobedience"* receives *"a just"* (fair) *"recompense"* (punishment). Accordingly, those who sinned under the Law in Old Testament times received a just punishment, which many times resulted in physical death. Here are a few of the many examples: (1) Nadab and Abihu lost their physical lives by offering *"strange fire before the Lord"* (Leviticus 10:1-2) (2) When Korah questioned Moses' and Aaron's authority, God took the lives of Korah and his followers (Numbers 16:1-50) (3) Achan and his entire household died as a result of Achan's sin (Joshua 7:24-26). Obviously, physical punishment resulted when the Law was transgressed. This fact is extremely important to remember, for in Hebrews 2:3 we read:

> *how shall we escape if we neglect so great a salvation? After it was at the first spoken through the Lord, it was confirmed to us by those who heard,* (Hebrews 2:3)

This verse is <u>not</u> referring to "escaping" hell. This passage deals with these Hebrew Christians, who were no longer bound by Law as a result of the new covenant, avoiding the judgment of Jerusalem in A.D. 70 and thereby "escaping" physical death.

To prove my point, we need only consider the historical background of this time period. As long as the church was viewed as a Jewish sect, the Roman Empire could tolerate its practices. Jews were not required to worship the Emperor, nor were Christians—so long as a majority of Christians were Jews. For the first 30 years after the church's birth, this was the case. However, things changed after a large number of Gentiles submitted to Jesus. The Roman government suddenly demanded Emperor worship from believers, which the church opposed. In A.D. 64, while Nero was Emperor of Rome, much of Rome burned to the ground. The Romans blamed Nero, accusing him of arson. Nero, naturally, shifted the blame to Christians. Because believers refused to worship the Emperor, he could accuse them of desiring to destroy the Empire. As a result, the Romans launched a wave of intense persecution against the church.

Then, around A.D. 64 to A.D. 66, the Jews rebelled against Rome and regained control of Jerusalem—which meant that the Jews regulated everything that occurred in and around the city. Suddenly, the Hebrew Christians living in the area were pressured to offer sacrifices in the temple (to live by the Law). Thus, the recipients of this epistle faced a dilemma. To them, at least, the solution seemed obvious: They could denounce Christ, place themselves under the sacrificial system in the temple, thereby alleviating the persecution from the unbelieving Jews, and recommit themselves to Christ after the persecution ceased. But this idea contained two major flaws. First, Hebrews 6:4-6 teaches that if a believer could denounce Christ and lose his/her salvation, he/she could never gain it back. Second, the Romans would soon destroy Jerusalem, along with the temple. (As we learned earlier, Titus, a Roman general, destroyed the city and temple in A.D. 70—and many unbelieving Jews lost their lives. However, no Hebrew Christian died in the takeover. As a result of reading this epistle, along with Luke 21:20-24, they had all disavowed temple worship and fled from Jerusalem by the time Titus arrived.)

Now back to Hebrews 2:3, where the writer states, *"how shall we escape if we neglect so great a salvation?"* From the information relating to the historical background of this time period, it is clear that the writer is not speaking of "escaping" hell. Rather, he is emphasizing that if the believing Jews *"neglect"* their *"salvation"* and return to Judaism, they will not *"escape"* physical death in A.D. 70. Consequently, this phrase in Hebrews 2:3 is not teaching that believers can lose their salvation. Are you seeing the importance of studying the historical background of a book before attempting to interpret its content?

Let's examine this same phrase again, focusing on the word *"neglect."* *"How shall we escape if we neglect so great a salvation."* Does this statement mean that believers can lose their salvation through negligence? This same word is used in 1Timothy 4:14, where Paul writes to Timothy: *"Do not neglect the spiritual gift within you."* What if Timothy had neglected his spiritual gift? Would it have been taken away? Not according to Romans 11:29, *"for the gifts and the calling of God are irrevocable."* Therefore, if you have a spiritual gift (and you have one if you know Jesus—1Peter 4:10), your gift cannot be removed. No doubt, if you walk in blatant sin (and refuse to confess and turn from your sin), the Lord may not implement your gift for a season. But, the gift that He bestowed to you cannot be taken away. Neither can you lose your *"salvation,"* even if you should *"neglect"* it (Hebrews 2:3).

The phrase, *"so great a salvation"* (v.3), actually points to the superiority of the new covenant (grace) over the old covenant (Law). As new covenant believers, these Hebrew Christians needed to comprehend the superiority of grace over Law and flee legalism altogether. The writer will emphasize this superiority throughout much of this fascinating epistle, so it will

These Hebrew Christians needed to comprehend the superiority of grace over Law and flee legalism altogether.

be exciting to observe as he develops (and validates) his argument.

The writer next states, *"After it was at the first spoken through the Lord, it was confirmed to us by those who heard"* (Hebrews 2:3). What was *"first spoken through the Lord"*? The gospel, of course! Jesus said, *"I am the way, and the truth, and the life; no one comes to the Father, but through Me"* (John 14:6). The gospel was *"first spoken through"* Jesus Christ, but it was *"confirmed to"* the writer, as well as his readers, *"by those who heard."* This sequence of events tells us that the author of Hebrews was neither one of the eleven apostles nor Paul. He had to be someone, therefore, who heard the gospel through one of the original eleven or Paul. But what does the writer mean when he records, *"it was confirmed to us by those who heard"*? Try to imagine the excitement surrounding Acts 2, after the Holy Spirit fell on those who believed. The original eleven apostles were suddenly empowered to carry their message to the world. But as they traveled, proclaiming this gospel, some people questioned their authority. For this reason God bore *"witness"* through them by *"signs…wonders…miracles and by gifts of the Holy Spirit"* (Hebrews 2:4):

> *God also bearing witness with them, both by signs and wonders and by various miracles and by gifts of the Holy Spirit according to His own will.* (Hebrews 2:4)

Stated differently, the visible (and miraculous) manifestation of God's power through the apostles (who proclaimed the truth) confirmed and validated their message. This endorsement protected the people of that day from impostors who posed as servants of Christ. In the last days, however, the Antichrist, through the power of Satan, will perform an abundance of miracles solely to deceive the unredeemed (2Thessalonians 2:8-12). Thus, the proper litmus test (for any messenger) is the exhibition of *"the fruit of the Spirit"* (Galatians 5:22-23) and the proclamation of truth—not merely the physical manifestation of the miraculous.

In Hebrews 2:5 we read:

> *For He did not subject to angels the world to come, concerning which we are speaking.* (Hebrews 2:5)

The phrase, *"the world to come"* (v.5), refers to the Millennium—the one thousand years that we, the church, along with Tribulation saints, will reign with Christ (Revelation 20:4). The earth will experience an abundance of topographical changes during this fascinating season of time (Zechariah 14:4-11; Isaiah 30:23-26; 35:1-2; 55:12-13; 65:17-25; Joel 2:21-27; 3:18). Hence, the writer is saying that angels will not rule during the Millennium—*"For He did not subject to angels the world to come"* (Hebrews 2:5).

The writer continues by stating:

> *But one has testified somewhere, saying, "WHAT IS MAN, THAT THOU REMEMBEREST HIM?"* (Hebrews 2:6)

As you read this passage, did you wonder if the writer knew the address (location) of the Scriptures referenced? I believe he did, for in verses 6-8 he quotes directly from the Septuagint, a Greek translation of the Hebrew Old Testament. In fact, he quotes Psalm 8:4-6, a Psalm of David. I believe the author chose his words to say, "Hey, God wrote the entire Bible, so somewhere in it one has said…" What has been concluded here will be confirmed to even a greater degree when we study Hebrews 4:4.

In Hebrews 2:6, the writer also quotes David asking, *"What is man, that Thou rememberest him? Or the son of man, that Thou are concerned about him?"* The word *"man"* makes reference to man, of course, but some think the phrase, *"the son of man,"* refers to Jesus. I disagree, for God refers to Ezekiel as *"son of man"* in Ezekiel 2:1. So both *"man"* and *"the son of man"* refer to mankind. Also, the word *"concerned"* (Hebrews 2:6) means much more than just thinking about man. It means the Father is actively involved in what is occurring with mankind. Even though man possesses a free will to choose as he pleases, even choose to repent and believe while depraved, God is sovereign enough to bring about His desired end.

Hebrews 2:7 is much food for thought:

> "*THOU HAST MADE HIM FOR A LITTLE WHILE LOWER THAN THE ANGELS; THOU HAST CROWNED HIM WITH GLORY AND HONOR, AND HAST APPOINTED HIM OVER THE WORKS OF THY HANDS;*" (Hebrews 2:7)

Have you considered that God has made mankind "*a little while lower than the angels*"? This state will not last forever, for we will eventually "*judge angels*" (1Corinthians 6:3).

God has also "*crowned*" mankind "*with glory and honor*" and "*appointed him over the works of* [His] *hands*" (Hebrews 2:7). This blessing was granted in Genesis 1:28 when He gave man dominion over the earth. When Adam and Eve sinned, however, mankind lost this dominion. Thus, in the Millennium (the one thousand year reign of Christ), mankind will regain dominion and once again rule over "*the works of*" God's "*hands.*" Man will also be "*crowned…with glory and honor,*" and "*all things*" will be "*put…in subjection under his* [man's] *feet*" (Hebrews 2:8). As was stated earlier, this condition does not exist today because of Adam and Eve's sin ("*But now we do not yet see all things subjected to him*"—v.8). It will exist, therefore, when we reign with Christ in the Millennium.

Let's take a moment to summarize what we have covered. Believers have authority over the powers of darkness, and Satan is nothing more than "*a roaring lion*" (1Peter 5:8). But, we do not yet reign over the works of God's hands to the degree that Adam and Eve originally reigned in the garden. This restoration of authority will not occur until the Millennium, when we will reign "*with Christ for a thousand years*" (Revelation 20:4).

Hebrews 2:9 is intriguing indeed:

> But we do see Him who has been made for a little while lower than the angels, namely, Jesus, because of the suffering of death crowned with glory and honor, that by the grace of God He might taste death for everyone. (Hebrews 2:9)

He has always been and will always be God, yet Jesus took on humanity to die for sinful mankind.

Yes, "*Jesus*" was "*made for a little while lower than the angels.*" The reason: He became a man. It took a sinless man to die for the sin of lost mankind. But, He was God-man at His First Coming. He has always been and will always be God, yet Jesus took on humanity to die for sinful mankind. Of course, He performed miracles (through the Father) while on earth—all of which were spin-offs of His nature. His goal, however, was to die, "*that by the grace of God He might taste death for everyone*" (v.9). The fact that Jesus tasted "*death*" means that He literally died. Note as well that He tasted "*death for everyone,*" confirming that all the sin of mankind was placed on the Father's sinless Son. Consequently, He died for everyone—not just those who receive Him as Savior. He took on all the pain and agony of believers and unbelievers alike. "*God*" performed this work because of His "*grace,*" but in so doing "*crowned*" Jesus "*with glory and honor*" (v.9). We too will receive "*an eternal weight of glory*" for the suffering we encounter as believers (2Corinthians 4:17). Wonderful!

The Father's work through the cross "*was fitting for Him*":

> For it was fitting for Him, for whom are all things, and through whom are all things, in bringing many sons to glory, to perfect the author of their salvation through sufferings. (Hebrews 2:10)

The word *"fitting"* means "proper." So the cross was properly sanctioned by the Father; it was an act in accordance with His character. Because *"God is love"* (1John 4:8, 16), He loved man enough to offer the supreme sacrifice—His Son.

Notice the phrase, *"for whom are all things"* (Hebrews 2:10). *"All things"* are for the Father, a truth that is evident from the Scriptures. In fact, at the end of the Millennium, the final enemy, *"death,"* will be destroyed (1Corinthians 15:25-26). Then *"all things"* will be summed up *"in Christ"* (Ephesians 1:10), at which time Christ will present *"all things"* to the Father (1Corinthians 15:24, 28). Thus, during the Eternal Order, God will *"be all in all"* (1Corinthians 15:28).

Also notice the phrase, *"through whom are all things"* (Hebrews 2:10). The writer is saying that *"all things"* were created *"through"* the Father, for the Father spoke them into existence (Genesis 1:3). Because Jesus is the *"Word"* of God (John 1:1-3), He (Jesus) *"created...all things"* (Colossians 1:16)—but the Father was the source behind Jesus' activity. Therefore, *"through"* the Father *"all things"* were created (Hebrews 2:10).

What Jesus accomplished on the cross allowed *"many sons"* to be brought *"to glory"* (Hebrews 2:10). *"Christ in"* us is *"the hope of glory"* (Colossians 1:27), because Jesus is the *"glory"* of God (Hebrews 1:3; John 1:14). As a result, when Jesus takes up residence in us (Galatians 2:20), the glory of God takes up residence in us, and we are made into the most holy and perfect saints imaginable. Through this avenue God has brought *"many sons to glory"* subsequent to their exercising personal repentance and faith while depraved. In fact, the only thing not yet glorified is your body, which will reach its final glorified state at the Rapture of the church (1Thessalonians 4:14-17).

Notice also that *"the author"* of our *"salvation,"* Jesus, was perfected through what He suffered (Hebrews 2:10). (Hebrews 5:8 will confirm this same truth later in the study.) These verses by no means indicate that Jesus sinned or was at some point imperfect. He has always been perfect and sinless (that is, with the exception of when He became sin on the cross—2Corinthians 5:21) and will remain perfect and sinless throughout eternity. Hebrews 2:10 basically teaches, therefore, that through dying on the cross, Jesus fulfilled His commission as God's perfect sacrifice. Understand as well that the word *"author"* means "leader" or "pioneer." Consequently, if your leader suffered, will you suffer? You bet (1Peter 4:12-13)! But all of our suffering is used for *"good"* (Romans 8:28; Psalm 119:71), preparing us to reign *"with Christ"* (Revelation 20:4).

Do you realize that when Jesus comes to live in us, He *"sanctifies"* us? Hebrews 2:11 addresses this subject, so let's read the verse and discuss its content:

> *For both He who sanctifies and those who are sanctified are all from one Father, for which reason He is not ashamed to call them brethren* (Hebrews 2:11)

What we do is not who we are, even though who we are has a tremendous impact on what we do.

As Hebrews 10:10 will verify later, Jesus totally *"sanctifies"* our person (our soul and spirit) when we are made new—subsequent to our repenting and believing while depraved. For that reason, we are not lowly sinners saved by grace, but rather saints who need to learn to act like saints. It is not surprising, therefore, that the term *"sanctified"* in the phrase, *"and those who are sanctified"* (v.11), can be rendered "being sanctified"—pointing to our behavior. Thus, although we were totally sanctified in our person at the point of justification (salvation), our behavior is continually being *"sanctified"* (being made holy) as we mature in the faith—verifying that what we do is not who we are, even though who we are has a tremendous impact on what we do. In other words, we are not lowly sinners saved by grace, but saints who sometimes sin. Unquestionably, the Father accepts us into His family as holy and perfect children who are *"the righteousness of"* Himself (2Corinthians 5:21)—all the while realizing that we are children with behavioral flaws that are in the process of being *"sanctified"*—being made holy. What grace!

Also note that because we have the same *"Father," "He"* (Jesus) *"is not ashamed to call"* us *"brethren"*—to refer to us as His brothers (Hebrews 2:11). Wow!

The next two verses are pretty basic. Verse 12 points to Jesus' ministry while on earth—He proclaimed the *"name"* of the Father. Consequently, since the Father's *"name"* has to do with the Father's person (His identity), Jesus proclaimed Who the Father is. Verse 13 states that Jesus, as well as His brethren, put their *"trust"* in the Father. But verse 14 needs special attention:

> *Since then the children share in flesh and blood, He Himself likewise also partook of the same,*
> *that through death He might render powerless him who had the power of death, that is, the*
> *devil;* (Hebrews 2:14)

We learned earlier that Adam and Eve lost their dominion through sin. From that point Satan became *"the god"* (notice the small "g") *"of this world"* (2Corinthians 4:4; Ephesians 6:12; 1John 5:19). Death was his domain, for he possessed *"the power of death"* (Hebrews 2:14). If man chooses to remain under the control of the world system, and refuses to accept Christ, he will be separated from his Creator for all eternity. Because believers *"share in flesh and blood"* (v.14), Jesus took on *"the same"* (an earthly body) so *"through death He might render powerless him who had the power of death"* (Satan).

Jesus possesses eternal life, the resurrection verifying that His kind of life is greater than death. Therefore, when Christ died, He took *"the keys of death"* from Satan (Revelation 1:17-18) and walked straight through his domain (death). When a man accepts Christ, he receives Christ's type of *"life"* (John 10:10; Colossians 3:4)—*"life"* with no beginning or end, *"life"* that is greater than death. For this reason the writer records:

> *and might deliver those who through fear of death were subject to slavery all their lives.*
> (Hebrews 2:15)

We should no longer *"fear…death"* (v.15), for the moment our bodies die, our spirits and souls go to be *"with the Lord"* (2Corinthians 5:8). So, through Christ, we are delivered from that which we have feared and been enslaved—the *"fear"* and dominion *"of death"* (Hebrews 2:15).

We can now comprehend why Jesus possessed *"joy"* while going to *"the cross"* (Hebrews 12:2). He realized, for starters, that His death and resurrection would: (1) Give all New Testament believers the capacity (through His life inside them) to see Satan overcome (1John 5:4) (2) Allow their spirits and souls to enter heaven when their bodies ceased operating (2Corinthians 5:8) (3) Cause their bodies to one day be resurrected in glory (1Corinthians 15:50-55). Thank you Jesus!!

In Hebrews 2:16 we find:

> *For assuredly He does not give help to angels, but He gives help to the descendant of Abraham.*
> (Hebrews 2:16)

The first phrase of this verse clearly states that Jesus did not die for angels. After all, fallen angels can never be redeemed. Now, follow these next few statements carefully. Jesus died that man might be redeemed, thus Jesus is greater than the redeemed. In the area of redemption, the redeemed are greater than those to whom no redemption is offered. Consequently, Jesus is greater than angels. The writer has made his point: Jesus is to be worshipped, not angels, confirming that the new covenant (grace), instituted by Christ, is greater than the old covenant (Law), given to Moses through angels. Undoubtedly, these Hebrew Christians needed to relinquish the idea of returning to the sacrificial system in Jerusalem.

The second phrase in verse 16 reads, *"but He gives help to the descendant of Abraham."* This phrase can actually be interpreted *"but of the seed of Abraham He took on."* No doubt, Jesus became a Jew to fulfill the very special office of kinsman redeemer—a topic mentioned in Leviticus 25:25. If a Jew lost his material possessions, his creditors could make him their slave. His nearest of kin, however, if he so desired, could pay the debt and secure his relative's freedom. This practice of freeing the enslaved is why it was necessary that Jesus be born a descendant of Abraham. The Jews were given the Law but could not keep the Law (Galatians 3:24; Romans 3:20). Their *"sin"* held them in bondage (John 8:34), but Jesus held the price of redemption. His innocent blood paid the debt in full (1Peter 1:18-19). Through repentance and faith in Christ, therefore, a Jew could be released from his/her bondage to enjoy all the benefits associated with belonging to God's family.

Do you realize that Gentiles become spiritual descendants of Abraham through faith in Christ (Galatians 3:29)? Like Israel, we held a sin debt we could not pay. Jesus, our brother, became a man (God-man), paid our sin debt, and set us free. As was required of the kinsman redeemer, Jesus had to desire to pay the redemption price. John 10:18 states that Jesus laid down His life freely, which proves that He endured the cross voluntarily. Isn't He a wonderful Savior?!

Because Jesus laid down His life freely, it is obvious that He endured the cross voluntarily. Isn't He a wonderful Savior?!

Doesn't this motivate you to know as much about Him as you possibly can? Note: Gentiles becoming spiritual descendants of Abraham through faith doesn't mean that the physical nation of Israel is no longer God's chosen people—a subject addressed in numerous resources available through this ministry.

According to Hebrews 2:17, Jesus *"had to be made like His brethren in all things"*:

> *Therefore, He had to be made like His brethren in all things, that He might become a merciful and faithful high priest in things pertaining to God, to make propitiation for the sins of the people.* (Hebrews 2:17)

Jesus took on flesh and became a male Jew. He became God-man in other words. Why was this taking on of flesh required? Jesus took on humanity so He could *"become a merciful and faithful high priest"* (v.17); only male Jews could become priests. Jesus is *"merciful"* in that He has been tempted as we are tempted and can thus identify with our trials. He is *"faithful"* because He suffered and remained true to the Father. (Notice that Jesus became a *"high priest"*—which means that He had not always been a *"high priest."* We will discuss this topic in more detail later in the course.)

Jesus became a *"high priest...to make propitiation for the sins of the people"* (v.17). *"Propitiation"* means "to appease—to satisfy—to pardon." Jesus' blood (and subsequent death) satisfied the Father in that it paid the price of man's redemption—the Father, in turn, accepting anyone who receives His Son through faith.

The writer provides even more wonderful news in verse 18:

> *For since He Himself was tempted in that which He has suffered, He is able to come to the aid of those who are tempted.* (Hebrews 2:18)

Because Jesus *"was tempted"* as we are tempted, *"He is able to come to the aid of those who are tempted"* (v.18). Isn't that encouraging? When temptations arise, we can rest assured that our Savior understands and that His provision of abundant grace will see us through. We will address this magnificent truth in more detail when we study Hebrews 4:14-16, but you might want to preview those verses. They will be well worth your time.

Next week, in Hebrews 3, we will learn more about our wonderful High Priest. Come back ready to be blessed. Isn't Hebrews an amazing book?

Hebrews 3 Questions

First Day

A word of warning: This week's material is some of the most difficult and lengthy in the entire course—but some of the most exciting. Remember to have fun as you do your work—a big smile and happy eyes!

So far, the writer has spent much time proving that Jesus is greater than angels, the agency through which Moses received the Law. Now he will prove (in verses 1-6) that Jesus is greater than Moses, the man who received the Law. Substantiating this truth is critical, for the Jews considered no one greater than Moses.

1.   Read Hebrews 3. How does the writer refer to his readers in verse 1? Consequently, was this epistle written to believers or unbelievers? If you have accepted Christ, are you *"holy,"* or are you a lowly sinner saved by grace? What do Ephesians 1:4, 5:27, and Colossians 1:22 say about this? Do we have *"a heavenly calling,"* as did these believers (v.1; Philippians 3:20; Ephesians 2:6)? On what, then, should we *"set"* our minds (Colossians 3:2)? How do you go about setting *"your mind on the things above"*?

2.   In verse 1, we are told to *"consider Jesus."* The word *"consider"* means "to perceive clearly, to understand fully, to make a careful diligent consideration." How does this definition tie in with Paul's words in Philippians 3:10? What would happen in our lives if we truly, intimately knew the heart of Christ?

3.   An apostle is "one sent as a messenger or agent, the bearer of a commission." What then was Jesus' responsibility as *"the Apostle...of our confession"* (v.1)?

4.   A high priest had the responsibility of interceding for man in God's presence; he was man's representative before God. What then is Jesus' responsibility as the *"High Priest of our confession"* (v.1)? What do Hebrews 7:25 and 8:1 add to this wonderful truth?

5.   What tribe was the priestly tribe of Israel (Numbers 18:6)? To what tribe did Moses belong (Exodus 2:1-2, 10)? Was Moses a high priest? If not, who among his relatives served in this office (Exodus 28:1)? Who then is the greater, Jesus or Moses? We will find in Hebrews 7:11 and 17-22 that Jesus is a high *"priest"* of *"the order of Melchizedek,"* an order of higher rank than that of Aaron's priesthood. If this ranking is fact, and unadulterated truth, is Jesus' priesthood greater than the priesthood associated with the Law? Why should this truth have convinced these readers to abandon the Law?

Second Day

1.   Read Hebrews 3. Don't forget to pray. What does verse 2 say about Jesus? What does it say about Moses? How did Moses disobey (Numbers 20:11-12), and what consequences did he reap from his sin? When was Moses allowed to enter Canaan (for assistance read Matthew 17:1-3)? What do these verses communicate regarding the character of our God, especially considering that Jesus' transfiguration took place in Canaan? Note that Hebrews 3:2 speaks only of Moses' obedience, not once mentioning a single shortcoming? What does this verify to you about your God?

2.   If both Jesus and Moses were *"faithful"* (v.2), why is Jesus, *"as the builder of the house"* (v.3), *"counted worthy of more glory than Moses"* (v.3), who is of *"the house"* (v.3)? How does this truth tie in with Colossians 1:16? What is it about the *"glory"* of Christ, when compared to the *"glory"* of Moses, that confirms Jesus' supremacy over Moses (Hebrews 1:3; John 1:14; Exodus 34:29-35; 2Corinthians 3:7-18)?

3. Verse 4 proves that Jesus *"is God."* Why? (Remember what we gleaned from Colossians 1:16 and Hebrews 1:8.)

4. Now look at verses 5 and 6. How does the fact that *"Moses was faithful in all His* [God's] *house as a servant,"* while Jesus was a *"faithful...Son over"* God's *"house,"* verify that Jesus is greater than Moses? Verse 5 also states that Moses gave *"a testimony of those things which were to be spoken later."* What does this phrase mean? (Read Deuteronomy 18:18 for more details.)

5. Notice the phrase, *"whose house we are"* (v.6). All believers from Genesis 1:1 to Revelation 22:21 become members *"of the household of the faith"* (Hebrews 3:2-6, Galatians 6:10, and Ephesians 2:19 confirm this fact)—they do not become members of the church, which consists of believers beginning in Acts 2 and continuing until the Rapture. How can Jesus being over this *"household"* prove that Jesus is greater than Moses?

6. The last phrase of verse 6 states: *"if we hold fast our confidence and the boast of our hope firm until the end."* Does this verse teach that if we fail to hold on to our salvation we will lose our salvation? If not, what is this phrase communicating? Does God's Word contain passages which teach that a believer is secure in Christ? If so, which verses?

Third Day

Read Hebrews 3. Caution: Verses 7-19 are some of the most difficult, yet enlightening, passages we will study. Due to the challenging nature of the subject matter, I have included charts, defined a variety of terms, and provided additional background information. If the remainder of this week's questions appears overwhelming, don't be disheartened. Just relax, yet dig deeply. What we glean will pay huge dividends once we begin next week's material. The two chapters mesh together amazingly well!

God, through Moses, redeemed Israel from physical bondage in Egypt. Through Christ, God redeemed the Hebrew Christians, addressed in this epistle, from spiritual bondage to sin. As a result, they should not disobey as Israel disobeyed under Moses. The writer confronts this issue in verses 7-19. Read Hebrews 3, along with Numbers 13 and 14, if time permits.

Three new terms (expressions) of importance are <u>Redemption rest</u>, <u>Canaan rest</u>, and <u>Sabbath rest</u>. Only *"Sabbath rest"* is named in Scripture (Hebrews 4:9), but examples of all three are portrayed in God's Word. The body of Christ has adopted these "terms" or "expressions" to allow for differentiation between the three different rests.

• <u>Redemption rest</u>, in the case of the <u>nation</u> of Israel under Moses, points to <u>physical</u> redemption from Egypt. The nation was released from her bondage to the Egyptians as a result of responding (in faith) to God's promise of deliverance. Redemption rest, in the <u>individual</u> sense, points to God's <u>spiritual</u> redemption granted to those who repent and exercise faith while depraved. (The Old Testament believers looked forward to the Messiah's coming, whereas we look back to the fact that He came). This rest brings a person to see that *"the Lamb of God who takes away the sin of the world"* (John 1:29) provides <u>eternal</u> redemption once a depraved individual repents and believes. Redemption rest is the first and most basic of the three levels of rest.

• <u>Canaan rest</u>, in the case of the <u>nation</u> of Israel coming out of Egypt, points to <u>physical</u> rest from her enemies in Canaan. Joshua gave Israel Canaan rest (to a great degree at least) when he took the second generation of physically redeemed Israel into the Promised Land by faith (Joshua 21:44; 22:4; 23:1). Canaan rest, in the <u>individual</u> sense, results when the believer learns to trust God to consistently overcome the enemy. Read Deuteronomy 28:1 and 28:7 to see how this rest applied in the Old Testament and 1Peter 5:8-9 to understand how it applies in the New. Canaan rest is <u>not</u> addressing what occurs when a believer experiences physical death and is taken to heaven (as some have been misled to believe).

• *"Sabbath rest"* is named specifically in Hebrews 4:9 (and referenced on several occasions in Hebrews 3 and 4 as *"rest"*). This rest is the highest level—available to the spiritually mature only. Upon entering *"Sabbath rest,"* a believer understands that the essence of life is knowing (in a deep and meaningful way) the heart of God—not staying in a frenzy working for Him. This truth must be remembered if the remainder of the study is to be meaningful.

No doubt, Paul entered Sabbath rest. His ultimate goal was to *"know"* Christ (the Messiah) as intimately as possible (Philippians 3:10). As a result, he could view God as sovereign over every aspect of life (yet granting man the freedom of choice)—a subject addressed in much detail in the *God's Heart* series distributed by this ministry. Consequently, Paul could *"give thanks"* in all things (1Thessalonians 5:18) and *"rejoice always"* (1Thessalonians 5:16). This rest erases the idea that good works allow a believer to retain his/her salvation. Actually, *"Sabbath rest"* brings us to the place of yielding to the indwelling Christ (Galatians 2:20) to do the work through us (Philippians 2:13). Thus, we can truly *"rest."* *"Sabbath rest"* was made available through God resting on the seventh day of creation (Hebrews 4:9-10). It will become increasingly obvious why the term *"Today"* is used in Psalm 95:7 and Hebrews 3 and 4 in association with this *"rest."*

The following page should grant additional insight into the Scriptural definition of *"rest."* Look up all verses and digest as much as you can before continuing.

The Three Types of Rest Offered to The First and Second Generations of Physically Redeemed Israel

	Redemption Rest: Rest from physical bondage In Egypt	Canaan Rest: Rest that came with trusting God to overcome the enemy	Sabbath Rest: The rest that comes with true spiritual maturity; the abundant life associated with knowing the Creator intimately
First generation of physically redeemed Israel (those 20 years and older in Numbers 14:26-30)	Entered Exodus 6:6, 15:13	Failed to enter Numbers 14:26-30 Numbers 20:8-12 Hebrews 3:17	Failed to enter Hebrews 3:18-19 Note: Of course, only the spiritually redeemed of the first generation who came out of Egypt had the option of entering this rest.
Second generation of physically redeemed Israel (those under 20 years of age in Numbers 14:26-30)	Entered Exodus 6:6, 15:13	Entered Joshua 21:44, 22:4, 23:1	Failed to enter Hebrews 4:8 Note: Of course, only the spiritually redeemed of the second generation who came out of Egypt had the option of entering this rest.

Note: Some of the first generation of physically redeemed Israel (those 20 years and older--Numbers 14:29) who sinned in the wilderness, and died in the wilderness, were spiritually redeemed (men like Moses for instance). So just because the first generation of physically redeemed Israel, outside of Joshua and Caleb (Numbers 14:30), died in the wilderness, does not mean that all who died physically were spiritually lost (remember that Moses appeared to Jesus at the Transfiguration in Matthew 17:1-3, which means that he was not spiritually lost).

The Three Types of Rest Offered to the Spiritually Redeemed Hebrew Christians Addressed in the Book of Hebrews, as well as all Spiritually Redeemed of all Time

	Redemption Rest: Rest from physical bondage In Egypt	Canaan Rest: Rest that comes with trusting God to overcome the enemy	Sabbath Rest: The rest that comes with true spiritual maturity; the abundant life associated with knowing the Creator intimately
Believers addressed in the book of Hebrews	Entered Hebrews 3:1 Colossians 1:13 Ephesians 4:32	Had begun to enter but had failed to fully enter Hebrews 10:32-35	Encouraged to enter Hebrews 4:9-11
All believers of all time	Entered God grants rest from spiritual bondage to sin when faith and repentance are exercised while depraved. Hebrews 11:6	Encouraged to enter Deuteronomy 28:1, 7 1Peter 5:8-10 2Corinthians 10:3-5 Romans 12:21	Encouraged to enter Psalm 95:7-11 (Spoken by David in the Old Testament--thus Sabbath Rest was offered to Old Testament believers) Hebrews 4:9-11 (Sabbath Rest has been available to all believers since the seventh day of creation when God rested--Genesis 2:2)

Make sure that you have looked up all Scripture references on the preceding chart before moving forward. Also be sure to notice the difference between the words "physical redemption" and "spiritual redemption" throughout the remainder of the course. This difference is so very, very important!

Answer the following questions, based on the preceding information.

1. Moses delivered Israel from what type of bondage? These Hebrew Christians were delivered from what type of bondage through Christ?

2. List the three types of rest that God's Word portrays. Which of the three rests is specifically named in the Scriptures, and where? Which of these rests points to the rest associated with overcoming the enemy?

3. Which rest results when a believer progresses to spiritual maturity? Why is the word *"Today"* used in association with this rest? What advantage does this rest have over the other two rests?

4. Which rest results when a believer realizes that he is delivered from spiritual bondage to sin?

5. How does 1John 2:12-14 tie in with these three types of rest?

Fourth Day

1. Read Hebrews 3, along with Numbers 13 and 14 if time permits. The quote in Hebrews 3:7-11 is found in which Psalm? From verses 7-11, why was God *"provoked"* with His people? What two locations are not mentioned in Hebrews 3:8 that are named in Psalm 95:8? Read Exodus 17:1-7 and Numbers 20:2-13 to find out what occurred in these localities. What did you find? If Exodus 17:1-7 took place at the beginning of the wilderness wanderings, and Numbers 20:2-13 occurred at the end, how does your knowledge of this fact affect your view of the phrase, *"They always go astray in their heart"* (Hebrews 3:10)? These sins kept the first generation of physically redeemed Israel from entering which type of rest?

2. What type of redemption had Israel experienced while coming out of Egypt (Exodus 6:6; 15:13)? Was it possible for the nation to return to Egypt (Exodus 13:17; 14:13)? When Israel desired to return to the land from which she had been freed (Numbers 14:1-4), how did God respond (Numbers 14:28-29)? What does this response communicate regarding the thoroughness and finality of God's redemption?

3. According to Hebrews 3:10 and Numbers 14:29, with which generation of <u>physically</u> redeemed Israel was God *"angry"*? What would happen to this particular generation (Numbers 14:29)? Taking into consideration the historical background of this epistle, why would the writer mention Israel's disobedience and resulting death while attempting to persuade his readers to abandon the Law?

4. Again, where did Moses die (Deuteronomy 34:4-5)? Why did he die (Numbers 20:1-12)? Since he was part of the generation of Israel that died in the wilderness, did he lose his salvation? (Read Matthew 17:1-3 for assistance.) Could these unalterable truths verify that a portion of the Jews who experienced physical death in the wilderness were spiritually redeemed? What does this input communicate to you?

5. Why were Joshua and Caleb allowed to escape physical death and enter Canaan? (The answer is in Numbers 14.) Realize that their obedience kept them from committing any specific sin relating to the promises concerning the land. What type of rest did the second generation of <u>physically</u> redeemed Israel enter under Joshua's leadership? (See Joshua 21:44; 22:4; 23:1—also refer to the chart included with Third Day's questions.) Read Hebrews 4:8-9 (also refer to the chart) to see what type of rest the second generation of <u>physically</u> redeemed Israel failed to enter under Joshua's leadership. What did you find? Remember your findings for future reference.

Fifth Day

1.   Read Hebrews 3. This series of questions should begin to tie things together. Verse 12 is directed toward the Hebrew Christians, the *"brethren"* contemplating going back under the sacrificial system in Jerusalem. The writer first says, *"Take care."* Why would he make such a statement? He then describes what happened to Israel in the wilderness—*"lest there should be in any one of you an evil, unbelieving heart, in falling away from the living God."* Were the Jews in the wilderness physically redeemed from Egypt when they fell? When they sinned in this manner, did God send them back to Egypt (did they lose their physical redemption), or did they die in the wilderness? Could then a spiritually redeemed individual develop *"an evil, unbelieving heart"* and fall *"away from the living God"* (v.12)—in other words, lose his/her <u>fellowship</u> (notice that I did not say relationship) with God? If so, how does this loss occur?

2.   In light of the historical background of this book, what would happen to these Hebrew Christians (in A.D. 70) if they failed to abandon the Law? (Hint: It would be the same thing that had happened to physically redeemed Israel when they chose to disobey.) Do you see the point the writer is making? Since all of the Jews who died in the wilderness were not spiritually lost (remember Moses), could the believers addressed in Hebrews die a physical death as a result of disobedience and yet remain spiritually redeemed? Taking into consideration what verses 7-11 teach regarding the first generation of physically redeemed Israel, why would the writer pen verse 12 to these Jews who were spiritually redeemed and part of the church? Does verse 12 then teach that these Hebrew Christians would lose their salvation should they fail to separate themselves from the temple sacrifices? If not, what point is the writer making?

3.   According to verse 13, how could these Hebrew Christians overcome the temptation of going back into Judaism? Again, from our earlier study, to which time period does the word *"Today"* refer? The word *"hardened"* in verse 13 means "to be hardened morally, to make stubborn." What causes a believer to become hardened, and how is this condition overcome? Notice that *"sin"* is described as deceitful (v.13). What does this input communicate to you?

4. Verse 14 is very similar to verse 6. Is this passage teaching that a believer can lose his/her salvation? If not, why not? (Be sure to notice that the word *"assurance"* is used and not "salvation.")

Sixth Day

1. Read Hebrews 3. Considering what we have studied in this chapter, what is the writer communicating in verse 15? Who *"provoked"* God *"when they had heard"* (v.16)? How long was God *"angry"* with Israel (v.17)? How does this truth tie in with what we learned from Psalm 95:8? What happened to *"those who sinned...in the wilderness"* (Hebrews 3:17)? Similarly, what would have happened to these Hebrew Christians had they returned to the sacrificial system in Jerusalem?

2. According to verses 18 and 19, why was the first generation of physically redeemed Israel not allowed to enter either Canaan rest or Sabbath rest? How can you make sure that you enter into Sabbath rest?

3. This week's lesson should answer several questions that went previously unanswered. Be sure to read every word of the lesson before going to next week's material. You may even want to read it two to three times. It is one of the most important lessons in the entire course. As you read, write down any new insights below. Next week's material is much shorter—I promise!

Hebrews 3 Lesson

This chapter proves that even though Moses and Jesus were both faithful, Jesus was, and is, greater than Moses. The author shows that many Israelites under Moses' authority walked in disobedience and reaped the consequence of physical death. The Hebrew Christians addressed in this epistle had Jesus as their leader. Would they, like those under Moses, disobey and reap physical death?

The writer has already proven that Jesus is greater than angels, so in verses 1-6 he will prove that Jesus is greater than Moses. Why is he compelled to do so? Let's suppose you had asked a Jew of Jesus' day to describe Moses. He would have said, "Moses is the most faithful Jew of all Jews—He is even greater than angels. Moses is the man used by God to deliver His people from Egypt. He performed miracle after miracle until Pharaoh finally released our people to return to Canaan. On Mount Sinai he received tablets of stone—stones on which the Law had been etched by the finger of God. He saw God's glory, and his face even shone with the radiance of this glory when he returned to the people. You see, no one is greater than Moses." We now understand why the writer of Hebrews is moved to illustrate Jesus' superiority over this great leader of Israel in the first six verses of chapter 3.

The readers are referred to as *"holy brethren"* (v.1), verifying that this epistle was written to Hebrew Christians:

> *Therefore, holy brethren, partakers of a heavenly calling, consider Jesus, the Apostle and High Priest of our confession.* (Hebrews 3:1)

The fact that the writer calls his readers *"holy brethren"* tells us that the author knew something very special. He knew that the cross had removed their sin and allowed a holy God to justify them—to make them *"holy."* In fact, once they repented and believed while depraved, they were made into *"new"* creations (2Corinthians 5:17), *"holy and blameless"* children of God (Ephesians 1:4; 5:27; Colossians 1:22).

These Hebrew believers were not worthless sinners saved by grace, but *"holy"* saints who were contemplating walking in disobedience. Obviously, as was stated earlier in the course, what we do is not who we are, even though who we are has a tremendous impact on what we do. (For more input on the subject of who we are as New Testament believers, refer to the portion of the course titled *Romans 1-8* that addresses Romans 5:1. If you do not have a copy of this resource, one can be obtained through this ministry.)

These Hebrew believers were not worthless sinners saved by grace.

These Hebrew believers had also received *"a heavenly calling"* (Hebrews 3:1). Since we have received this same *"calling,"* and since *"our citizenship is in heaven"* (Philippians 3:20; Ephesians 2:6), on what should we set our minds? They should be *"set...on the things above"* (Colossians 3:2)! We *"set"* our minds *"on the things above"* (Colossians 3:2) by feasting on God's Word, which is transformed from information to revelation through the power of the Holy Spirit. This revelation, in turn, increases our ability to view life from God's perspective (from the heavenly perspective—read 2Corinthians 4:18), which greatly affects the choices we make as believers. Point being: The *"heavenly calling"* that these readers received through Jesus was much greater than the calling of the earthly temple with its sacrificial system. Thus, they should abandon the idea of going back under the Law by choosing grace over anything the unbelieving Jews sent their way. We too should discard whatever hinders our living from the heavenly perspective.

In Hebrews 3:1, we are told to *"consider Jesus."* The word *"consider"* means "to perceive clearly, to understand fully, to make a careful diligent consideration." Consequently, our ultimate goal is to *"consider"* (perceive clearly) the heart of Christ (Philippians 3:10). When this occurs, we begin understanding the deeper things of God and our lives are forever transformed.

Do you realize that Jesus is an *"Apostle"* (v.1)? An *"apostle"* is defined as "one sent as a messenger or agent, the bearer of a commission." Therefore, Jesus is God's representative to man. But His Apostleship (during His First Coming) was different from that of the twelve apostles. He not only communicated a message from the Father, but His death and resurrection ushered in a new dispensation, the dispensation, or age, of grace. The twelve apostles carried the message of this new dispensation to the world. Because the dispensation of Law was established

The writer continues to confirm the supremacy of Christ over the earthly sacrificial system.

through Moses and the dispensation of grace came through Jesus, the fact that grace replaced the Law (John 1:17) also illustrates that Jesus is greater than Moses. Are you seeing how the writer continues to confirm the supremacy of Christ over the earthly sacrificial system?

Jesus is also the *"High Priest of our confession"* (Hebrews 3:1). A high priest (under the Law) had the responsibility of interceding for man before God; he was man's representative in God's presence. Isn't it comforting to know that Jesus is *"at the right hand of"* the Father, interceding for us, and serving as our Representative (Hebrews 7:25; 8:1)? Moses was from the tribe of Levi (Exodus 2:1-2, 10), the priestly tribe (Numbers 18:6)—but he was not a priest. Only Aaron and his descendants could serve *"as priest"* (Exodus 28:1). Jesus is a *"priest"* of *"the order of Melchizedek,"* an "order" of higher rank than the priesthood associated with the Law (Hebrews 7:11, 17-22). Thus, Jesus is greater than Moses. The priesthood of Christ will be studied in more detail later, but for now we can take comfort in knowing that Jesus is in heaven (at this very moment) serving as our *"High Priest"* (Hebrews 3:1).

We know also that both Jesus and Moses were *"faithful"* to the Father:

> *He was faithful to Him who appointed Him, as Moses also was in all His house.* (Hebrews 3:2)

Moses, however, sinned in the wilderness and was not allowed to enter Canaan with Joshua and the second generation of physically redeemed Israel (Numbers 20:11-12). Moses later entered the land when Jesus was *"transfigured"* (Matthew 17:1-3), but Jesus' faithfulness supersedes Moses'. Also, Moses was *"faithful...in"* God's *"house"* (Hebrews 3:2), but *"the builder of"* that *"house"* is Jesus:

> *For He has been counted worthy of more glory than Moses, by just so much as the builder of the house has more honor than the house.* (Hebrews 3:3)

Since *"the builder of"* a *"house"* is always greater *"than the house"* (and those who live in it—v.3), Jesus is greater than Moses. Consequently, Jesus *"has been counted worthy of more glory than Moses"* (v.3) because Jesus is *"the glory of"* God (Hebrews 1:3; John 1:14). Thus, the *"glory"* on Moses' *"face"* soon faded (Exodus 34:29-35; 2Corinthians 3:7-18). Undeniably, God's Word confirms the supremacy of Christ from cover to cover—as evidenced by what the writer addresses next.

The fact that Jesus *"created...all things"* is confirmed in Hebrews 3:4 as well as Colossians 1:16:

> *For every house is built by someone, but the builder of all things is God.* (Hebrews 3:4)

> *For by Him* [Jesus] *all things were created, both in the heavens and on earth, visible and invisible, whether thrones or dominions or rulers or authorities — all things have been created by Him and for Him.* (Colossians 1:16)

If Jesus *"built"* (created) the *"house,"* and Moses is a member of that *"house,"* then Jesus created Moses. So Jesus is greater than Moses. (Notice that the writer implies that Jesus *"is God"* in Hebrews 3:4. This truth dovetails nicely with what we learned in Hebrews 1:8.)

Moses was *"a servant"* *"in…His* [God's] *house"* (v.5), *"but Christ was faithful as a Son over His* [God's] *house"* (v.6):

> *Now Moses was faithful in all His house as a servant, for a testimony of those things which were to be spoken later;* (Hebrews 3:5)

> *but Christ was faithful as a Son over His house whose house we are, if we hold fast our confidence and the boast of our hope firm until the end.* (Hebrews 3:6)

Since *"a Son"* is greater than *"a servant,"* Jesus is greater than Moses. Verse 5 also states that Moses gave *"a testimony of those things which were to be spoken later."* Moses' testimony in Deuteronomy 18:18, therefore, mentions *"a prophet"* who would *"speak"* on the Father's behalf. This *"prophet"* was (and is) the second Person of the Trinity (Jesus) Who later spoke the words of God to the nation of Israel.

Hebrews 3:6 states, *"…whose house we are…."* All believers (from Genesis 1:1 through Revelation 22:21) become members of the household of faith. Moses was a member of the household of faith (along with all Old Testament believers—Hebrews 3:2-5). New Testament believers are members as well (Galatians 6:10; Ephesians 2:19), but only New Testament believers (those who live between Acts 2 and the Rapture) make up the church, the *"body"* of Christ (Ephesians 5:22-33). Because Jesus is the Son of God *"over"* all believers, again we observe that Jesus is much greater than Moses. After all, Moses only led the physical Jewish nation.

The last portion of Hebrews 3:6 needs special attention: *"whose house we are, if we hold fast our confidence and the boast of our hope firm until the end."* Is the writer advocating that good works ensure our salvation, *"firm until the end"*? Is he teaching that we can lose our salvation if we don't hold on? If so, we must work to keep what we have in Christ. A problem exists with this mindset. If we could work enough to keep our salvation, we could have worked enough to have attained it. Thankfully, this predicament is not what verse 6 is communicating.

> *If we could work enough to keep our salvation, we could have worked enough to have attained it.*

The verse basically states that the continuance of fruit in our lives confirms (to all around us) that we are believers. Thus, if these readers held *"fast"* their *"confidence and the boast of"* their *"hope,"* the unbelieving Jews would continue to realize they were Christians. This realization would result in further persecution, but their faithful *"High Priest"* (Hebrews 3:1) would see them through (Hebrews 2:18). However, even if their fruit diminished for a season (if they failed to *"hold fast"* their *"confidence and the boast of"* their *"hope"*), their salvation would not have been jeopardized.

In contrast, the person who (quote) *"falls away,"* and stays away, never knew Christ in the first place (1John 2:19). This person, unlike the spiritually regenerated, will not receive God's chastening while living in sin (Hebrews 12:5-8). Therefore, Hebrews 3:6 deals with believers losing their *"confidence and the boast of"* their *"hope,"* which they can forfeit in a heartbeat by entertaining disobedience. This verse does not teach that believers can lose their salvation.

Clearly, Hebrews 3 does not teach that these readers would have lost their salvation had they returned to the temple sacrifices. Rather, the writer is encouraging them to go on to spiritual maturity. (To take a closer look at the security of the believer, study passages such as John 6:39, John 10:29, Philippians 1:6, Ephesians 1:13, Hebrews 7:25, Jude 1, Jude 24, etc.)

The writer has proven that Jesus is greater than Moses (Hebrews 3:1-6). But consider that

Jehovah, through Moses, delivered Israel from physical bondage, which resulted in their physical redemption. Through Christ, on the other hand, the Father delivered these Hebrew Christians from spiritual bondage, which resulted in their spiritual redemption. That being true, they should not disobey as Israel disobeyed under Moses. The author addresses this issue in verses 7-19.

Verse 7 begins by confirming that the Scriptures are inspired, absolute truth:

> *Therefore, just as the Holy Spirit says, "*TODAY IF YOU HEAR HIS VOICE, *(Hebrews 3:7)*

God's Word must be truth if *"the Holy Spirit,"* the third person of the Trinity, communicated it to man (v.7a; 2Peter 1:20-21). Before studying verses 7b-19, however, we must realize that three levels of rest are available to the believer: (1) Redemption rest (2) Canaan rest (3) Sabbath rest. These rests were defined and illustrated in the Third Day's questions of this week's material. A review might be necessary before continuing.

What the course states about these three levels of rest is confirmed in 1John 2:12-14:

> *I am writing to you, little children, because your sins are forgiven you for His name's sake. I am writing to you, fathers, because you know Him who has been from the beginning. I am writing to you, young men, because you have overcome the evil one. I have written to you, children, because you know the Father. I have written to you, fathers, because you know Him who has been from the beginning. I have written to you, young men, because you are strong, and the word of God abides in you, and you have overcome the evil one.* (1John 2:12-14)

Here we find that *"little children"* (those new in the faith) know their *"sins are forgiven"* (v.12) and *"know the Father"* as their God (v.13). They have entered Redemption rest. The *"young men,"* those more mature in the Lord, *"have overcome the evil one"* (vv.13-14) and entered Canaan rest (rest from the enemy). The *"fathers,"* the seasoned believers, *"know"* the heart of *"Him who has been from the beginning"* (vv.13-14). They *"know"* the heart of Christ (have intimacy with Christ) and have entered Sabbath rest. Our <u>ultimate</u> goal, therefore, is not to realize that our *"sins are forgiven"* (Redemption rest), nor to learn how to trust God to *"overcome the evil one"* (Canaan rest), but to *"know"* (intimately) the heart of God's Son (Sabbath rest). Intimacy with the Father is attained only through establishing intimacy with His Son (John 14:7 and 9).

To continue with our original topic (the fact that these Hebrew Christians should not disobey as Israel disobeyed under Moses), we need to examine Hebrews 3:7b-11 (a quote from Psalm 95:7-11) as closely as time permits.

In Hebrews 3:7b, the writer states, *"Today if you hear His voice...."* Because the word *"Today"* is used in Hebrews 3:7, 13, 15, and twice in Hebrews 4:7, we would be wise to determine its meaning.

These Hebrew Christians were living in a period known as *"Today."* In Hebrews 4 we will discover that *"Today"* points to the span of time in which Sabbath rest is made available to believers. But when did *"Today"* begin? Evidently *"Today"* began when God rested on *"the seventh day"* of creation (Genesis 2:2; Hebrews 4:4), the Sabbath (since "Sabbath" means a rest from activity), because as early as Exodus 20:8-11 the Lord commanded that His people rest one day of the week—on the *"sabbath."* This command painted a physical picture of what God desired for all believers in the spiritual realm—true *"Sabbath rest"* which continues *"Today"* (Hebrews 4:7-9). Thus, all followers of Jehovah have had access to *"Sabbath rest,"* the *"rest"* that God entered at the completion of *"His works"* (Genesis 2:2; Hebrews 4:4).

*A*ll followers of Jehovah have had access to "Sabbath rest."

Because Sabbath rest is offered to all believers does not mean that all will enter. (Review the materials associated with Third Day's questions.) Scripture will confirm this fact as we examine Israel's experiences in the wilderness. The Hebrew Christians addressed in this epistle were not to respond individually as Israel had responded collectively—by refusing to act on God's promises.

As has already been verified, Hebrews 3:7b-11 is a quote from Psalm 95:7-11. Notice that Psalm 95:8, unlike Hebrews 3:8, mentions *"Meribah"* and *"Massah"*:

> *Do not harden your hearts, as at Meribah, as in the day of Massah in the wilderness;* (Psalm 95:8)

> *Do not harden your hearts as when they provoked Me, AS IN THE DAY OF TRIAL IN THE WILDERNESS,* (Hebrews 3:8)

How does this detail relate to our study? The Israelites, at the <u>beginning</u> of their journey from Egypt, complained because of a lack of *"water"* (Exodus 17:1-7). Moses obeyed God by striking *"the rock,"* and *"water"* came forth. God was *"provoked,"* however, over Israel's lack of faith (Hebrews 3:8). As a result, the place was named *"Massah"* (meaning 'test') and *"Meribah"* (meaning "quarrel"). A similar occurrence transpired toward the <u>end</u> of the wilderness wanderings (Numbers 20:2-13). In this instance, Moses disobeyed by striking *"the rock twice"* (Numbers 20:11) instead of speaking *"to the rock"* (Numbers 20:8). Because of this disobedience, both Moses and Aaron died in the wilderness (Numbers 20:12). Why? They sinned by bringing forth water in their own strength (Numbers 20:10). This place too was named *"Meribah"* (Numbers 20:13), meaning "quarrel." The writer's point in Hebrews 3:7-11 is that throughout the wilderness wanderings, from <u>beginning</u> to <u>end</u>, the nation of Israel provoked God to anger.

The writer again speaks of how sin (Hebrews 3:9-10) kept the Israelites from entering Sabbath *"rest"* (v.11). (These sins prevented this first generation of physically redeemed Israel from entering into Canaan rest as well.) Notice that Israel tested God *"for forty years"* (v.9), the duration of the wilderness wanderings—verifying what was addressed in the previous paragraph:

> *Where your fathers tried Me BY TESTING Me, AND SAW MY WORKS FOR FORTY YEARS.* (Hebrews 3:9)

The church, when this epistle was penned, had existed for almost the same length of time—A.D. 30 to A.D. 64, 65, or 66—at least 34 years. Would these Hebrew Christians, being part of the church, test God through disobedience as did the first generation of physically redeemed Israel?

The Israelites had been redeemed physically from Egypt (Exodus 6:6; 15:13), and because of their physical redemption could never return (Exodus 13:17; 14:13). In fact, God allowed them to experience physical death in the wilderness rather than have them backtrack to their original place of bondage (Numbers 14:1-4; Numbers 14:29).

Undeniably, the *"generation"* of Israel that left Egypt (*"this generation"*—Hebrews 3:10) was responsible for provoking God to anger in the wilderness:

> *"THEREFORE I WAS ANGRY WITH <u>THIS GENERATION</u>, AND SAID, 'THEY ALWAYS GO ASTRAY IN THEIR HEART; AND THEY DID NOT KNOW MY WAYS';* (Hebrews 3:10—emphasis added)

They would *"not enter"* God's *"rest"*:

> *As I swore in My wrath, 'THEY SHALL NOT ENTER MY REST.'"* (Hebrews 3:11)

This first *"generation"* (v.10) of physically redeemed Israel (*"from twenty years old and upward"*—Numbers 14:29) died in the wilderness because of *"an evil, unbelieving heart"* (Hebrews 3:12)—or as is stated in Hebrews 3:19, *"unbelief"*:

Take care, brethren, lest there should be in any one of you <u>an evil, unbelieving heart</u>, in falling away from the living God. (Hebrews 3:12—emphasis added)

An *"unbelieving heart"* (v.12) in this case points to their refusal, as a result of a lack of faith, to act on God's promise. God had promised that the land was theirs for the taking. None of these Jews doubted that God was capable of destroying their enemies, for they had observed God annihilate the Egyptians. However, they believed that He wouldn't. Thus, unbelief is not believing that God can't come through in the clutch, but believing that He won't.

We should sit up and take notice here, for these Hebrew Christians were encouraged to refrain from doing individually what the nation of Israel had done collectively. Due to a lack of faith, Israel missed out on many of the blessings she could have known as a result of being physically redeemed from Egyptian bondage. By failing to go on to spiritual maturity, New Testament believers similarly miss out on blessings that could be theirs as a result of being spiritually redeemed from their bondage to sin.

Think on this as well. Moses, the man of God, died in the wilderness (Deuteronomy 34:4-5) due to disobedience (Numbers 20:12). Aaron died also (Numbers 20:28-29) because of disobedience (Numbers 20:24). But their loss of physical life was no indication that their spiritual status had been annulled—that they had lost their salvation. How can we be certain of this fact? Moses appeared to Jesus at the Transfiguration (Matthew 17:1-3). Consequently, not all the physically redeemed from Egypt who died physically in the wilderness died spiritually unredeemed. Also, realize that Joshua and Caleb escaped physical death in the wilderness (Numbers 14:30) because they were not guilty of any specific sin associated with the promises regarding the land. However, they did sin in general ways. Comprehending this difference is extremely important for properly viewing this chapter.

Not all the physically redeemed from Egypt, who died physically in the wilderness, died spiritually unredeemed.

The writer is using Israel's past failures to encourage his readers to press on to spiritual maturity—to Sabbath rest. Should they refuse, they would lose their physical lives (not their salvation) due to unbelief (as was the case with all believers, twenty years old and up, who came out of Egypt—with the exception of Joshua and Caleb). Unbelief here points to these Hebrew Christians' refusal to appropriate (apply) God's promises.

Putting all of this information into its historical framework, we can conclude the following: If these Hebrew Christians refused to go on to spiritual maturity (to Sabbath rest) and returned to the temple sacrifices in order to ward off persecution from the unbelieving Jews, they would lose their physical lives in the Roman destruction of Jerusalem in A.D. 70. Jesus spoke of this destruction in Matthew 24:2, Luke 21:6, and Luke 21:20-24. These believers (who had been redeemed spiritually) faced a critical decision. They could return to the sacrificial system, remain immature, and die when the Romans destroyed Jerusalem. Or, they could progress to spiritual maturity and dwell in Sabbath rest—by separating themselves from legalism and allowing God's Spirit, truth, and grace to carry them through. In this case, they would be spared from physical death at the hands of the Romans.

Read Hebrews 3:12 once again:

Take care, brethren, lest there should be in any one of you an evil, unbelieving heart, in falling away from the living God. (Hebrews 3:12)

The first time I read this passage I said, "I had better hang on to my salvation with all that is within me. If I don't, I will lose it by falling away." A closer examination of this passage reveals something totally different. Let me explain.

We have already learned that God ensures that one who has been redeemed can never return to his/her original place of bondage. He confirmed this truth through His dealings with Israel. She could never, under any circumstance, return to Egypt—regardless of how much she complained and rebelled in the wilderness (Exodus 13:17; 14:13). Therefore, these Hebrew Christians are encouraged to *"Take care"* (Hebrews 3:12). The writer is asking them to respond differently than the first generation of physically redeemed Israel. Upon receiving the report from the twelve spies (Numbers 13-14), Israel responded with *"an evil, unbelieving heart"* and fell *"away from the living God"* (Hebrews 3:12)—lost their fellowship with God. (Israel's fall resulted from her thinking that it was Israel's responsibility to kill the giants in Canaan. They had forgotten that this responsibility was God's alone.) Had they been redeemed physically? Of course! Did God send them back to Egypt? No way! Can then a spiritually redeemed individual have *"an evil, unbelieving heart"* and fall *"away from the living God"* (v.12)—in other words, lose his/her fellowship with God? Yes! How does this *"falling away"* occur? It occurs when a believer refuses to go on to spiritual maturity and, in turn, fails to appropriate God's promises. If these readers compromised, they would reap the same consequences as that of the first generation of physically redeemed Israel. They would die a physical death—not in the wilderness, but at the hands of the Romans. Their salvation, nonetheless, would remain intact. After all, Jesus *"is able to save forever those who"* are His (Hebrews 7:25).

Have you previously considered the similarities between the Israel that came out of Egypt and the Hebrew Christians to whom this epistle was written? When faced with the wilderness trials, the first generation of physically redeemed Israel desired to return to Egypt, the place from which they had been <u>physically</u> redeemed. When persecuted by the unbelieving Jews, these spiritually redeemed Hebrew Christians desired to return to Judaism, the place from which they had been <u>spiritually</u> redeemed. Isn't God's Word fascinating!?

This section verifies, beyond doubt, that spiritually redeemed individuals can forfeit blessings through disobedience. Their disobedience, however, does <u>not</u> result in a loss of salvation.

How could these Hebrew Christians overcome the temptation of returning to Judaism? Hebrews 3:13 has the answer:

> *But encourage one another day after day, as long as it is still called "Today," lest any one of you be hardened by the deceitfulness of sin.* (Hebrews 3:13)

These readers were to *"encourage one another"* to go on to spiritual maturity *"as long as it is still called Today"* (v.13). Simply stated, if they remained immature, they would not enter into Sabbath rest. Consequently, they would *"be hardened by the deceitfulness of sin"* (v.13). The word *"hardened"* means "to be hardened morally, to make stubborn." Yes, a brother's unconfessed sin hampers his ability to hear from God. Thus, he cannot appropriate God's promises. This lack of maturity negatively impacts his behavior, many times causing him to act as if he is spiritually unredeemed. He lives in this state until he chooses to repent and confess his sin, at which time fellowship with God (not relationship with God) is restored. Special note: Sin is deceitful (v.13). It may look appealing on the surface but ushers in pain, agony, and despair in the end.

Verse 14 is similar to verse 6.

> *For we have become partakers of Christ, if we hold fast the beginning of our assurance firm until the end;* (Hebrews 3:14)

Since we can't do anything to save ourselves, we can't do anything to keep ourselves saved.

(You might first want to review the portion of the lesson that deals with verse 6.) Notice that the writer does <u>not</u> say, "For we have become partakers of Christ, if we hold fast the beginning of our <u>salvation</u> firm until the end." Since we can't do anything to save ourselves, we can't do anything to keep ourselves saved. We know too that the person who (quote) "falls away" and stays away, all the while enjoying his/her sin void of God's chastening, never knew Christ in the first place (1John 2:19). Hebrews 3:14, therefore, isn't teaching that it is our responsibility to keep ourselves saved. Rather, it addresses the fruit that should be manifested from our lives as we progress to spiritual maturity. If we *"hold...our assurance* [or confidence] *firm until the end,"* those around us will clearly see that we are believers (v.14). Know too that the phrase, *"we have become"* (v.14), is in the perfect tense. The perfect tense indicates past action, completed action, with a resulting state of being. Thus, these Hebrew Christians could not lose what they had received from God the moment they repented and exercised faith while depraved. They were partakers of Christ—it was a done deal, a sealed pact, and nothing could alter their status with the Creator. As a result, the writer encourages them to go on to spiritual maturity so they can *"hold fast"* their *"assurance."* In this way, fruit would be manifested in and through their lives by means of Christ's indwelling presence. They most definitely were not being encouraged to mature so they could hold to their salvation!

The writer, consequently, communicates the following in verse 14: "That we *'have become partakers of Christ'* will become obvious to our observers if we *'hold fast the beginning of our assurance firm until the end.'"*

If these believers rejected this exhortation, a loss of salvation would <u>not</u> result. Just as the Israelites died physically in the wilderness (some of whom were spiritually redeemed), these Hebrew Christians would die in A.D. 70 should they refuse to pursue Sabbath rest. The word *"assurance"* (v.14) means "the quality of confidence which leads one to stand under, endure, or undertake anything." If these readers would stand in faith (in Christ's strength, of course), the fruit of their salvation would become obvious to all. In other words, those observing their lives would know that they were followers of Jesus. If this fruit diminished, it would be difficult to distinguish them from the unbelieving Jews. This verse addresses the evidence of salvation, not salvation itself.

The writer again quotes Psalm 95:7-8 in verse 15:

> *while it is said,* "TODAY IF YOU HEAR HIS VOICE, DO NOT HARDEN YOUR HEARTS,
> AS WHEN THEY PROVOKED ME." (Hebrews 3:15)

This passage emphasizes the importance of going on to spiritual maturity, to Sabbath rest, *"Today."* After all, this epistle was written in A.D. 64-66. Since Rome destroyed Jerusalem in A.D. 70, the time was very short. These believers needed to progress to spiritual maturity and forget the idea of going back under the sacrificial system in Jerusalem. They needed to do it quickly; in fact, they needed to do it *"Today."* The writer then asks *"who provoked"* God in the wilderness (v.16). He answers his question with *"those who came out of Egypt led by Moses"* (v.16). In fact, their sin caused God to be *"angry"* with them *"for forty years"* (v.17). Their sin also brought on physical death (v.17). Because of disobedience (v.18) and *"unbelief"* (v.19), they did not experience Canaan *"rest"* from their enemies (which their children later experienced to a great degree through Joshua's leadership), nor Sabbath rest (the rest which results from spiritual maturity). By no means did God send this first generation of physically redeemed Israel back to Egypt. And by no means did those who were spiritually redeemed, yet died in the wilderness, lose their salvation.

This section of Hebrews should greatly encourage us. It allows believers to understand that sin does not result in a loss of salvation, even though it hampers our quest for spiritual maturity and its accompanying "rest." Yes, Sabbath rest is the goal, only to be attained through intimacy with Christ.

> *S*in does not result in a loss of salvation, even though it hampers our quest for spiritual maturity.

Next week's questions and lesson are much shorter, which will provide ample opportunity to review this week's material if necessary. We are building a foundation to support the wealth of truth contained in Hebrews 5-13. Foundations take considerable time and effort, but are well worth our time. Press on!

Hebrews 4 Questions

First Day

You might need to refer to last week's materials as you answer this week's questions. Comprehending what the writer is communicating here, and how it relates to Hebrews 3, is extremely important. Take your time and digest all you can.

    1. Read Hebrews 4. Considering the historical setting of this book, what did these believers have to *"fear"* (v.1) should they disregard Sabbath *"rest"* (spiritual maturity)?

    2. How many, and who, had *"preached"* the *"good news"* to these believers (v.2)? (Hint: Who carried the good news to the world after Jesus' resurrection?) Who, and how many, had *"preached"* the *"good news"* to Israel (Numbers 13:4-16, 23-27)? Why did the *"good news"* that Israel heard fail to *"profit them"* (Hebrews 4:2)? How did this failure on Israel's part apply to those addressed in the book of Hebrews?

    3. How does verse 3 confirm that Sabbath *"rest"* is available to New Testament believers? How long have God's *"works"* been *"finished"* (v.3)? How does this truth relate to statements in verse 4 (as well as what we studied last week concerning God's rest on the seventh day of creation)? How does this truth nullify the error that a person is saved by grace but kept by works? What is the major problem with believing that a person is saved by grace but kept by works?

Second Day

    1. Read Hebrews 4. Don't forget to pray. Verses 5 and 6 reinforce what we studied earlier. Why did the first generation of physically redeemed Israel fail to *"enter"* God's *"rest"*? (Note: Neither did they enter Canaan rest—review the chart under Week 3's Third Day's questions.)

2.   Compare Hebrews 4:7 with Hebrews 3:7.   Why can these passages be used to confirm the inspiration and dual authorship of Scripture?   How do 2Peter 1:20-21 and 2Timothy 3:16 relate?

3.   According to verse 7, what famous Old Testament believer encouraged the redeemed to enter Sabbath rest *"Today"*?   Did he live before or after Joshua?   What type of *"rest"* did Israel enter (to a great degree, at least) under Joshua (Joshua 21:44; 22:4; 23:1-13)?   What type of *"rest"* did Israel fail to enter under Joshua (Hebrews 4:8)?   If Sabbath rest remained available <u>after</u> Joshua brought the second generation of physically redeemed Israel into Canaan, how does this availability tie in with verse 9?   The word *"remains"* (v.9) is critically important.   Could the writer be saying that *"Sabbath rest"* has been available to all believers of all time?   If so, why?

Third Day

1.   Read Hebrews 4.   From verse 10, what transpires in believers once they enter Sabbath *"rest."*   How does this input encourage you?

2.   Why must we *"be diligent"* if we are to *"enter"* Sabbath *"rest"* (v.11)?   (The word *"diligent"* means "eager or earnest.")   Does the phrase, *"lest anyone fall through following the same example of disobedience"* (v.11), mean that these Hebrew Christians would lose their salvation, fall away from Christ (so to speak), should they fail to *"enter"* Sabbath *"rest"*?   If not, what does it mean?

3.   Stephen and Paul entered Sabbath rest.   Read Acts 7:54-60, 1Thessalonians 5:16-18, and 2Corinthians 4:7-18 to observe how this rest impacted their lives.   What impresses you most about these men?

Fourth Day

1. Read Hebrews 4. Verse 12 gives a description of *"the word of God."* What does it communicate? Have you found God's *"word"* to be *"living and active"* (v.12)? If so, why? When did the Scriptures last reveal *"the thoughts and intentions"* of your *"heart"* (v.12)? Did you like what you saw? If not, how did you respond?

2. According to verse 13, how much does God know about our inward thoughts and motives? How should this truth have impacted these readers who were contemplating resubmitting themselves to the Law? How does this truth impact you?

3. Since God knows our hearts even better than we know our hearts, what encouragement do you draw from the fact that Jesus is our *"great high priest"* (v.14) Who *"intercedes for us"* (Romans 8:34)? Where is our high priest seated (Hebrews 1:3), and what did He pass *"through"* to get there (Hebrews 4:14)?

4. Does verse 14 teach that we are to *"hold fast our"* salvation? If not, what is it communicating? What dilemma would we face should we be required to *"hold fast our"* salvation?

Fifth Day

1.   Read Hebrews 4. Why should knowing that Jesus sympathizes with the believer's pain and trials (*"weaknesses"*—v.15) have encourage these Hebrew Christians to refrain from buckling under the pressure from the unbelieving Jews?   Why could Jesus *"sympathize with"* their *"weaknesses"* (v.15)?   Did He *"sin"* when He was *"tempted"* (v.15)?   Why should this input have invigorated these Hebrew Christians?   How does this knowledge affect your perception of Christ?

2.   Verse 15 states that Jesus was *"tempted in all things as we are, yet without sin."* Does this verse teach that He was tempted to drive a Ferrari 95 miles per hour in a 45 mile per hour zone? If not, how does 1John 2:16 relate to this subject matter?

Sixth Day

1.   Read Hebrews 4. How do you define *"grace"*? According to verse 16, with what attitude are believers to *"draw near...the throne of grace"*?   Why can we (all New Testament beleivers) approach the Father's *"throne"* in this manner?   Why do you need *"mercy and...grace...in time of need"*?

2.   Be sure to read all of this week's lesson. Record any new insights below.

Hebrews 4 Lesson

The input regarding *"rest"* from Hebrews 3 must remain at the forefront of our minds for proper interpretation of Hebrews 4. Note verse 1:

> *Therefore, let us fear lest, while a promise remains of entering His rest, any one of you should seem to have come short of it.* (Hebrews 4:1)

The writer begins by instructing his readers to *"fear lest"* they *"come short"* (v.1) *"of entering"* God's *"rest"* (Sabbath *"rest"*—v.9). The verb *"fear"* means "to be fearfully anxious." Should spiritual maturity (Sabbath *"rest"*) be bypassed, they had good reason to be *"fearfully anxious."* They would die at the hands of the Romans in A.D. 70!!

Like Israel, these Hebrew Christians *"had good news preached to"* them (v.2):

> *For indeed we have had good news preached to us, just as they also; but the word they heard did not profit them, because it was not united by faith in those who heard.* (Hebrews 4:2)

Israel had *"heard"* *"good news"* (Hebrews 4:2) when the twelve spies reported that Canaan was flowing *"with milk and honey"* (Numbers 13:27). Due to their lack of *"faith,"* however, *"the word they heard did not profit them"* (Hebrews 4:2). As a result, they died in the wilderness. Thus, the first generation of physically redeemed Israel not only failed to enter Canaan rest (failed to trust God to destroy their enemies in Canaan), but failed to enter Sabbath rest as well—the rest granted to the spiritually redeemed who progress to spiritual maturity. (Just think of what their children reaped from their disobedience.) The Hebrew Christians addressed in this epistle were in danger of experiencing a similar result. They had heard the *"good news"* of the gospel through the twelve apostles but would die physically should they remain immature by circumventing Sabbath rest.

Because the Israelites were content in the wilderness, they refused to enter Canaan under Moses' leadership. Yes, they complained about their living conditions, but all their needs were met through God's supernatural provision. They had fresh manna every morning, their clothing never wore out, and God told them where to go and how fast to get there. To think of trading this lifestyle for a lifestyle of war seemed absurd. Do you find yourself avoiding the battles necessary for spiritual growth, as did the Israelites?

Hebrews 4:3 verifies that the recipients of this epistle had access to Sabbath *"rest"*:

> *For we who have believed enter that rest, just as He has said, "AS I SWORE IN MY WRATH, THEY SHALL NOT ENTER MY REST," although His works were finished from the foundation of the world.* (Hebrews 4:3)

The word *"enter"* (v.3) is a present-tense verb since this *"rest"* is (has been, and will always be) available to the redeemed of all time. Sabbath *"rest"* occurs when a believer rests *"from his works, as God did from His"* (vv.4, 10). We learned last week that after God created the heavens and the earth, and all things in them, He *"rested"* (Genesis 2:2). We must learn to do the same.

The phrase, *"although His works were finished from the foundation of the world"* (Hebrews 4:3), is extremely interesting. No doubt, *"God…rested on the seventh day"* (Genesis 2:2). In fact, the Rabbis taught that since no evening was associated with *"the seventh day"* of creation (Genesis 2:1-3), unlike the other six days of the week (Genesis 1:23 for example), that God's *"rest"* continues throughout eternity. Certainly, everything He does is done in a state of *"rest."* We can *"rest"* as well, for

To enter Sabbath "rest" requires the maturity to realize that we can't live the Christian life.

the God Who lives in *"rest"* lives in us (Galatians 2:20; Colossians 1:16). Thus, to enter Sabbath *"rest"* requires the maturity to realize that we can't live the Christian life. Victorious living is experienced through one means only—through yielding to Jesus, Who is inside us living in *"rest."* Wow! This realization results in no more doing things "for" God, but trusting Him to do the impossible "through us" as we yield to, and therefore live by, His life! No wonder Paul records in Romans 6:13:

> *Neither yield ye your members as instruments of unrighteousness unto sin: but yield yourselves unto God, as those that are alive from the dead, and your members as instruments of righteousness unto God.* (Romans 6:13 KJV—emphasis added)

Unquestionably, the ultimate experience in the Christian life is yielding, on a moment-by-moment basis, to the God Who has become our most trusted Ally. Consequently, intimacy with Jesus is the only means through which Sabbath *"rest"* can be realized.

We must allow God's truth to override the lie that we were saved by grace but are being kept by deeds performed <u>for</u> God. This falsehood has caused many "God-fearing" men and women to live in heartbreaking defeat and despair. If we are kept by works, we must define the number (and kinds) of works necessary to keep ourselves saved. This definition is unattainable since the Scriptures don't specify. Why don't they provide such information? The answer is simple. It isn't our responsibility to keep ourselves saved! So give up on the idea of performing good deeds to maintain your salvation. Enjoy Christ's indwelling presence (Galatians 2:20; Philippians 3:10)—and *"rest."* Christ's work is a finished work!!

It isn't our responsibility to keep ourselves saved!

Before moving to verse 5, notice the phrase, *"For He has thus said somewhere concerning the seventh day"* (v.4). Again, as in Hebrews 2:6, the writer is stating that God wrote the entire Bible and in it spoke these words. He was not, of course, experiencing a memory lapse.

As a result of disobedience, every member of the first generation of physically redeemed Israel (outside of Joshua and Caleb) failed to enter Canaan *"rest."* Neither did they enter Sabbath *"rest"* (Hebrews 4:5-6). This fact, by no stretch of the imagination, means that Sabbath *"rest"* was not available. All believers have had opportunity to enter this *"rest,"* but they have had to go on to spiritual maturity before experiencing it.

Note that David is mentioned in Hebrews 4:7:

> *He again fixes a certain day, "Today," saying through David after so long a time just as has been said before, "TODAY IF YOU HEAR HIS VOICE, DO NOT HARDEN YOUR HEARTS."* (Hebrews 4:7)

God confirmed through *"David"* that Sabbath rest remained available in David's day. (Notice that David uses the term *"Today"*—Hebrews 4:7; Psalm 95:7.) I find it interesting that David is mentioned. He was the man who, when facing Goliath, probably thought, "How can I miss him?" (Read 1Samuel 17:26.) King Saul, however, as a result of fear, must have thought, "How can I hit him?" (Read 1Samuel 17:11.) Two totally different perspectives were demonstrated during this crisis. Why so? David knew about, and lived in, Sabbath rest. Thus, he viewed life from God's perspective as a result of knowing God's heart. (Read Psalm 27:8.)

Notice that Hebrews 4:7 credits *"David"* with speaking what is stated in Psalm 95:7-11, while Hebrews 3:7 credits *"the Holy Spirit."* These acknowledgements line up perfectly with 2Peter 1:20-21, confirming the dual authorship of Scripture. Obviously, God's Word is inspired (2Timothy 3:16).

Even though Joshua brought the second generation of physically redeemed Israel across the Jordan and into Canaan *"rest"* (*"rest,"* to a great degree at least, from their enemies—Joshua

21:44; 22:4; 23:1-13), he did not lead them into Sabbath *"rest"* (spiritual maturity). This fact is confirmed in the first phrase of Hebrews 4:8:

> *For if Joshua had given them rest, He would not have spoken of another day after that.*
> (Hebrews 4:8)

Notice the last phrase of the same verse: *"He would not have spoken of another day after that."* David lived after Joshua. Consequently, God's offer of Sabbath rest through David (v.7) came after Joshua had led Israel into the land. Thus, the phrase, *"another day after that"* (v.8).

We should memorize verse 9:

> *There remains therefore a Sabbath rest for the people of God.* (Hebrews 4:9)

What a statement! Did you notice the word *"remains"*? If *"Sabbath rest"* (v.9) was available in David's day (v.7), then *"Sabbath rest"* (v.9) is available to God's people *"Today"* (v.7). Why? As we learned in last week's material, it has "remained" available since Genesis 2.

Oh, to rest!!: No more working for God, but watching God perform His work through us (Philippians 2:13; 1Corinthians 15:10) as we face the variables of our day. No more involving ourselves with busyness to the point of exhaustion, but spending time with Him, just Him, for the purpose of knowing His heart. When we seek His heart, we have the awesome privilege of watching Him change lives through us—while we rest. But before we can walk in this manner, we must recognize that we can do nothing to save ourselves or retain our salvation. Christ's work performed in our lives, subsequent to our repenting and believing while depraved, is a completed work. Therefore, we can *"rest from"* our *"works, as God did from His"* (v.10):

> *For the one who has entered His rest has himself also rested from his works, as God did from His.* (Hebrews 4:10)

Sabbath *"rest"* results from seeking it wholeheartedly and diligently:

> *Let us therefore be diligent to enter that rest, lest anyone fall through following the same example of disobedience.* (Hebrews 4:11)

"Diligent" means "eager or earnest"— so only those who earnestly seek to establish intimacy with the Creator will know this *"rest."* Most believers, on the other hand, spend more time doing things <u>for Him</u> than communing with Him. The Hebrew Christians addressed in this epistle were guilty of this sin. As a result, they had failed to enter into Sabbath rest. Thus, they had followed *"the same example of disobedience"* displayed by the first generation of physically redeemed Israel (v.11). They would *"fall"* (v.11) if this issue was not rectified. In fact, their sin, as was the case with Israel, would result in physical death (in A.D. 70). To see clearly how Sabbath rest can positively influence believers, review the death of Stephen (Acts 7:54-60) and the words of Paul (1Thessalonians 5:16-18 and 2Corinthians 4:7-18).

Hebrews 4:12 gives a description of *"the word of God"* along with its impact on the spiritually hungry heart:

> *For the word of God is living and active and sharper than any two-edged sword, and piercing as far as the division of soul and spirit, of both joints and marrow, and able to judge the thoughts and intentions of the heart.* (Hebrews 4:12)

First, God's Word is *"living"*—God-breathed, which explains why we can memorize a verse of Scripture, quote it for years, and later see it in a fresh, new, and exciting way. The *"word"* is also *"active."* Once written on the passionate heart (mind), it (coupled with the Holy Spirit) transforms the lives of its possessors. It is also *"sharper than a two-edged sword."* Let me illustrate.

One fall a friend gave me a Buck Knife and suggested that we go camping. My chestnut tree was producing a bumper crop, so I took some chestnuts along, eager to see if my new knife could remove the shells surrounding their cores. Later, at the camp sight, I began the removal process. At one point, my thumb became extremely sensitive—the thumb that had helped hold the chestnuts as I made each stroke—the thumb that had come in contact (ever-so-slightly) with the blade of the knife. God's Word is much the same. It is a *"two-edged sword"* (v.12). As it touches our hearts, it makes them exceptionally sensitive. Thus, it pierces *"as far as the division of soul and spirit,"* as well as the *"joints and marrow"*—deep into our innermost being—and is *"able to judge the thoughts and intentions of the heart"* (v.12). Yes, God's Word can reveal our motives in a heartbeat. Is it any wonder that those who walk out of fellowship with the Father (and refuse to repent) find God's Word so overwhelmingly offensive?

These Hebrew Christians needed to prayerfully read (and meditate upon) God's Word for it to perform its perfect work within their hearts. Should they do so, conviction would result. They would then reject Law for a life of Sabbath rest. If not, and because God knows *"the thoughts and intentions of the heart"* (v.12), He would bring chastening (Hebrews 12:5-10). As a result, they would die physically in the destruction of A.D. 70. Yes, God loves believers enough to, in some instances, take them home when they wallow in sin (read 1Corinthians 11:27-30 for confirmation).

The writer next records:

> *And there is no creature hidden from His sight, but all things are open and laid bare to the eyes of Him with whom we have to do.* (Hebrews 4:13)

As a result of knowing *"all things,"* nothing can be concealed from God (v.13). The Creator understands the intent of every motive and word. These Hebrew Christians could not hide their unwise plans. God knew their hearts. Therefore, they needed to repent, receive a steady diet of God's Word, and allow Him to bring them to maturity.

Since the Father examines our motives and understands our *"thoughts"* (Hebrews 4:12), how can He possess such an awareness and remain faithful to His people? He can do so because of our *"great high priest,"* Jesus Christ:

> *Since then we have a great high priest who has passed through the heavens, Jesus the Son of God, let us hold fast our confession.* (Hebrews 4:14)

Under the sacrificial system associated with the Law, a high priest would enter God's presence (in a temple on earth) on behalf of Israel. Our *"high priest,"* on the other hand, *"passed through the heavens"* (the atmospheric heavens—v.14) to take His seat *"at the right hand of the Majesty on high"* (Hebrews 1:3). What is His role as He sits in this position of power? He prays for the redeemed. In other words, He has assumed an intercessory role for us (Romans 8:34).

Knowing Jesus' role should have caused these Hebrew Christians to *"hold fast"* their *"confession"* (Hebrews 4:14) and pursue spiritual maturity:

> *Since then we have a great high priest who has passed through the heavens, Jesus the Son of God, let us hold fast our confession.* (Hebrews 4:14)

Notice that the writer does not say, "let us hold fast our salvation" (v.14). The security of their salvation is not in question here. Besides, should a believer be required to hold to his/her salvation for the purpose of retaining it would mean that he/she could have done something to attain it. The writer is encouraging these believers to walk away from Law and *"hold fast"* their

The security of their salvation is not in question here.

original *"confession"* (that Jesus is the Son of God and Messiah) which had brought on the persecution from the unbelieving Jews in the first place.

The knowledge that Jesus knew (and understood) their pain should have caused these believers to *"hold fast"* their *"confession"* (v.14). After all, He was *"tempted in all things as"* they were, *"yet"* lived *"without sin"* (v.15):

> *For we do not have a high priest who cannot sympathize with our weaknesses, but One who*
> *has been tempted in all things as we are, yet without sin.* (Hebrews 4:15)

Jesus knows our pain as well, but we need to be careful when applying this verse to our day and age. He was never *"tempted"* to steal an automobile, since Henry Ford did not yet exist. But He may have been *"tempted"* to steal another means of transportation, like a camel—a temptation that is not common to us (unless, of course, you desire to live in the slow lane and wear a turban—Ha). Jesus faced temptation in the general areas that all believers are *"tempted"*—*"the lust of the flesh and the lust of the eyes and the boastful pride of life"* (1John 2:16). The writer encourages these Hebrew Christians to reflect on the fact that Jesus knew their struggles, for He had been where they were. I am certain that He was *"tempted"* to compromise His message and follow the majority. Because He rejected such thinking, and because He intercedes for those who struggle in this same area, the recipients of this epistle could take courage and stand firm (in His strength of course).

Grace can be defined as "the power to do God's will." Therefore, victory is inevitable once grace is received and implemented. Thus, the readers were encouraged to *"draw near with confidence to the throne of grace"*:

> *Let us therefore draw near with confidence to the throne of grace, that we may receive mercy and*
> *may find grace to help in time of need.* (Hebrews 4:16)

Why could they approach the Father's *"throne"* *"with confidence"*? Jesus serves as our *"great high priest"*—He is our representative before the Father (v.14). He also understands *"our weaknesses"* (v.15). Since the *"throne"* is where *"mercy and...grace"* are abundantly supplied to the New Testament believer, these Hebrew Christians needed to approach it rather than the sacrificial system in Jerusalem. Only God's *"grace"* could sufficiently empower them once they chose to obey (read 1Corinthians 15:10).

Next week we will study more about Christ as our *"high priest."* Come back ready to learn.

Hebrews 5 Questions

First Day

1. Read Hebrews 5. Considering what the writer discussed in Hebrews 4:14-16, what does he begin to prove concerning Jesus' priesthood in Hebrews 5? According to verses 1-3, what were some of the duties associated with the office of *"high priest"*? Why was it required that a *"high priest"* be a man (vv.1-2)?

2. According to verse 4, through what means did a high priest receive his office? Through what means did Aaron receive his position as a high priest (Exodus 28:1)? What happened to those who attempted to appoint themselves to this office (Numbers 16:1-35)?

3. What do verses 5 and 6 teach regarding the manner in which Jesus became a *"high priest"*? How long will He serve in this position (v.6)? Of what *"order"* is Jesus' priesthood (v.6)? Does this mean that the priesthood changed when Jesus became a high priest? If the Melchizedekian priesthood is eternal, whereas the Aaronic priesthood was temporary, which priesthood is the greater? Remember this answer for future reference.

Second Day

1. Read Hebrews 5. In what way does verse 7 confirm Christ's humanity? From verse 1, why was it necessary that Jesus become a man?

2. The *"prayers and supplications"* mentioned in verse 7 were the *"prayers"* that Jesus prayed at *"Gethsemane"* (Matthew 26:36-44) before the crucifixion. In your opinion, what was Jesus' greatest concern in going to the cross? The fact that Jesus had never, throughout eternity past, been spiritually separated from the Father should assist you in properly answering the previous question. Why would taking on the *"sin"* of man (2Corinthians 5:21) temporarily separate Him from the Father?

3. Realizing that darkness fell upon the land when Jesus took on the sin of man, did Jesus first die physically or spiritually? (Read Matthew 27:45-46 and Luke 23:44-46.) How do these same verses confirm that Jesus was resurrected spiritually before He died physically?

4. According to Luke 24:1-5, when was Jesus bodily resurrected from the grave? Was this resurrection before or after His spiritual resurrection? What does 1Corinthians 15:12-17 communicate regarding the importance of the bodily resurrection of Christ? No doubt, His bodily resurrection verified that His spiritual resurrection occurred previously (while on the cross). What does the bodily resurrection of Christ say about Who He is?

5. If the word *"piety"* in verse 7 means "reverence," or "reverent submission," what does this verse communicate concerning the manner in which Jesus submitted to the Father's will? Why did the Hebrew Christians addressed in this epistle need this reminder?

Third Day

1. Read Hebrews 5. From verse 8, how did Jesus learn *"obedience"*? How will we learn obedience? Considering that Jesus is our high priest, why was it important that He experience pain in the same areas that we experience pain? According to 2Corinthians 1:3-4, in what areas can you minister most effectively?

2. Why was Jesus sent to earth (John 12:27)? When Jesus fulfilled His mission (through the Father's strength), what did He become *"to those who obey Him"* (v.9)? So, is your salvation temporary or *"eternal"* (v.9)? Why should this truth encourage you?

3. Does the phrase, *"to all those who obey Him"* (v.9), communicate that salvation is by works? How do passages such as Ephesians 2:8-9, Titus 3:5, Hebrews 11:6, and Romans 5:1 confirm that salvation is *"by grace...through faith"*? If the word *"source"* (Hebrews 5:9) means "author," what does this verse say about Jesus?

Fourth Day

1. Read Hebrews 5. According to the first phrase of verse 10, what did *"God"* do for Jesus? Of what *"order"* is Jesus' priesthood? Considering what we addressed in verses 5 and 6, why is Jesus' priesthood greater than that of Aaron's? Why then should the readers abandon the sacrificial system in Jerusalem and go on to spiritual maturity?

2. The first phrase in verse 11 states, *"Concerning him we have much to say."* Who is the *"him"* in this passage? Why was the writer unable to discuss *"him"* in more detail (v.11)? When did *"sin"* last cause you to *"become dull of hearing"*?

Fifth Day

1. Read Hebrews 5. How does verse 12 confirm that these Hebrew Christians knew much more than they were applying? What happens when a person fails to apply what he or she already knows (v.12; Hebrews 2:1)? Has studying this subject increased your passion to apply the truth that is already yours? If so, how?

2. What type of nourishment did these believers need (v.12), and how are such believers classified (v.13)? The words, *"not accustomed"* (v.13), mean "inexperienced or unskillful." Thus, these Hebrew Christians were inexperienced and unskilled in their handling of the Word of God. If the *"word of God"* is the believer's sole offensive weapon against the schemes of the enemy (Ephesians 6:17), why could the inexperience of these readers explain their lack of boldness?

3. The *"solid food"* of the Word (the meat) is for what group of believers (v.14)? Are you interested in learning to *"discern good and evil"*? Was Paul concerned about such matters (Philippians 1:9-10)? What would have happened differently had these Hebrew Christians possessed the ability *"to discern good and evil"* (Hebrews 5:14)? What will be necessary for this ability to become a reality in your life?

Sixth Day

1. Read Hebrews 5. Read this week's lesson and record all new insights. Rest assured that God is honoring the time you are devoting to His Word!

Hebrews 5 Lesson

The writer will now prove that Jesus' priesthood is greater than that of Aaron's. He will address this topic through Hebrews 7. He actually began speaking of Christ's priesthood in Hebrews 4:14-16, so you may want to review those notes before continuing.

In Hebrews 5:1, we find that *"every high priest taken from among men"* served *"on behalf of men."* Consequently, a *"high priest"* was required to be a man since he served as a mediator between God and man. His responsibilities also included ministering to the needs of the people. Notice too that he was *"appointed,"* and that his responsibilities included offering *"gifts and sacrifices for sins."*

Because the high priest associated with the Law was a man, he could understand the weaknesses of his fellow man (v.2). He could *"deal gently with"* those who struggled with sin since he was subject to the same weaknesses. In fact, when he offered *"sacrifices for"* the *"sins"* of *"the people,"* he would also *"offer sacrifices for...himself"*—for his own *"sins"* (v.3), confirming the degree to which he could relate to those he represented.

An extremely important point must be addressed here for proper understanding. The point is: Every high priest was appointed *"by God"*— *"no one"* took this *"honor to himself"*:

> *And no one takes the honor to himself, but receives it when he is called by God, even as Aaron was.* (Hebrews 5:4)

Thus, Aaron was appointed as high priest (Exodus 28:1), and only his descendants could serve in this capacity after him. Anyone who attempted to appoint himself to this special office reaped horrible consequences—read Numbers 16:1-35. Jesus was also appointed. In fact, the Father appointed *"Christ"* (v.5) as *"high priest,"* not just temporarily, but *"forever"* (v.6). Why could He do so? Christ's priesthood is of *"the order of Melchizedek"* (vv.5-6), a priesthood which is perpetual.

Scripture mentions only two priesthoods: Aaronic and Melchizedekian. We will study the Melchizedekian priesthood in more detail in Hebrews 7, but for now just know that the priesthood changed when Christ became high priest—and His term is forever. (The Melchizedekian priesthood is eternal; the Aaronic was temporary). No doubt, Christ's priesthood is greater than that of Aaron's.

Notice the phrase, *"In the days of His flesh"* (v.7). This phrase confirms Christ's humanity, which was a prerequisite to His fulfilling the office of *"high priest"* (v.1). At Gethsemane Jesus *"offered up both prayers and supplications"* to the Father *"with loud crying and tears"* (v.7; Matthew 26:36-44). (To supplicate is to cry for mercy or favor in the midst of trying circumstances.) He asked the Father *"to save Him from death"* (v.7), but the words *"from death"* actually mean "out of death." Jesus was not seeking deliverance from the physical pain of the cross, for the cross was the main purpose of His coming (John 12:27). Evidently, He was asking the Father to raise Him from both the physical and spiritual deaths He would endure on the cross. I believe too that spiritual separation from the Father—spiritual death—was Christ's greatest concern. From eternity past He and His Father had lived in perpetual, unbroken, uninterrupted fellowship. For Jesus to even think of being separated from Him for one moment must have produced agony beyond anything we can imagine. Compared to this suffering, the pain involved in Jesus' physical death must have seemed less than significant.

Do you realize that Jesus died spiritually before He died physically?

Let's take a closer look at the cross. Do you realize that Jesus died spiritually before He died physically? Read Matthew 27:45-46 to see that *"darkness fell upon all the land"* from *"the sixth hour"* (noon) *"until the ninth hour"* (3 p.m.), at which time Jesus said, *"My God, My God, why hast Thou forsaken Me?"* This order of events means that from noon until 3 p.m., God the Father turned His back on the Son. The Father had no alternative since His holiness prohibits Him from communing with sin (it was during this time that the sin of all mankind was placed on Christ—2Corinthians 5:21; 1John 2:2). In fact, for the first (and last) time in their existence the Father and Son broke fellowship. Thus, Jesus died spiritually, for "death" in Scripture can mean separation as well as extinction—depending on the context. But the good news is that Jesus was resurrected spiritually even before He died physically, as verified by Luke 23:44-46. There we find that immediately after *"the ninth hour"* (3 p.m.), after His *"spirit"* had been resurrected (Luke 23:44-46), Jesus said, *"Father, into Thy hands I commit My spirit"* (v.46). He then died physically: *"And having said this, He breathed His last"* (v.46). Three days later, *"on the first day of the week"* (Luke 24:1-5), Jesus' bodily resurrection occurred.

To comprehend the significance of the bodily resurrection of Christ, read 1Corinthians 15:12-17. No doubt, Jesus' bodily resurrection confirmed that His spiritual resurrection had occurred previously. It also confirmed, beyond doubt, that He is the holy Son of God.

Previous input should bring encouragement as we examine the last phrase of Hebrews 5:7, *"and He was heard because of His piety."* *"Piety"* means "reverence," which confirms that Jesus honored the Father for Who He is. It is translated in at least one version as *"reverent submission."* As a result, Jesus could say, "Father, your will be done, regardless of the cost." These Hebrew Christians needed this reminder, and so do we.

If Jesus *"learned obedience from the things which He suffered"* (v.8), so will you and I:

> *Although He was a Son, He learned obedience from the things which He suffered.* (Hebrews 5:8)

Unquestionably, pain brings us to a deeper place of surrender. As society dives headlong into sin, rejecting God's truth and those who love Him, I suffer. In fact, I am grieved to the core. But as I observe what society is reaping, I am more determined than ever to walk in compliance with God's will. Consequently, like Jesus, we learn obedience through suffering. Pain also gives us an ability to sympathize with those who are experiencing adversity. No wonder Paul went so far as to say that we minister most effectively in the areas we have experienced pain (2Corinthians 1:3-4). Since Jesus' suffering (as God-man) was the most intense known to man, He can sympathize as we walk through the valleys of life. Realizing He understands our pain, therefore, should make us extremely thankful that He is our high priest. Again, these Hebrew Christians needed to heed God's message in this epistle and turn from sin.

Jesus fulfilled His objective, for He was sent for a specific purpose—to die (John 12:27). When He did so (and was raised from the dead), His mission was completed. Thus, He became *"the source of eternal salvation"* for all who *"obey"* (Hebrews 5:9). Don't allow the phrase, *"those who obey Him"* (v.9), to bring confusion. The writer is not saying that we are saved through the avenue of good works. Passages such as Ephesians 2:8-9, Titus 3:5, Hebrews 11:6, and Romans 5:1 confirm that God grants salvation only *"by grace...through faith"*—faith exercised while depraved. Notice that the *"salvation"* He supplies is *"eternal"* (Hebrews 5:9), not temporary. No doubt, the believer is secure in his/her relationship with the Son.

> *The writer is not saying that we are saved through the avenue of good works.*

Did you notice the word *"source"* (Hebrews 5:9)? This word means "author." Jesus, therefore, is the reason *"eternal salvation"* could be offered to man. No wonder Paul pursued His heart with a passion second to none (Philippians 3:10).

Since Christ fulfilled His mission (through the Father's strength), *"God"* has *"designated"* Him *"as a high priest according to the order of Melchizedek"* (Hebrews 5:10). Because Jesus is a better priest than the priests who served under the Aaronic priesthood (His priesthood is eternal while theirs was temporary), these readers are encouraged to abandon the old covenant (Law) and walk by faith. If they failed to do so, they would be swept away in the destruction of A.D. 70.

In verse 11, the writer states, *"Concerning him we have much to say."* But who is the *"him"* in this case—Jesus or Melchizedek? It seems to be Melchizedek. And why was the writer unable to discuss Melchizedek in more detail? These Hebrew believers had *"become dull of hearing"* (v.11). Why had they *"become dull of hearing"*? They had sinned by contemplating going back under Law to avoid the persecution from the unbelieving Jews. Without a doubt, sin always hampers our ability to hear God's voice.

Clearly, these believers had been taught "the *elementary principles of the oracles of God*" (v.12). They had known Christ long enough to have become *"teachers"* (v.12), but their compromise had retarded their spiritual growth. (When we fail to apply what we know, we many times forget what we have previously learned—remember Hebrews 2:1.) These Hebrew Christians had digressed to *"milk"* only, for *"solid food"* (meat) would have been too much for them to bear (v.12). How are such believers classified? They are babes, or infants, for they are *"not accustomed to the word of righteousness"* (v.13). The words, *"not accustomed,"* mean "inexperienced or unskillful." If God's Word is the believer's only offensive weapon against Satan's schemes (Ephesians 6:17), one who is inexperienced or unskilled in the truth will not stand. Consequently, these readers were becoming weak in the faith, which always results in compromise. They needed to repent of their sin and go on to spiritual maturity.

When believers fail to consistently *"practice"* God's Word, they lose their ability *"to discern good and evil"* (v.14). Thus, one of the greatest assets of graduating from milk to meat, and becoming mature, is the "capacity" to distinguish right from wrong. We can also choose the *"excellent"* over the good (read Philippians 1:9-10). This "capacity" to choose rightly allows us to live life from God's vantage point—the true meaning of wisdom. These Hebrew Christians had lost the ability to perceive their circumstances from God's perspective. Why? They were no longer walking in truth. Consequently, when persecution arose, they assumed their only alternative was to succumb to the pressure and compromise. An inability to withstand adversity will overtake us as well unless we prayerfully feast on the meat of God's Word.

> *We can choose the "excellent" over the good.*

Let's consider an example that ties in well here. I used to raise Hampshire hogs (pigs). My dad taught agriculture at my high school (and farmed in his spare time)—so I came by my profession honestly. I soon discovered that a baby pig dies if it doesn't drink its mother's first milk—the special milk she produces the few hours after delivery. Believers are the same. Either new Christians drink the milk of the Word soon after salvation, or they may never experience the abundant *"life"* of John 10:10. Another observation: I never saw a newborn pig that did not hunger for its mother's milk. In the same way, a person who is legitimately born again will hunger for truth. But one of the most intriguing scenarios comes about during the weaning process. Had we not separated the young pigs from their mother, and placed them on meat products (fish and other high-powered protein), they would have nursed her the remainder of their days. What would they have grown up to be? They would have become RUNTS!! Conclusion: If you don't want to be a runt, progress to the *"meat"* of the Word. These Hebrew Christians were babes who needed to make the tough choice of progressing to spiritual maturity.

Next week we will study that famous chapter known as Hebrews 6. We are growing, so be encouraged!!

Hebrews 6 Questions

First Day

I would venture to say that no section of Scripture has stirred more debate than Hebrews 6:1-8. Remember to plug these passages into the historical setting of this book.

1.   Read Hebrews 6. Don't forget to pray. What were these believers to leave (v.1)? What were they to *"press on to"* (v.1)? How does this subject matter relate to what we studied in Hebrews 5:10-14?

2.   What type of *"foundation"* were these believers not to *"again"* lay (vv.1-2)? Have you always viewed the topics that make up this *"foundation"* as *"the elementary teaching about the Christ"* (v.1)? If not, why not? Considering what is stated in verses 1 and 2, have you yet graduated from *"elementary"* school? If not, what can you do about it?

3.   What does the writer mean by the words, *"repentance from dead works and of faith toward God"*? What Scriptures back up your answers?

4.   What does the writer mean by the words, *"instruction about washings, and laying on of hands"* (v.2)? What Scriptures back up your answers?

5.   What does the writer mean by the words, *"the resurrection of the dead, and eternal judgment"* (v.2)? What Scriptures back up your answers?

Second Day

1.　Read Hebrews 6.　What does verse 3 communicate to you?　How do verses 1 and 2, along with verse 3, confirm that this epistle was written to believers?

2.　Do verses 4 and 5 describe a believer or an unbeliever?　Why?　Note: The word *"tasted"* (verses 4 and 5) is from the same Greek root word used in Hebrews 2:9 to describe Jesus' *"death"* (*"that…He might taste death for everyone"*).　Also, the word *"partakers"* (Hebrews 6:4) is from the same Greek root word used in Hebrews 2:14 to describe the fact that Jesus *"partook"* of *"flesh and blood."*

3.　If verses 4 and 5 describe a believer, is it possible for us to lose our salvation and gain it back at a later date (v.6)?　If not, why not?　Considering the historical background of this book, why did the readers need to be reminded of this truth?

4.　What do 2Corinthians 5:17, Ephesians 1:13, Romans 8:35-39, John 10:29, and Hebrews 9:15 communicate regarding the security of the believer?　If it were possible to lose our salvation (through performing a single or series of unrighteous deeds), could we gain it back through good works?　How does Titus 3:5 tie in here?　Also, if our acts of sin could cause us to lose our salvation, how many, and what kind, would bring it about?

Third Day

1. Read Hebrews 6. In verses 7-8, the writer compares the fruit produced in a mature believer with the fruit of a believer who has compromised. As you study these verses, be sure to notice that the believer's fruit is emphasized and not the believer. What happens when a believer goes on to maturity and allows God to bear fruit through him/her (v.7)? What happens if a believer disobeys God and does not go on to maturity (v.8)? Is it the believer or the fruit of the believer that burns in this instance (v.8)? How does verse 8 tie in with Romans 8:1, 2Corinthians 5:10, and 1Corinthians 3:10-15?

2. What was the writer *"convinced of"* in verse 9? Why does verse 9 confirm that these readers were believers? How does verse 10 verify that the readers were believers?

3. What are the readers encouraged to do in verse 11? Was this *"diligence"* (v.11) for the purpose of holding on to their salvation or for the purpose of receiving a reward as a result of persevering (in God's strength, of course)? According to verse 12, who were they to imitate? Name some of the men of whom the writer might have been thinking. (For a hint, read Hebrews 11.)

Fourth Day

1. Read Hebrews 6. What great Old Testament believer is mentioned in verse 13? Did he live before or after the Law was established? Was he motivated by *"the promise"* of God or by Law (v.13)? What encouragement could these Hebrew Christians draw from Abraham's example?

2. Was Abraham required to wait for the fulfillment of God's *"promise"* regarding Isaac (v.15; Genesis 12:2-4)? According to Genesis 12:2-4 and Genesis 17:1-8, what was the minimum number of years that Abraham had to wait—considering that Isaac, the fulfillment of the first portion of the promise, was born sometime after Genesis 17:1-8? Why would the writer desire that his readers consider this subject matter?

3. What does verse 16 state about *"an oath"*? Did God seal His promise to Abraham with *"an oath"* (vv.13-14)? Has God remained faithful to the promise (and oath) that He made to Abraham? Now read verses 16-20. Did God make an oath when stating that Jesus would be *"a high priest forever according to the order of Melchizedek"* (vv.16, 17, and 20; Psalm 110:4; Hebrews 5:5-6)? (Remember this answer for future reference, especially when we study Hebrews 7:21.) As a result of this truth, with what degree of certainty could these readers view Christ as their true and faithful high priest? How should knowing this truth have affected their attitude toward the high priest and sacrificial system in Jerusalem?

Fifth Day

1. Read Hebrews 6. Is it possible *"for God to lie"* (v.18)? Why should this truth bring hope to the believer? How does this answer tie in with the phrase, *"we who have fled for refuge in laying hold of the hope set before us"* (v.18)?

2. This *"hope"* (v.18) serves what purpose in the life of a believer (v.19)? If an *"anchor"* prevents a boat from drifting, what is the writer communicating to his readers in verse 19? Where is this *"anchor"* positioned (v.19)? Considering the answer to the previous question, along with Hebrews 5:9, do you think this *"anchor"* is sufficient to hold the New Testament believer?

3. According to verses 19 and 20, Jesus entered inside *"the veil"* as a *"forerunner for us."* Challenge question: How do Ephesians 2:6 and 2Corinthians 5:8 tie in with this wonderful truth?

4. Again, what is *"the order"* of Christ's priesthood (v.20)? How long will He serve as our *"high priest"* (v.20)? Why would knowing this truth have encouraged these believers, especially in light of what we studied in Hebrews 4:14-15 and Hebrews 5:9?

Sixth Day

1. Read Hebrews 6. Read the entire lesson associated with this week's material and record any new insights.

Hebrews 6 Lesson

Before these Hebrew Christians could comprehend the significance of Christ's priesthood, a priesthood of the order of Melchizedek, they had to mature (Hebrews 5:10-14). So, guess what the writer addresses first as he leads them into the deeper truths of God? He addresses the issue of the security of the believer! This fact confirms what I have thought for years—that until we have settled this fundamental doctrinal issue, we will never walk in the assurance and rest available to all who believe. Hang on! It is going to be an eventful journey.

Hebrews 6:1-8 has stirred much debate within the body of Christ. Some people view these verses to be teaching that believers can lose their salvation. Others perceive them as validating the security of the believer (that believers cannot lose their salvation). Still others perceive them as describing unbelievers. Which perception is correct? Before we decide, we must: (1) Study the verses in question from a literal (and contextual) standpoint (2) Plug our findings into the historical setting of the book. By God's grace, this we will do.

The first phrase in Hebrews 6:1 states, "*Therefore leaving the elementary teaching about the Christ*":

> *Therefore leaving the elementary teaching about the Christ, let us press on to maturity, not laying again a foundation of repentance from dead works and of faith toward God, of instruction about washings, and laying on of hands, and the resurrection of the dead, and eternal judgment.* (Hebrews 6:1-2)

The word *"elementary"* actually means "the word of the beginning." The recipients of this letter knew the basics of the faith but had grown stagnant (review Hebrews 5:12). Thus, they were encouraged by the writer to *"press on to maturity"* (v.1). Hence, the readers were believers. Consequently, the school of thought that views these passages as addressing unbelievers must be incorrect—as will become increasingly apparent as we progress through verses 2-8.

The last portion of verse 1 and all of verse 2 list *"the elementary teaching"* these believers should have left behind: (1) *"repentance from dead works"* (2) *"faith toward God"* (3) *"instruction about washings"* (4) *"laying on of hands"* (5) *"the resurrection of the dead"* (6) *"eternal judgment."* Again, these theological issues are the basics of the faith that they should have grown past. We will take each of these six categories and discuss them in more detail.

(1) *"repentance from dead works"*

Because a New Testament believer is *"not under law, but under grace"* (Romans 6:14), these Hebrew Christians were to view anything associated with the temple sacrifices as *"dead works"*— and repent. That they considered returning to the sacrificial system confirmed their need to go on to spiritual maturity. They were to appropriate the fact that *"deeds...done in righteousness"* could not save them (Titus 3:5).

(2) *"faith toward God"*

These readers had accepted Christ through exercising personal repentance and *"faith"* (Ephesians 2:8-9) while depraved (while spiritually unregenerated). The *"faith"* to function in a particular area of spiritual gifting (1Peter 4:10), however, is a gift from God (Romans 12:3)— bestowed to New Testament believers when they are made new—subsequent to their exercising personal repentance and *"faith"* (Ephesians 2:8-9) while depraved. Therefore, the personal *"faith"* we exercised while depraved (Ephesians 2:8-9) differs from the gift of *"faith"* (Romans 12:3) we received when we were placed in Christ and made new. This truth is foundational. The recipients of this epistle were viewing faith from an incorrect vantage point. They were contemplating the impossible—giving up their faith (and salvation), reattaching themselves to the Law, and later, after the persecution from the unbelieving Jews subsided, exercising faith and being saved a second time. We will soon find that if we could lose our salvation, we could never gain it back. Consequently, what the readers were considering was totally unworkable.

(3) *"instruction about washings"*

The *"washings"* mentioned here are evidently the same as those addressed in Hebrews 9:10. They had to do with the ceremonial immersions associated with the Law and were worthless in bringing a believer to maturity. If the word *"washings"* does not refer to these immersions, but refers to Christian baptism, these readers needed to be baptized. Water baptism was the final act that severed a Hebrew Christian from Judaism. (Technically, under Israeli law, a Jewish believer was not reckoned a Christian until he was water baptized.)

This technicality meant that once these believers were water baptized, their faith would be known to even a greater degree among the unbelieving Jews. Persecution would then greatly intensify. If water baptism was refused, on the other hand, they would carry a guilty *"conscience"* toward *"God"* based on 1Peter 3:21—they would house shame for not severing ties with Judaism and proclaiming publicly (and to the greatest degree possible) their faith in Christ. Thus, according to 1Peter 3:21, water *"baptism"* would *"save"* them from carrying a guilty *"conscience,"* not "save" them from going to hell.

Next consider that both 1Peter and the epistle to the Hebrews were written to Jewish believers. How does this input relate to the Jewish believers addressed in the book of Hebrews? If they refused water baptism, and as a result failed to sever ties with Judaism, they would not only carry a guilty conscience, but would not be "saved" (in the physical sense) from the destruction of A.D. 70. Obviously, 1Peter 3:21 does <u>not</u> teach that water baptism "saves" us in the spiritual sense. In fact, no verse in God's Word communicates such an idea. Water baptism, rather, is a visible picture of what has already occurred spiritually in the life of a believer. The *Romans 1-8* study (distributed by this ministry) addresses this subject in greater detail.

(4) *"laying on of hands"*

Under the Law, priests and other leaders were commissioned through the laying on of *"hands"* (Numbers 8:10; Numbers 27:23). The recipients of this epistle were to grow past discussing such issues and press on to maturity.

(5) *"the resurrection of the dead"*

Jesus has been resurrected. This truth is the foundation of the Christian faith (1Corinthians 15:12-14). Some Hebrew Christians had been Pharisees as unbelievers (Pharisees believed in the resurrection of the dead). Other Hebrew Christians had been Sadducees as unbelievers (Sadducees, prior to exercising faith in Christ, did <u>not</u> believe in the *"resurrection"* of the dead— Luke 20:27). This fundamental truth was to be accepted by all believers even though the unbelieving Jews failed to acknowledge Christ's resurrection.

(6) *"eternal judgment"*

God will judge every person who rejects Christ (John 3:36). This fact cannot be denied. But, these believers were probably facing such questions as, "How can God be a loving God and send the unredeemed to hell?" A friend once explained *"eternal judgment"* in this manner: If lost mankind desires to exchange God's truth for a life of agony (both on the earth and later in hell), God loves them enough to grant them their desires. This explanation, which can never be accepted by those who choose to disbelieve, forever settles the issue. God is love (1John 4:8,

16). He will never force His love upon anyone—for forced love is no love at all. Actually, it is a crime (a subject covered in much detail in the *God's Heart* series distributed by this ministry). These Hebrew Christians needed to go on to spiritual maturity and allow those who had rejected Jesus to grapple with the elementary issues that truth alone can resolve.

The writer stated earlier (in Hebrews 6:1) that he, along with the recipients of this epistle, should *"press on to maturity."* He then records in verse 3 that such would occur *"if God permits"*:

> *And this we shall do, if God permits.* (Hebrews 6:3)

Indeed, all spiritual growth and maturity come from God. The redeemed, however, must pursue this spiritual growth and maturity before it is permitted. This fact confirms that: (1) Man possesses the freedom of choice (2) God, being a God of love (1John 4:8, 16), will never force His will upon anyone.

Conclusion: These believers could either pursue spiritual maturity or remain babes (Hebrews 5:13). If their choice was maturity, God's grace would bring about the change as they yielded to Christ's life within (Galatians 2:20; Colossians 1:27).

Passages such as Hebrews 6:4-6 have been debated for centuries, but actually are not difficult at all:

> *For in the case of those who have once been enlightened and have tasted of the heavenly gift and have been made partakers of the Holy Spirit, and have tasted the good word of God and the powers of the age to come, and then have fallen away, it is impossible to renew them again to repentance, since they again crucify to themselves the Son of God, and put Him to open shame.* (Hebrews 6:4-6)

The people described here are believers—not unbelievers. Having *"been enlightened"* (v.4), they had since *"endured"* much persecution for their faith (Hebrews 10:32). Why would they have been persecuted if they were not true believers? They had also *"tasted of the heavenly gift"* (Hebrews 6:4), as Jesus tasted *"death for everyone"* (Hebrews 2:9). Because Jesus tasted *"death"* and actually died (Hebrews 2:9), these readers, in tasting *"the heavenly gift"* (Hebrews 6:4), had actually received *"the heavenly gift."* The *"heavenly gift"* (Hebrews 6:4) in this instance is salvation (John 4:10), granted to New Testament believers who have exercised repentance and faith while depraved.

These readers had also become *"partakers of the Holy Spirit"* (Hebrews 6:4), just as Jesus *"partook"* of *"flesh and blood"* (Hebrews 2:14). Therefore, because Jesus literally took on *"flesh and blood"* (Hebrews 2:14), those addressed here had literally partaken *"of the Holy Spirit"* (Hebrews 6:4)—were born again. They had also *"tasted the good word of God"* (v.5) through the prophets who lived in their day. And finally, they had *"tasted...the powers of the age to come"* (v.5). The phrase, *"age to come,"* points to the Millennium. Because the recipients of this epistle were believers, they would reign *"with Christ for a thousand years"* (Revelation 20:4). Consequently, since they were one with Christ, they had already *"tasted"* of *"the powers of"* that *"age"* even before it had officially begun (Hebrews 6:5).

These Hebrew Christians had erroneously assumed that they could walk away from the faith and later, after the persecution from the unbelieving Jews had ceased, reattach themselves to Christ. But can believers lose their salvation (fall away) and gain it back at a later date? Hebrews 6:6 deems this loss and recovery an impossibility! Why? For this scenario to transpire, Jesus would have to be re-crucified (v.6). Yet, Jesus can be crucified only *"once"* (Hebrews 10:10). Thus, the situation described in verses 4-6 is hypothetical. If a man thinks he can lose his salvation one day and gain it back the next, he must somehow arrange for Jesus to die a second time. This second crucifixion, obviously, can never occur. The only hope for these Hebrew Christians was to proceed to spiritual maturity and accept God's grace to see them through.

Let's take a moment to discuss the impossibility of believers losing their salvation. Should the loss of salvation be possible, we must somehow define the number of sins required for this loss to transpire. Can you define the number? If they commit one sin, will they lose it? Are two sins enough? What about ten, or twenty? How many? And what kinds of sins must be committed? Lying, stealing, or even adultery—are they severe enough to bring it about? Do you see my point? If we cannot define such matters, how can believers who do not feel secure in Christ (and base their security on works) ever possess peace? They cannot!! Even worse, no unbeliever will desire what the apprehensive and anxious believer has in Christ. Can you see the need to settle this issue once and for all?! Thanks to the full counsel of God's Word, it is settled. Consider the following.

We are secure in Christ!! We have been placed *"in Christ"* (2Corinthians 5:17) and *"sealed in Him with the Holy Spirit of promise"* (Ephesians 1:13). Christ is *"in the Father"* (John 14:10), and we are *"in Christ"* (2Corinthians 5:17)—so we are in the Father as well. How secure does that make us? It makes us as secure as secure can be!! Nothing will ever *"separate us from the love of Christ"* (Romans 8:35-39), and nothing can *"snatch"* us *"out of the Father's hand"* (John 10:29). This security is why the writer states that Christ *"is able to save forever those who"* are His, *"since He always lives to make intercession for them"* (Hebrews 7:25). Consider this fact as well: If we could lose our salvation through works, we could have gained it through works—a topic addressed earlier in the course. But salvation through works is impossible (Titus 3:5).

In Hebrews 6:7-8, the writer compares the fruit produced in the believer who goes on to spiritual maturity with the fruit of a believer who has compromised:

> *For ground that drinks the rain which often falls upon it and brings forth vegetation useful to those for whose sake it is also tilled, receives a blessing from God; but if it yields thorns and thistles, it is worthless and close to being cursed, and it ends up being burned.* (Hebrews 6:7-8)

As you study these verses, be sure to notice that the believer's fruit is emphasized and not the believer. If a believer obeys God and goes on to spiritual maturity, good fruit will be manifested, as when the *"ground...drinks the rain"* and *"vegetation"* breaks forth (v.7). If a believer disobeys God and does not mature, he will yield bad fruit—*"thorns and thistles"* (v.8). Accordingly, the thorns and thistles are *"burned"* (v.8). (Note: Only the thorns and thistles are destroyed when a field is burned—not the ground itself. The ground produces vegetation soon afterwards.) Therefore, these verses do not teach that the believer who yields bad fruit burns in hell. Only his/her fruit *"is burned,"* as validated by 1Corinthians 3:10-15.

We must possess an accurate view of the believer's judgment.

To properly understand Hebrews 6:7-8, we must possess an accurate view of the believer's judgment. Did you realize that every New Testament saint will *"appear before the judgment seat of Christ"* (2Corinthians 5:10)? This judgment is for rewards—not condemnation (Romans 8:1). This same judgment is addressed in 1Corinthians 3:10-15. If a *"man's work"* (fruit) *"remains"* after being tested by *"fire,"* he will *"receive a reward."* (This *"reward"* is the *"blessing from God"* addressed in Hebrews 6:7). If his *"work"* (fruit) *"is burned up, he shall suffer loss,"* but will *"be saved, yet so as through fire"* (1Corinthians 3:15). Had these Hebrew Christians returned to the sacrificial system in Jerusalem, they would have positioned themselves to receive fewer rewards at the judgment seat of Christ. Hebrews 6 deals with this loss of rewards, not with whether or not these believers could lose their salvation. Had they disobeyed God, returned to the Law and died in Jerusalem, their salvation would have remained intact. Keep in mind what we have learned regarding the security of the believer. Also remember that believers reap *"the consequences"* of their sin in this life even though forgiven (Colossians 3:25).

The writer states that he is *"convinced of better things concerning"* these Hebrew Christians, *"things that accompany salvation"* (Hebrews 6:9). These statements again confirm that he is addressing believers. He is not saying that they must perform good deeds to gain, regain, or even maintain their salvation. He is dealing specifically with the fruit that would be manifested through their yielding to Christ. Thus the phrase, *"things that accompany salvation"* (v.9), refers to the fruit that Christ would produce in and through them as they matured in the faith. Knowing that God had made them into *"holy brethren"* (review the lesson on Hebrews 3:1), the writer realized that they would act in a manner consistent with their identity should they refrain from compromise. By doing so, they would grow past *"the elementary teaching"* mentioned in Hebrews 6:1-2, and God's fruit exhibited through their lives would be brilliantly manifested as they basked in Sabbath rest.

These readers are reminded that God would not *"forget"* their ministry *"to the saints"* (believers) in the past and the present:

> *For God is not unjust so as to forget your work and the love which you have shown toward His name, in having ministered and in still ministering to the saints.* (Hebrews 6:10)

Tying this passage to verse 7, these deeds obviously will bring rewards and blessings at the judgment seat of Christ. The writer desires that they show *"diligence"* (earnestness or zeal), for only then could they reap the full benefit of their salvation— *"realize the full assurance of hope until the end"* (v.11) as they faced the trials before them:

> *And we desire that each one of you show the same diligence so as to realize the full assurance of hope until the end,* (Hebrews 6:11)

Again, they were not to be diligent for the purpose of holding to their salvation, but to receive a reward as a result of persevering—in God's strength, of course. They were *"not"* to *"be sluggish"* (slothful, lazy), *"but imitators of those who through faith and patience inherit the promises"*:

> *that you may not be sluggish, but imitators of those who through faith and patience inherit the promises.* (Hebrews 6:12)

Clearly, the writer is saying: "Look guys, appropriate your faith and all will be well. But returning to Law will bring nothing but heartache and physical death—not loss of salvation. Take time to consider how previous believers persevered when confronted with similar difficulties."

In Hebrews 11, the writer will mention a long list of believers who persevered under trial. For now he mentions only *"Abraham"* (Hebrews 6:13-15), the father of the Jewish nation and a man beloved of Jews everywhere. Because he lived <u>before</u> the Law and the Levitical priesthood were established, he lived a life of faith apart from the Law:

> *For the promise to Abraham or to his descendants that he would be heir of the world was not through the Law, but through the righteousness of faith.* (Romans 4:13)

Abraham's example could encourage these Hebrew Christians, for he walked in a manner pleasing to God, motivated totally by God's promise. Keep this example in mind as we proceed.

Abraham knew God's *"promise"*—the *"promise"* relating to Isaac and his future descendants:

> *For when God made the promise to Abraham, since He could swear by no one greater, He swore by Himself, saying, "I WILL SURELY BLESS YOU, AND I WILL SURELY MULTIPLY YOU."* (Hebrews 6:13-14)

He understood well that the terms of the *"promise"* were unconditional. For God to remain true and faithful, under no circumstance could He violate His Word.

Note that when God *"made"* this *"promise,"* He later *"swore by Himself"* (Hebrews 6:13). This swearing means that He made an oath, an oath being "the confirmation of a compact, guaranteeing the discharge of liabilities." Thus, an oath guarantees the fulfillment of the conditions of a promise. Considering that the initiator of *"the promise"* and oath is *"greater"* than all (v.13), and *"cannot lie"* (Titus 1:2), Abraham could rest assured that what God had promised would be fulfilled.

But what was the promise, and what was the oath? God initially gave the promise to Abraham in Genesis 12:2:

> *And I will make you a great nation, and I will bless you, and make your name great; and so*
> *you shall be a blessing;* (Genesis 12:2)

Abraham *"was seventy-five years old"* when the promise was made (Genesis 12:4), but the oath did not come until later. Hebrews 6:14 seems to be a direct quote from Genesis 22:17, so I assume that this is when the oath was introduced—after Abraham had obeyed by placing Isaac on the altar (read Genesis 22:16-17 to see if you agree). If, instead, the writer is referring to God's statements in Genesis 17:1-8 (when Abraham *"was ninety-nine years old"*—the year before Isaac was born), it makes no difference. Either way, Abraham was forced to wait at least 25 years—the time between Genesis 12:2 and Isaac's birth—before beginning to receive what God had guaranteed. The writer's point is that Abraham had to exercise patience to receive even the first portion of the promise—Isaac.

Has God remained faithful to the balance of His promise? He certainly has! In fact, through Isaac, Abraham's son, the Jewish nation has multiplied tremendously. Jesus was born a Jew as part of this promise as well (Galatians 3:16). Also consider that Abraham is the spiritual father of all who believe, both Jews and Gentiles (Romans 4:13; Galatians 3:7, 29). Yes, what God says He will do, He will do.

Abraham exercised much patience in waiting for the fulfillment of even the first portion of the promise:

> *And thus, having patiently waited, he obtained the promise.* (Hebrews 6:15)

These Hebrew Christians could take courage in this, for if Abraham walked with the Lord amidst uncertainties, obeying without Laws and rituals, so could they. The writer, in other words, is saying, "Consider Abraham, stop thinking about going back under the hollow sacrificial system in Jerusalem, and walk on in faith! Abraham persevered by establishing intimacy with God and going on to maturity. So must you!"

The writer seems to speak of a different *"oath"* in verses 16-20—God's *"oath"* associated with Christ's priesthood. (Tie verse 17 in with verses 18-20 and see if you agree.) Christ's priesthood (of *"the order of Melchizedek"*) is not a new topic; it was introduced in Hebrews 5:5-10. When man makes *"an oath,"* he swears by someone *"greater than"* himself:

> *For men swear by one greater than themselves, and with them an oath given as confirmation is*
> *an end of every dispute.* (Hebrews 6:16)

This *"oath"* confirms man's determination to fulfill the promise, and thus the *"dispute"* ends (v.16). Because God is God of all, He could swear by no one greater than Himself. Therefore when He, the God of all truth, sealed this *"promise...with an oath"* (v.17), its fulfillment was sealed as well:

> *In the same way God, desiring even more to show to the heirs of the promise the*
> *unchangeableness of His purpose, interposed with an oath,* (Hebrews 6:17)

Also consider Psalm 110:4:

> *The Lord has sworn and will not change His mind, "Thou art a priest forever according to the order of Melchizedek." (Psalm 110:4)*

Did you notice that God attached an oath to this promise? (Hebrews 7:21 will further confirm this truth.) So Christ's priesthood most definitely was *"interposed with an oath"* (Hebrews 6:17). Remember this *"oath"* for future reference.

Jesus is the believer's *"hope"* (1Timothy 1:1), along with *"the gospel"* that He presented to man (Colossians 1:23). Consequently, it is the good news of Christ's gospel that brings *"hope"* to our souls:

> *in order that by two unchangeable things, in which it is impossible for God to lie, we may have strong encouragement, we who have fled for refuge in laying hold of the hope set before us.*
> (Hebrews 6:18)

This *"hope"* is our *"refuge"* (v.18), guaranteeing victory both in this life and the life to come. Because *"it is impossible for God to lie"* (v.18), all who have laid *"hold of"* this *"hope"* (through *"laying hold"* of Christ) should be strongly encouraged (v.18). First, the believer's *"hope,"* being *"an anchor,"* adds stability to the soul:

> *This hope we have as an anchor of the soul, a hope both sure and steadfast and one which enters within the veil, where Jesus has entered as a forerunner for us, having become a high priest forever according to the order of Melchizedek. (Hebrews 6:19-20)*

Since this *"anchor"* of *"hope"* is positioned *"within the veil"* (v.19), where Jesus resides (v.20), it is hooked solidly and can never be removed. Therefore, if these Hebrew Christians would appropriate their faith, and resulting hope, Christ could prevent them from drifting back into Judaism. Second, Christ is a *"forerunner for us, having become a high priest forever according to the order of Melchizedek"* (v.20). By using the word *"forerunner,"* the writer suggests that others would follow Christ into the presence of God. Thus, while New Testament saints are still on earth, somehow (and I don't pretend to understand everything associated with this wonderful truth) they are also *"seated...in the heavenly places, in Christ Jesus"* (Ephesians 2:6). Later, after their bodies cease to operate, their spirits and souls will join Christ in heaven (2Corinthians 5:8). As a result, these believers are encouraged to walk in hope as they wait for the fulfillment of God's promises both in this life and the life to come.

As their eternal *"high priest,"* even as *"a high priest...according to the order of Melchizedek"* (v.20), Christ would be their *"source of eternal salvation"* (Hebrews 5:9)—not a salvation that could be lost and regained. Jesus had *"entered"* inside *"the veil"* of the tabernacle in heaven (Hebrews 6:19-20), and, as their high priest, understood their *"weaknesses"* (Hebrews 4:14-15). This knowledge should encourage them to go boldly *"to the throne of grace,"* to *"receive mercy and...find grace to help in time of need"* (Hebrews 4:16). If they did so, they would grow in their intimacy with Christ, which would result in spiritual maturity, which would bring discernment, which would allow them to see their need to forever abandon rules and regulations for a life lived in the leading and fellowship of the Holy Spirit.

*E*ternal salvation cannot be lost and regained.

To return to Judaism made absolutely no sense, for the sacrificial system in Jerusalem was totally obsolete. They were to follow Abraham's example and continue in faith—regardless of the circumstances. From the background information included in the **Introduction**, we realize that this path was their path of choice.

For sure, the book of Hebrews is filled with meaty theology that is well worth our time. Much good news, therefore, awaits us.

Hebrews 7 Questions

First Day

1.   Read Hebrews 7. This chapter addresses the priesthood of Christ and how it, being of the order of Melchizedek, supersedes the Aaronic priesthood. How is Melchizedek described in verse 1? What two offices did Melchizedek hold (v.1)? Challenge question: Did Aaron or any of his descendants hold the office of both *"king"* and *"priest"*? Jesus holds what offices today (1Timothy 1:17; Revelation 15:3; 1Chronicles 17:11-12; Hebrews 5:5-6)? Zechariah 6:12-13 speaks of Christ during the Millennium (His one thousand year reign on earth). What offices will He, as *"Branch,"* occupy? From what geographical location will He rule (Psalm 2:6-8)? How is this truth regarding Christ similar to what we studied regarding Melchizedek?

2.   Read Genesis 14 to understand the phrase, *"who met Abraham as he was returning from the slaughter of the kings and blessed him"* (v.1). Who blessed whom when Abraham and Melchizedek met? Who then was the greater, Abraham or Melchizedek? If Melchizedek was a *"priest,"* what does verse 1 communicate regarding the purpose of the priesthood?

3.   According to Hebrews 7:2, what did Abraham do with a portion of the *"spoils"*? Remember your answer for future reference. The translation of Melchizedek's name is given in verse 2. What does it mean? Taking into consideration Psalm 76:2, and tying it in with Hebrews 7:2, Melchizedek was *"king"* over what city?

Second Day

1. Read Hebrews 7. Don't forget to pray. How is Melchizedek described in verse 3? Does this description of Melchizedek mean that he had no *"father"* or *"mother,"* no *"beginning of days nor end of life"*? Or could it point to the fact that this information is not included in the Scriptures? Read Exodus 28:1, Numbers 18:7, and Ezra 2:61-63, and record what was required of a man before he could function as high priest under the Law. Based on this input, why would the writer describe Melchizedek as he does in Hebrews 7:3 if his goal was to prove that Christ's priesthood, after the order of Melchizedek, is greater than the Aaronic priesthood?

2. Keep in mind that Melchizedek was a type of Christ, and was *"made like the Son of God"* (v.3). This fact confirms that he was not the Son of God. Jesus did not become a man (God-man) until He was conceived of the Holy Spirit in Mary's womb. How does this truth, along with Hebrews 5:1, confirm that Melchizedek could not have been Christ?

3. According to Genesis 14:20 and Hebrews 7:4, what did Abraham do with a portion of the *"spoils"*? From Hebrews 7:5, along with Numbers 18:21 and 26, who received tithes under the Law, and from whom did they receive them? How do verses 4 and 5 of Hebrews 7 confirm that Christ's priesthood, after the order of Melchizedek, is greater than Aaron's priesthood—the obsolete priesthood associated with the Law?

4. How do verses 6 and 7 confirm that Christ's priesthood, of the order of Melchizedek, is greater than the Aaronic priesthood?

Third Day

1. Read Hebrews 7. What does verse 8 say about those who received *"tithes"* under the Law? How does this same verse describe Melchizedek? In what way does this validate the superiority of Christ's priesthood (being of the order of Melchizedek)? (Remember that Melchizedek *"lives on"* in the sense that his genealogy is not recorded in Scripture. He, being a man, experienced physical death.)

2. How do verses 9 and 10 confirm that Christ's priesthood, of the order of *"Melchizedek,"* is greater than the priesthood associated with the Law?

3. From verse 11, why was it necessary *"for another priest to arise according to the order of Melchizedek"?* How does this truth relate to Romans 3:20, Romans 3:28, Romans 5:20, Galatians 2:21, Galatians 3:11, Galatians 3:21, and Philippians 3:9? Who was this other priest?

4. According to verse 12 of Hebrews 7, what must occur *"when the priesthood is changed"?* Does the Melchizedekian priesthood, therefore, need the Mosaic Law to carry out its purpose? How can we know this? (Don't make this question more difficult than it actually is.) According to Romans 8:2, under what *"law"*—*"law"* here meaning "principle"—does the Melchizedekian priesthood function (Romans 8:2)?

Fourth Day

1. Read Hebrews 7. What do verses 13 and 14 of Hebrews 7 say about the lineage of Christ? Taking this input, along with what is communicated in Numbers 3:6-10, could Jesus have served as high priest under the Mosaic Law? If not, why not?

2. What do verses 15, 16, and 17 of Hebrews 7 state about Christ's priesthood and its duration? If verse 17 is a quote from Psalm 110:4, and if David wrote this psalm, what does this make David?

3. What does verse 18 of Hebrews 7 state about the Law? How does this input regarding the Law tie in with Romans 6:14? Does the Law then serve a purpose? If so, what purpose (Galatians 3:24)?

4. How often could God be approached under the Law, and who could approach Him (Leviticus 16:2, 29-34)? How often can we who believe approach Him now (Hebrews 4:14-16)? How does this wonderful truth relate to Hebrews 7:19?

Fifth Day

1. Read Hebrews 7. From verses 20-22, list even more reasons why Jesus' priesthood is superior to that of the priests who served under the Law. How does this input relate to what we studied in Hebrews 6:16-20?

2. Verses 23 and 24 of Hebrews 7 give yet another reason why Jesus' priesthood is superior to the Aaronic priesthood. What is that reason? The word *"forever"* in verse 25 means "completely." Tying these facts in with the phrase, *"He always lives to make intercession for them"* (v.25), what conclusions do you draw? Would you say that you are secure in Christ if you are a believer? If so, why? If not, why not?

3. Verses 26-28 of Hebrews 7 contrast Jesus with the priests who ministered under the Law. Take your time and list every difference addressed in these passages.

Sixth Day

1. Read Hebrews 7. Read this week's lesson and record any new insights. Make sure to digest as much of the lesson as possible. It is rich!

Hebrews 7 Lesson

This chapter deals with the priesthood of Christ and how it, being of the order of Melchizedek, supersedes the Aaronic priesthood.

Scripture doesn't provide an abundance of information regarding Melchizedek, but we do know that he was *"king of Salem"* (Jerusalem), and God's *"priest"*:

> *For this Melchizedek, king of Salem, priest of the Most High God, who met Abraham as he was returning from the slaughter of the kings and blessed him,* (Hebrews 7:1)

Melchizedek was both *"king"* and *"priest,"* an honor that no priest under the Levitical system received. Jesus is both *"King"* (1Timothy 1:17; Revelation 15:3; 1Chronicles 17:11-12) and *"priest"* (Hebrews 5:5-7) and will reign over the earth (Zechariah 6:12-13; Zechariah 14:9; Psalm 72:8) during the Millennium. Jesus also will rule from Jerusalem (Psalm 2:6-8)—as was the case with Melchizedek. Obviously then, Melchizedek was a type of Christ, although he was not (nor ever will be) equal with Christ.

Did you notice that Melchizedek was *"priest of the Most High God"* (v.1; Genesis 14:18-20)? None is greater than our God!! None!! He is the sovereign Ruler over the entire universe, and not just over Israel. In fact, the name used for *"God"* (*"God Most High"*—Genesis 14:18-20) is *El Elyon*, a more universal name. Because Melchizedek served as *"priest of the Most High God"* (Hebrews 1:1), he was a priest to all nations. The Levitical priests, on the other hand, ministered to the nation of Israel alone. Therefore, if Jesus' priesthood is of the order of Melchizedek, and not of the order of Aaron, He can minister to all nationalities, not just to Jews. Wonderful!!

"Abraham," the father of the Jewish nation, is again mentioned in the last half of Hebrews 7:1. If you read all of Genesis 14, you will understand why. There Abraham came to the defense of Lot, who had been taken captive during the battle of the five kings against the four. After Abraham defeated the kings and rescued Lot, along with the spoils of battle, Melchizedek met Abraham and *"blessed him"* (Genesis 14:17-20). Abraham responded by giving Melchizedek *"a tenth of"* the spoils (Genesis 14:20). Since it is impossible to digest Hebrews 7 without this backdrop, remember its location and use it for future reference.

Because Melchizedek *"blessed"* Abraham when he returned *"from the slaughter of the kings"* (Hebrews 7:1), Melchizedek was greater than Abraham. From this situation, we can see that one of the main purposes of his priesthood was to issue blessings on mankind. Abraham also gave Melchizedek *"a tenth…of…the spoils"* (v.2), which will be discussed in more detail later. But notice that verse 2 gives the meaning (translation) of Melchizedek's name:

> *to whom also Abraham apportioned a tenth part of all the spoils, was first of all, by the translation of his name, king of righteousness, and then also king of Salem, which is king of peace.* (Hebrews 7:2)

Melchizedek, his personal *"name,"* means *"king of righteousness."* *"Melchizedek"* as a title, however, means *"king of Salem."* Since *"Salem"* means "peaceful," Melchizedek's title was *"king of peace."* Note: *"Salem,"* in Psalm 76:2, is Jerusalem. Therefore, Melchizedek was *"king"* over the city of Jerusalem (Hebrews 7:1-2).

In verse 3 we find that Melchizedek was:

> *Without father, without mother, without genealogy, having neither beginning of days nor end of life, but made like the Son of God, he abides a priest perpetually.* (Hebrews 7:3)

That he is described as having neither *"father"* nor *"mother"* does not mean that he had no father or mother, but rather that Scripture does not record his genealogy. This lack of record verifies that his lineage could not be traced back to any particular individual. The Law, on the other hand, required that a man trace his lineage back to Aaron before serving as priest (Exodus 28:1; Numbers 18:7; Ezra 2:61-63). Thus, under the Aaronic priesthood, a man became priest through pedigree. Under the Melchizedekian priesthood, on the other hand, a man became priest by divine appointment. Consequently, because Scripture gives no account of Melchizedek's birth, genealogy, or death, he is also described as *"having neither beginning of days nor end of life"* (Hebrews 7:3). In this regard (because Scripture does not record his birth or death) he was *"made like the Son of God"* and *"abides a priest perpetually"* (Hebrews 7:3). The writer, by no stretch of the imagination, is indicating that Melchizedek did not die.

In light of the fact that Jesus possesses eternal life, life with no beginning or end, it is easy to see how Melchizedek could be a <u>type</u> of Christ. Think on the following as well: Melchizedek is said to abide as *"a priest perpetually"* (v.3) in the sense that Scripture does not record his death—pointing to the fact that Christ's priesthood, unlike Aaron's, will continue throughout eternity. What amazing news!! This truth will serve us well while studying the remainder of this epistle. Melchizedek, as a <u>type</u> of Christ, was *"made <u>like</u> the Son of God"* (v.3—emphasis added). He was not, therefore, the Son of God.

Melchizedek was a *"man"* (v.4), since all priests were *"taken from among men"* (Hebrews 5:1). Jesus, Who is God (Hebrews 1:8), did not become a man (God-man) until He was conceived of the Holy Spirit in His mother's womb. This difference is another reason why Melchizedek (a man who lived during Old Testament times) could not have been Christ.

Remember, Melchizedek received *"a tenth of the choicest spoils"* from Abraham (Genesis 14:20; Hebrews 7:4), which validates the superiority of Melchizedek's priesthood. How so? Aaron, a descendant of Abraham and *"Levi"* (Hebrews 7:5), served under a priestly order that received tithes from the sons of Abraham (v.5). Because Melchizedek received tithes from Abraham, and *"blessed"* Abraham (v.6), he was *"greater"* than Abraham (v.7). If Melchizedek was *"greater"* than Abraham, then Melchizedek's priesthood was superior to Aaron's, Aaron being Abraham's offspring.

Ponder this thought as well: Under Aaron's priesthood *"mortal men receive tithes"* (v.8), meaning that these priests eventually died. Melchizedek, as a type of Christ, *"lives on"* (v.8) in the sense that Scripture does not record his death. (Actually, the Melchizedekian priesthood *"lives on"*—not Melchizedek himself. Verse 8 is not stating that Melchizedek avoided physical death.) Jesus Christ is the only high priest Who serves eternally, of Whom Melchizedek is a picture. The fact that *"Levi"* was in Abraham's *"loins"* (gene pool) when *"Abraham...paid tithes"* to Melchizedek (vv.9-10) confirms that Melchizedek's priesthood, and thus Christ's priesthood, is greater than Aaron's (the Levitical priesthood).

Had Aaron's priesthood—the Levitical priesthood established under the Mosaic Law—made the worshipper perfect, there would have been no *"need"* to establish another *"priesthood"*:

> *Now if perfection was through the Levitical priesthood (for on the basis of it the people received the Law), what further need was there for another priest to arise according to the order of Melchizedek, and not be designated according to the order of Aaron?* (Hebrews 7:11)

Since the Law brought perfection to no one (Romans 3:20, 28; 5:20; Galatians 2:21; 3:11, 21; Philippians 3:9), God established a different *"priesthood,"* a *"priesthood...according to the order of Melchizedek"* (Hebrews 7:11). Christ serves as high priest in this new order. Notice too that *"when the priesthood is changed,"* the *"law"* under which it functions changes as well (v.12). The Melchizedekian priesthood existed as far back as Genesis 14 and functioned without the Mosaic Law—the Mosaic Law and the Levitical priesthood were not established until later. This chronological sequence confirms that the Melchizedekian order can function void of Law. So the writer records:

> *For when the priesthood is changed, of necessity there takes place a change of law also,"*
> (Hebrews 7:12)

His message: This different priesthood does not need the Mosaic Law to carry out its purpose.

Also consider that the Levitical priesthood was so closely linked to the moral Law given to Moses that one could not function without the other. When God gave the Law, He presented His righteous standard to man. God knew, however, that man was incapable of keeping this Law, for it was given to bring conviction of *"sin"* (Romans 3:20)—to allow man in his depravity to see his need for a Savior (Galatians 3:24). Because man could not keep the Law, God instituted a priesthood and sacrificial system through which man could receive atonement (covering) for sins committed under the Law. (Note: The offerings presented by the priests only atoned for, or covered, man's sin; they did not remove man's sin.) An imperfect system cannot bring *"perfection"* (Hebrews 7:11).

However, this system served the special purpose of verifying that the solution to man's dilemma was a perfect priest who could remove man's sin. In fact, the inferior system was a picture of what Christ would accomplish as our High Priest!! Thus, the Mosaic Law presented the problem while the Levitical system illustrated the solution that it simply could not provide. Jesus is the solution!! But if the priesthood was to be changed from the Levitical priesthood to Christ's, a priesthood according to the order of Melchizedek (Hebrews 5:6), the law under which it operated had to be changed as well. Verse 12 exactly communicates this change: *"For when the priesthood is changed, of necessity there takes place a change of law also."* The fact that the New Testament believer is no longer under the Mosaic Law but under the liberating *"law of the Spirit"* (Romans 8:2) should cause all church saints everywhere to fall to their knees and worship.

Can you see what the writer is accomplishing? He is confirming that New Testament believers would be foolish to submit themselves to the statutes and ordinances of such an outdated, obsolete system as the Levitical system.

Jesus *"descended from"* the *"tribe"* of *"Judah,"* David's tribe (Romans 1:3), a *"tribe...from which no one has officiated at the altar"* (Hebrews 7:13-14). Aaron, however, was from the tribe of *"Levi"* (Exodus 6:16-20), which explains why Aaron's priesthood is called the Levitical (or Aaronic) priesthood. Only Aaron and his descendants could serve as priests under the Law (Exodus 28:1). The remaining Levites served as ministers to the priests (Numbers 3:6-10).

The fact that Jesus' and Aaron's tribes differed confirms that Jesus' priesthood is of a different order than Aaron's (Hebrews 7:13-14). Verse 15 describes Jesus as *"another priest"*—not an additional priest, but One different from that of the Aaronic priesthood—-Who would serve *"according to the likeness of Melchizedek"* (v.15). The old priesthood (the Aaronic priesthood) was based upon *"a law of physical requirement,"* but the new priesthood (Jesus's priesthood) is *"according to the power of an indestructible life"* (v.16). The old priesthood functioned with priests who descended

The new priesthood is carried out by a Priest Who lives eternally.

from Aaron and performed temporarily (until death), whereas the new priesthood is carried out by a Priest Who lives eternally. Consequently, the Priest who serves in the Melchizedekian order must be a man (God-man) who lives eternally—of which Melchizedek was a type. Because Jesus lives eternally, and is God-man, He serves as high priest perpetually. Thus, Jesus is *"a priest forever according to the order of Melchizedek"* (v.17)!

These verses confirm that David was a prophet. How so? The statement, *"Thou art a priest forever according to the order of Melchizedek"* (v.17) quotes Psalm 110:4. David, who wrote this psalm, obviously realized that the Aaronic priesthood would one day be replaced by Christ's priesthood, a priesthood *"according to the order of Melchizedek"* (v.17).

Note what the writer states in the next passage:

> *For, on the one hand, there is a setting aside of a former commandment because of its weakness and uselessness.* (Hebrews 7:18)

Do you comprehend what this means? The Law has been set *"aside"* in the life of a New

Testament believer. We are no longer *"under law, but under grace"* (Romans 6:14). But be careful here. We must not throw the baby out with the bathwater. The Law is weak and useless (Hebrews 7:18) in that it condemns you for your wrongs but cannot empower you to do right. Yet, the Law serves an extremely important function in the life of an unbeliever. It allows those who are without Christ to see their need for a Savior (Galatians 3:24; 1Timothy 1:9-10).

"The Law" could make *"nothing perfect"* (Hebrews 7:19). But after the old priesthood was laid aside, *"a better hope"* was established, a *"hope"* through which we can *"draw near to God"* (v.19). Considering that *"Jesus...is our hope"* (1Timothy 1:1), as well as our *"faithful high priest"* (Hebrews 2:17), God's *"throne"* is constantly accessible to us (Hebrews 4:14-16). Under the old system, only the high priest could approach God's presence one day of the year (on the Day of Atonement—Leviticus 16:2, 29-34). Through Jesus, we can have communication, association, relationship, kinship, union, and intimacy with our Father every moment of every day. Clearly, Jesus brought in *"a better hope"* (v.19).

Christ's priesthood is superior for several reasons, one of which is mentioned in Hebrews 7:20-21. It was confirmed with *"an oath"* (v.20) which stated that His priesthood is *"forever"* (v.21). God's Word alone would have been enough, but the *"oath"* confirmed the certainty of Christ's eternal priesthood. God would *"not change His mind"* (v.21). Neither Aaron nor the priests who served after him (under the old priesthood) received an *"oath"* from God (v.21). As a result, God could withdraw the Aaronic priesthood whenever He desired. Because *"Jesus has become the guarantee of a better covenant"* (v.22), He is responsible for carrying out the obligations of this *"better covenant."* We will address this topic in more depth when we study Hebrews 8.

Many advantages accompany Jesus' priesthood, for the priests under the Law served temporarily (v.23). Aaron died and was succeeded by Eleazar (Numbers 20:22-28). Eleazar then died and was succeeded by Phinehas (Joshua 24:33; Judges 20:28). Therefore, between the death of a high priest and the ordination of his successor, the priesthood was temporarily vacated. Not so with Jesus. He lives on, and his priesthood is permanent and uninterrupted:

> *but He, on the other hand, because He abides forever, holds His priesthood permanently.*
> (Hebrews 7:24)

Just think of what this permanence means! We who know Jesus are secure—we cannot lose our salvation:

> *Hence, also, He is able to save forever those who draw near to God through Him, since He always lives to make intercession for them.* (Hebrews 7:25)

The word *"forever"* means "completely." Our salvation is not a partially done project to be completed later. When we were justified (saved), our salvation (from the penalty of sin) was complete—*"forever."* We were made permanent members of God's family because our high priest is a perpetual priest Who *"always lives to make intercession for"* us (v.25). Thus, it is His responsibility to keep us saved—never ours!

Through Jesus we can also *"draw near to God"* (v.25). The Law was incapable of establishing intimacy between the worshipper and the Father. In fact, Exodus 20:19 records that Israel, after receiving the Ten Commandments from Jehovah, desired that Moses *"speak"* to them instead of God. Only through the Spirit of God, God's gift subsequent to our repenting and believing while depraved, can we call God, *"Abba! Father!"* (Romans 8:15-16)

Undoubtedly, Jesus does the saving, not those who believe in Him—*'He is able to save forever those who draw near to God through Him"* (v.25). Stated differently, it is our Lord's responsibility to save us and keep us saved—not ours. Basically, all we did was exercise personal repentance and faith while depraved (while spiritually unregenerated). In response, He caused us to be born again. Salvation, therefore, is a *"gift"*—not a result of our good deeds (Ephesians 2:8-9; Titus 3:5). After all, to exercise faith while depraved is not a work (read Romans 3:27-28, 4:5, and

Romans 9:32). Neither can we retain our salvation through good works, for it is retained *"forever"* through (and by) Christ!! Because He lives forever, He saves *"forever."* Hence, for us to lose our salvation, Jesus must cease to exist. But we have already confirmed that He is *"a priest forever"* (Hebrews 7:17). Clearly, the believer is safe, sealed, and secure in Christ.

*B*ecause He lives forever, He saves *"forever."*

Hebrews 7:26 describes Jesus as our *"high priest"*:

> *For it was fitting that we should have such a high priest, holy, innocent, undefiled, separated from sinners and exalted above the heavens;* (Hebrews 7:26)

Jesus differs from the Levitical priests in that He is *"holy," "innocent,"* and *"undefiled."* He has never sinned nor will He ever sin, whereas Levitical priests sinned regularly (v.27). He is also *"separated from sinners"* (v.26) in that His present ministry as high priest is in heaven, away from evil (He has been *"exalted above the heavens"*—v.26). Thus, Jesus' ministry as high priest did not begin until <u>after</u> His crucifixion. Consequently, He <u>became</u> a *"high priest"* (Hebrews 2:17), meaning that He has not always been a *"high priest."*

The writer continues describing Jesus' priesthood in Hebrews 7:27:

> *who does not need daily, like those high priests, to offer up sacrifices, first for His own sins, and then for the sins of the people, because this He did once for all when He offered up Himself.* (Hebrews 7:27)

Unlike the Levitical priests, Jesus is not required to *"offer up sacrifices...for His own sins"* (Hebrews 7:27). Why would He offer sacrifices for sins He never commits? Also, since Jesus died for *"all"* the *"sins"* of mankind (v.27), He was required to die only *"once"* (v.27). His sacrifice for mankind was final, unlike the sacrifices the Levitical priests offered *"daily"* on behalf *"of the people"* (v.27).

That Jesus' priesthood is superior to the priesthood associated with the Law becomes more and more apparent. Note verse 28:

> *For the Law appoints men as high priests who are weak, but the word of the oath, which came after the Law, appoints a Son, made perfect forever.* (Hebrews 7:28)

The Law appointed *"weak" "men as high priests"*— *"weak"* in the sense that they would die (v.28). These priests also sinned (v.27). But Jesus was appointed with an *"oath...after the Law"* was instituted (v.28). For this reason He is our eternal high priest. After all, He is the eternal resurrected *"Son"* who is *"made perfect forever"* (v.28).

Next week we will begin studying the sanctuary (tabernacle) in which Jesus ministers in heaven. We will also compare the new covenant (grace) with the old covenant (Law). The material will be very informative, so spend as much time as possible working through next week's questions and lesson. We are growing!!

Hebrews 8 Questions

First Day

1. Read Hebrews 8. Notice that much of what the writer states in verses 1-6 has been mentioned earlier. Are you, when given opportunities to share or teach, concerned about repeating yourself? If so, why? Was this a concern for Peter (2Peter 1:12-13)?

2. What is *"the main point"* the writer has been communicating (v.1)? Where is Jesus, even at this very moment, serving as *"high priest"* (v.1)? How do the following verses relate to Hebrews 8:1: Psalm 20:6; 44:3; 60:5; 63:8; 118:16; 138:7? Would you say you are secure *"in Christ"* (2Corinthians 5:17), or are you in danger of losing your salvation?

3. According to verse 1, what posture did Jesus assume when He entered heaven as our *"high priest"*? Did the earthly priests sit down, or were they up and about performing the duties of the priesthood? Would you say that Christ's sacrifice was superior to the sacrifices offered by the Levitical priests? If so, why?

Second Day

1. Read Hebrews 8. Where does Jesus *"minister"* today (v.2)? Where did the earthly priests minister (v.2)? Which ministry is the greater and why?

2. Refer to the diagram titled "The Earthly Tabernacle" located in the Reference Section. The earthly tabernacle consisted of three parts. List them. What was its length? What was its width? We will study the earthly tabernacle in more detail in Hebrews 9, so don't be concerned if you are somewhat confused. Exodus 25-31 and Exodus 35-40 describe it in detail, so you need to read these chapters as soon as possible (preferably in the Living Bible if you have not read them previously).

3. For what purpose was the *"high priest...appointed"* (v.3)? What did Jesus *"have...to offer"*? What did the Levitical priests *"offer"*? Which is the more excellent ministry?

Third Day

1. Read Hebrews 8. Where does Jesus now minister as high priest (vv.4-5)? Verse 4 states that Jesus would have been prohibited from serving as high priest under the Levitical system. Why? (You may need to review previous lessons to answer this question.)

2. What does verse 5 communicate concerning the earthly priesthood and *"tabernacle"*? How does this input relate to Exodus 25:40? Are you comprehending that the earthly priesthood and tabernacle were but *"a copy and shadow of the heavenly"* (v.5) priesthood and tabernacle?

3. From verse 6, why is Jesus' *"ministry"* greater than that of the priests who served under the Law? The new covenant was (and is) unconditional, meaning that God would fulfill His promise regardless of the peoples' response. The old covenant was different, for it was conditional (read Deuteronomy 27 and 28). From what you read, why does the writer state that the new *"covenant"* is *"enacted on better promises"* (v.6)?

Fourth Day

1. Read Hebrews 8. Don't forget to pray. If the *"first covenant"* was the Law, why did a need exist *"for a second"* covenant, the covenant of grace (v.7)? According to Romans 6:14, what covenant are you *"under"* as a New Testament believer? How does this encourage you?

2. Verses 8-12 are a quote from Jeremiah 31:31-34. Does this mean that Jeremiah viewed the old covenant as one day being replaced by the *"new"*? Have you realized that Old Testament believers understood the temporary nature of the old covenant? Why would the writer of Hebrews desire that his readers know this, especially considering their present situation?

3. According to verse 8, with whom would God make a *"new covenant"*? (The phrases, *"house of Israel"* and *"house of Judah,"* relate to how the Jewish nation was divided after the death of King Solomon, King David's son. *"The house of Israel"* inhabited the northern portion of Canaan, with Samaria as its capitol. *"The house of Judah"* inhabited to the southern portion of Canaan, with Jerusalem as its capitol. Sometimes, however, when speaking of these two groups jointly, God refers to them as *"Israel."*) Who is responsible for effecting (carrying out) the *"new covenant"* (v.8)? How does this encourage you?

Fifth Day

1. Read Hebrews 8. What *"covenant"* is mentioned in verse 9? How did Israel respond to this *"covenant"* (v.9)? What *"covenant"* do verses 10, 11, and 12 address? How do Ezekiel 11:19-20 and Ezekiel 36:26-27 relate to what is stated in Hebrews 8:10?

2. The members of the body of Christ (all Jewish and Gentile believers between Acts 2 and the Rapture of the church) have the Holy Spirit move inside them once they repent and believe. How does this truth relate to Paul's words in Romans 8:11, 1Corinthians 2:12 and 3:16, Galatians 2:20, and Colossians 1:27?

3. From verse 12, how many of the believer's *"sins"* does God *"remember"* now that the new covenant is in effect? Does this mean that God keeps no record of our sins (if we are believers)? How does this knowledge affect your attitude regarding Jesus' death on the cross?

Sixth Day

1. Read Hebrews 8. According to the first half of verse 13, what did the *"new covenant"* of grace do to the old covenant of Law? The writer then states that the old covenant *"is becoming obsolete and growing old"* and *"is ready to disappear"* (v.13). Considering the historical background of this book, what does this statement mean?

Hebrews 8 Lesson

In the first six verses of this chapter, the writer reviews much of what we have already studied. He, like Peter (2Peter 1:12-13), realized the importance of repetition. The writer reviews for a specific purpose: He wants his readers to know that the high priesthood of Jesus is the primary thrust of all he has said. He records and emphasizes many essential truths, but the fact that Jesus serves as *"high priest"* in heaven is the most important of all (Hebrews 8:1):

> *Now the main point in what has been said is this: we have such a high priest, who has taken*
> *His seat at the right hand of the throne of the Majesty in the heavens,* (Hebrews 8:1)

Jesus, as *"high priest…has taken His seat at the right hand of the throne of the Majesty in the heavens"* (v.1). Next consider the following. God's *"right hand"* is filled with limitless power (Psalm 20:6; 44:3; 60:5; 63:8; 118:16; 138:7) because of His *"Majesty"* (greatness). Therefore, no being is greater than our God—absolutely none. Because Jesus is seated securely at the Father's *"right hand"* (Hebrews 8:1), we are secure as well. After all, we are *"in Christ"* (2Corinthians 5:17). Consequently, for New Testament believers to lose their salvation, they would first have to fall out of Christ, and then fall out of heaven—also, Christ, our eternal *"high priest,"* would be required to die. This scenario is a total impossibility.

Notice too that Jesus sat down when He entered heaven as our *"high priest"* (Hebrews 8:1). Since the earthly priests' work was never done, they were constantly in motion. Not so with Jesus. He could sit down because His blood (and subsequent death) produced a finished work. As a result, the need for future sacrifices is nonexistent. The Jews contemplating returning to the Levitical system were to appropriate this remarkable truth and flee from the impending danger. This flight is exactly what they did, and none died in the destruction of Jerusalem in A.D. 70.

Christ, Who is seated as our high priest, encourages and empowers us by *"standing"* (rising to His feet) when we are in need (Acts 7:55). As Redeemer, His work is finished. Thus, He has sat down. But as Encourager, He is always available to empower and inspire in the heat of the battle. In fact, His life in us, when yielded to on a moment-by-moment basis, defeats the enemy every time.

Jesus ministers as high priest in the *"tabernacle"* in heaven, the *"tabernacle"* that *"the Lord pitched"*:

> *a minister in the sanctuary, and in the true tabernacle, which the Lord pitched, not man.*
> (Hebrews 8:2)

The Levitical priests ministered in a tabernacle built and pitched by *"man"* (Hebrews 8:2). This fact again confirms the supremacy of Jesus' ministry over that of the Levitical priests.

We find a detailed description of the earthly tabernacle in Exodus 25-31 and 35-40. I highly recommend that you read these Scriptures in the short-term. (Consider reading them first in the Living Bible if you have not studied them previously.) You will find that the earthly tabernacle was 150 feet long and 75 feet wide. It consisted of three parts: The outer court, the holy place, and the Holy of Holies. (Refer to the diagram titled "The Earthly Tabernacle" in the Reference Section.) We will study the earthly tabernacle in more detail in Hebrews 9.

A *"high priest is appointed to offer both gifts and sacrifices"*:

> *For every high priest is appointed to offer both gifts and sacrifices; hence it is necessary that this*
> *high priest also have something to offer.* (Hebrews 8:3)

This verse confirms that a difference exists between a gift offering and a sacrifice. Under the Law, gift offerings were made (through the priests) to display the worshipper's commitment and dedication to the Lord. Atonement (covering) for sin, however, was accomplished when the priests offered the blood of animals (sacrifices) on behalf of the person (or persons) who had disobeyed. As New Testament believers, we offer gifts of praise and adoration to God through our high priest, Jesus Christ (Ephesians 5:20; Colossians 3:17). Also, Jesus, as *"high priest,"* was required to *"offer"* a sacrifice for our sins (Hebrews 8:3). He, for His offering, offered His own sinless, perfect blood. Knowing that His blood is greater than the blood of animals, we also know that His ministry is greater than that of the Levitical priests.

Christ's priestly ministry is in heaven, not on earth (Hebrews 8:4):

> *Now if He were on earth, He would not be a priest at all, since there are those who offer the gifts according to the Law;* (Hebrews 8:4)

Jesus couldn't serve as *"priest"* under the Law (in the earthly tabernacle) because He descended from the tribe of Judah. If you remember, all earthly high priests descended from the tribe of Levi and were direct descendants of Aaron.

Note Hebrews 8:5:

> *who serve a copy and shadow of the heavenly things, just as Moses was warned by God when he was about to erect the tabernacle; for, "SEE," He says, "THAT YOU MAKE all things ACCORDING TO THE PATTERN WHICH WAS SHOWN YOU ON THE MOUNTAIN."*
> (Hebrews 8:5)

Because the earthly ministry of the Levitical priests is only *"a copy,"* a *"shadow"* (Hebrews 8:5) of Christ's ministry in heaven, God instructed Moses to build the earthly *"tabernacle...according to"* His *"pattern"* (Exodus 25:40)—*"the pattern"* of *"the tabernacle"* in heaven (Hebrews 8:5). Thus, the earthly *"tabernacle"* was only *"a copy,"* a *"shadow"* of the heavenly one (v.5). A shadow only confirms that an object exists. It also explains why the priests, who served in a sense as mediators between God and man, functioned ineffectively in comparison to Christ. They were but copies, or shadows, of the true Mediator, Jesus.

Considering everything we have studied, quite obviously the priestly ministry of Jesus is greater than that of the priests who served under the Law. In Hebrews 8:6, the writer adds even more punch to his argument:

> *But now He has obtained a more excellent ministry, by as much as He is also the mediator of a better covenant, which has been enacted on better promises.* (Hebrews 8:6)

The *"covenant"* associated with Christ's priesthood is *"better"* than the *"covenant"* under which the Levitical priests ministered. It is *"better"* because it is *"enacted on better promises"* (v.6). The Law was a conditional covenant. If the Jews obeyed, God would shower blessings. If they disobeyed, God would level curses (Deuteronomy 27-28 confirms this truth.) Keep these truths in mind as we address the following subject matter.

God entered into two types of covenants with Israel—conditional and unconditional. With a conditional covenant, the fulfillment of the conditions of the covenant is dependent upon the response of the individuals receiving the covenant—not its grantor. Certain conditions must be met by the recipients before the grantor is obligated to provide what was promised. The Mosaic covenant (the Law) was such a covenant. With an unconditional covenant, on the other hand, the grantor is required to fulfill the conditions prescribed in the covenant regardless of the recipients' response. No "if" is attached in this situation. The promises associated with the covenant are guaranteed based on the authority and integrity of the one enacting the covenant. As a result, the promises are fulfilled apart from the worthiness or response of the covenant's beneficiaries. Even so, conditioned blessings are associated with such an arrangement, blessings dependent on the response of the ones receiving the covenant. These conditioned blessings, however, do not make the original covenant conditional. The Abrahamic covenant is a prime example, being unconditional (Genesis 12:1-3). God would fulfill His promises to Abraham regardless of Abraham's response. Nevertheless, Abraham could miss out on many blessings should he choose to walk in disobedience. For instance, God promised to *"bless"* those who blessed Abraham and *"curse"* those who cursed him (Genesis 12:3). But the number of people cursing Abraham could be multiplied (thus making his life less enjoyable) should he lack compassion, love, and sensitivity toward his acquaintances. We too can reap consequences <u>in this life</u> from sins committed while believers (Colossians 3:25) even though Christ's blood, the blood of the unconditional new covenant, allowed God to forgive our past, present, and future sins.

The old covenant of Law was given to convict the <u>lost</u> (the depraved) of sin (Galatians 3:24). This truth lines up perfectly with 1Timothy 1:9-10: *"the law is not made for"* the *"righteous, but for...the ungodly."* The New Testament believer, therefore, is *"not under law, but under grace"* (Romans 6:14). This news is magnificent, for the Law was incapable of empowering the old self (the old man, Adamic nature, etc.—who we used to be) to overcome sin. The new covenant, on the other hand, being unconditional and based on God's grace, empowers us (the new man) in such a way that sin becomes more manageable as we mature in the faith. Because the new covenant is based on unconditional promises, whereas the promises under the old covenant were conditional, it is clear that the new *"covenant...has been enacted on better promises"* (Hebrews 8:6).

Moses mediated the old covenant, receiving the Law from God (through angels) and communicating it to the Jews. (Review notes on Hebrews 1:4.) Christ is the new covenant's *"mediator"* (1Timothy 2:5). Since Jesus is greater than Moses (review lesson on Hebrews 3:1-6), and since the new covenant is based on *"better promises"* (Hebrews 8:6), the new covenant supersedes the old. This new covenant is why we are no longer *"under law"* (Romans 6:14), for it (the new covenant) renders the old covenant null and void. We now live *"under grace"* (Romans 6:14).

The writer provides more input regarding the new covenant in Hebrews 8:7. He states:

> *For if that first covenant had been faultless, there would have been no occasion sought for a second.* (Hebrews 8:7)

Because the *"first covenant"* (Law) could neither save (Romans 3:20) nor bring victory over sin, it was replaced by a covenant that could. We are not only made righteous under the new covenant, but are also empowered to live righteously through yielding to Christ's indwelling presence. We will discuss this subject in more depth later in today's lesson.

> *W*e are empowered to live righteously through yielding to Christ's indwelling presence.

Hebrews 8:8-12 quotes Jeremiah 31:31-34. The writer shares these verses with his readers not to say that the *"new covenant"* is being totally fulfilled through the church (for it isn't), but to confirm that the Old Testament prophets knew about the new covenant long before it was enacted. They, therefore, understood the old covenant's temporary nature. I sense, then, that the writer is saying, "Even Jeremiah realized that the old covenant would be superseded by the new, so why even consider returning to the sacrificial system in Jerusalem—a totally obsolete and outdated means of worship?"

Hebrews 8:8 states that God found *"fault with them"*:

> *For finding fault with them, He says, "*BEHOLD, DAYS ARE COMING, SAYS THE LORD, WHEN I WILL EFFECT A NEW COVENANT WITH THE HOUSE OF ISRAEL AND WITH THE HOUSE OF JUDAH;*"* (Hebrews 8:8)

The *"them"* in this case refers to the Jews. Because God found *"fault with"* the Jews who lived prior to (and during) Jeremiah's day (Jeremiah lived generations after Moses), He (God) spoke of a day when He would *"effect a new covenant with the house of Israel and with the house of Judah"* (v.8). The phrases, *"house of Israel"* and *"house of Judah,"* relate to the division of the Jewish nation after the death of King Solomon, King David's son. The *"house of Israel"* inhabited the northern portion of Canaan—its capitol Samaria. The *"house of Judah"* lived to the south—its capitol Jerusalem. Sometimes, however, when speaking jointly of these two houses, God refers to them as *"Israel."* Note: The *"new covenant"* (v.8) will be fulfilled completely when the Jews (all the Jews dwelling on the earth at the end of the Tribulation) accept Jesus as Messiah. This ultimate fulfillment (a subject addressed in more detail shortly) doesn't mean that Jews and Gentiles are prevented from partaking of this covenant during the church age—the church having begun in Acts 2. Unquestionably, these readers were partakers of the *"new covenant"*—and so are we.

The *"new covenant"* is God's plan, not man's (Hebrews 8:8). Thus, God alone will carry out the terms of the covenant. Hence, when the depraved recognize their need for Christ (and exercise personal repentance and faith), God saves them through the avenue of the new covenant.

The new covenant is *"not like the covenant"* that God *"made"* with Israel in the days of Moses (v.9), a covenant which she broke (v.9). The new covenant allows the Law to be written on the *"minds"* and *"hearts"* of those who believe (vv.10-11—also read Ezekiel 11:19-20 and 36:26-27). All who enter this covenant have their sins forgiven. In fact, God remembers *"their sins no more"* (Hebrews 8:12). Therefore, Jesus' blood, as the perfect offering, removed our past, present, and future sins the moment we repented and exercised faith while depraved—something the offerings associated with the old covenant could never accomplish (Hebrews 10:4, 11). Undoubtedly, the new covenant *"has been enacted on better promises"* (Hebrews 8:6).

Because the members of the body of Christ (the body of Christ consisting of all Jews and Gentiles who believe between Acts 2 and the Rapture of the church) are beneficiaries of the new covenant, we now have the Law written on our *"hearts"* (Hebrews 8:10; Jeremiah 31:33). No wonder Paul taught that the *"Spirit"* now lives in New Testament believers (Romans 8:11; 1Corinthians 2:12; 3:16). He taught that Jesus lives inside them as well (Galatians 2:20; Colossians 1:27).

> *We now have the Law written on our hearts.*

Special note: As was stated earlier, the new covenant will not be fulfilled in totality until the end of the Tribulation—when every Jew living on the earth (at that time) will *"know the Lord"* (Hebrews 8:11) and have God's *"law"* written *"on their heart"* through the power of the Holy *"Spirit"* (Jeremiah 31:31-34) after accepting Christ as Savior. Ezekiel 11:17-20 and Ezekiel 36:24-27 confirm this truth as well. Even so, the church (which began in Acts 2, and is made up of Jews and Gentiles alike) partakes of the new covenant. These truths verify that the new covenant, though now in effect, will reach its ultimate fulfillment through the physical Jewish nation—not the church. Thus, Paul proclaims that a day will come when *"all Israel will be saved"* (Romans 11:26-27)—which will transpire in conjunction with Christ's Second Coming—at the end of the seven years of Tribulation and shortly before the beginning of the Millennium, Christ's reign on earth. In fact, at the end of the Tribulation, the remnant of Jews (living on the earth at that time) will call Christ back (Hosea 5:15; Zechariah 12:10). They will do so because *"all Israel"* (all Jews on the earth at that time) will choose to believe on Christ and enter into the *"new covenant"* (Jeremiah 31:31-34). Yes, a day will come when *"all Israel will be saved"* (Romans 11:26-27)—*"all Israel"* being *"all"* Jews on the earth at the end of the Tribulation.

The *"new covenant"* rendered the *"first"* (old) covenant *"obsolete"* (Hebrews 8:13):

> *When He said, "A new covenant," He has made the first obsolete. But whatever is becoming obsolete and growing old is ready to disappear.* (Hebrews 8:13)

The old covenant only atoned for sins (covered sins) when sacrifices were offered in faith. Consequently, if faith did not accompany a sacrifice, not even atonement resulted. The new covenant, on the other hand, totally removes the believer's sins (Hebrews 8:12):

> *"FOR I WILL BE MERCIFUL TO THEIR INIQUITIES, AND I WILL REMEMBER THEIR SINS NO MORE."* (Hebrews 8:12)

We will discuss this truth in more detail in the weeks ahead.
The writer states:

> *When He said, "A new covenant," He has made the first obsolete. But whatever is becoming obsolete and growing old is ready to disappear.* (Hebrews 8:13)

Why would he make such a declaration? When this epistle was penned, the temple had not yet been destroyed. As a result, the sacrificial system remained intact. The new covenant was in effect, but the unbelieving Jews continued to offer sacrifices according to old covenant regulations. When Titus destroyed the temple in A.D. 70, the sacrificial system was totally annihilated. Because the temple fell only a few years after Hebrews was written, we can understand why the writer would say, *"But whatever is becoming obsolete and growing old is ready to disappear"* (v.13).

Next week we will deal more specifically with the tabernacle employed under the old covenant and compare it with Christ's perfect offering in the tabernacle in heaven. You should be very much encouraged with your progress!

Hebrews 9 Questions

First Day

1. Read Hebrews 9. Don't forget to pray. Additional material is included in this week's study, but do your best to complete each day's assignment. What does the writer mention regarding *"the first covenant"* in verse 1? What do you know about these subjects?

2. From the diagram titled "The Earthly Tabernacle" located in the Reference Section, and from Exodus 27:18 (considering that a cubit is one and one-half feet), how long and how wide was the outer court of the tabernacle? From Exodus 27:1-8 and Exodus 40:29, along with Exodus 30:17-21 and Exodus 40:30-32, what pieces of furniture were located in the outer court? Find these pieces of furniture on the previously referenced diagram.

3. What two pieces of furniture are mentioned in Hebrews 9:2, Exodus 25:31-40, Exodus 25:23-30, and Exodus 40:22-24? Where were these pieces positioned within the tabernacle (v.2)? Refer to the diagram titled "The Earthly Tabernacle" if you need assistance.

4. What important part of the tabernacle is mentioned in Exodus 26:31-33 and Hebrews 9:3? What was located behind the *"second veil"* (Hebrews 9:3), which is labeled the "outer veil" on the diagram?

Second Day

1. Read Hebrews 9. What piece of furniture is mentioned first in verse 4 (it is also addressed in Exodus 30:1-10 and Exodus 37:25-29) Locate this object on the diagram of the tabernacle. If you read Hebrews 9:4 at face value only, it seems that *"the altar of incense"* was positioned inside the Holy of Holies. If this altar was situated there, the writer of Hebrews contradicts Exodus 40:26, which indicates that it was located in the holy place (*"in front of the veil"*). What could possibly solve our dilemma? The solution is simple, for both references are correct. Although the *"golden altar of incense"* was positioned in the holy place, just outside *"the veil,"* the smoke proceeding from the incense passed through *"the veil"* into the Holy of Holies. Thus, its ministry, though physically located in the holy place, was in the Holy of Holies in the presence of God. Apparent contradiction resolved! Write down any new insights below.

2.   What other piece of furniture is mentioned in Hebrews 9:4? (Also see Exodus 25:10-15.) Where was this object located (Hebrews 9:3-4)? What was placed inside it (v.4; Exodus 16:31-34; Numbers 17:10; Exodus 25:16; 31:18; Deuteronomy 9:9)?

3.   From verse 5, what was located *"above"* the ark of the covenant? Where did God *"meet with"* Israel (Exodus 25:22)? Challenge question: If the articles placed within the ark of the covenant represented Israel's rebellion (Exodus 16:1-30; Numbers 16:1-17:11; Exodus 32:1-20), and God met with Israel above the mercy seat (which was located on top of the ark of the covenant), what does this arrangement communicate regarding the heart of our God?

4.   From verses 6 and 7, Exodus 28:43, Exodus 35:19, and Leviticus 16:2, the regular priests could enter what part of the tabernacle? From these same verses, the high priest could enter what portion of the tabernacle? According to Hebrews 9:7, Exodus 30:7-8, and Leviticus 24:1-8, what were some of the high priest's responsibilities?

5.   From verse 7 and Leviticus 16:29-34, how often could the high priest enter the Holy of Holies? What did he take with him when he entered (Hebrews 9:7)? For whom was the *"blood"* offered on this day (v.7)? What types of sins were atoned for (covered) on this day (v.7)? When and how were the other types of sins dealt with under the Law?

Third Day

1.   Read Hebrews 9. Considering what we have been studying, what does verse 8 communicate to you? What does verse 9 say about the inefficiency of the Old Testament *"sacrifices"*?

2.   Verse 10 speaks of *"a time of reformation."* In your opinion, to what is the writer making reference? (Consider verses 11-14 before recording your answer.)

3. How is Jesus described in the first portion of verse 11? Where did He enter as *"high priest"* (v.11)? How do Acts 7:48-50 and Acts 17:24 validate this wonderful truth? Why should 2Corinthians 5:17 and Ephesians 2:6 now take on new meaning?

4. What occurred in King Herod's temple when Jesus died (Matthew 27:50-51)? According to 1Peter 2:9, New Testament believers are priests? What advantage do we have over the Levitical priests who served under the Law (Hebrews 4:16; 6:19; 10:19-20)? Can you see how a good working knowledge of the Old Testament makes the New Testament come alive? How do Paul's words of Romans 15:4 relate?

5. What did the Levitical high priest take into the Holy of Holies on the Day of Atonement (v.12a; Leviticus 16:11 and 15)? What did Jesus take into the tabernacle in heaven (Hebrews 9:12)? What type of *"redemption"* did Jesus obtain for us (Hebrews 9:12)? What do these answers communicate regarding the effectiveness of *"His...blood"* and your security as a believer?

6. According to verses 13 and 14, Christ's blood accomplished for the believer what animal blood could never achieve. What was it? Through what avenue did Jesus offer *"Himself...to God"* (v.14)? What would result if we offered ourselves in this manner?

Fourth Day

1. Read Hebrews 9. How does the first phrase of verse 15 describe Jesus? A *"mediator"* is one who intervenes between two parties to ratify a covenant, establish peace, or both. Jesus' death on the cross allows God to establish peace between Himself and those who choose (while depraved) to accept Christ as Savior. In this way, Jesus *"is the mediator of a new covenant."* Based on previous lessons, did the blood of the animals offered under the old covenant remove the Old Testament believer's sins? Through what avenue were those sins *("transgressions")* removed, or forgiven (v.15)? The *"new covenant,"* mentioned in verse 15, is also addressed in Jeremiah 31:31-34, Ezekiel 11:19-20, and Ezekiel 36:26-27. What encourages you most in these passages? Had you been one of the Hebrew Christians addressed in this epistle, what would you have been thinking by now?

2. The writer changes subjects in verses 16 and 17. Instead of continuing to address covenants as such, he makes statements regarding wills. (Note: The word *"covenant"* can actually be translated "will" in these two verses). The writer communicates how wills are initiated and, in turn, used to bring about binding agreements. He gives this illustration to confirm what Christ's death accomplished. So long as the initiator of the will is alive, he can change the will in any manner he desires. But once he dies, the will is binding, unalterable, and irrevocable. What does the fact that the mediator of the new covenant (Jesus) has died communicate regarding the certainty with which the conditions of the new covenant will be fulfilled?

3. Through the old covenant, God made a pact between Himself and man. From verses 18-20, did the One who made the covenant die, or did something else die instead? Consequently, what type of blood sealed the old covenant? According to verses 19 and 21, what was done with this blood? How was the new covenant sealed (Matthew 26:28)?

4. What does verse 22 state about *"blood"*? Once the old covenant was sealed with blood (animal blood), its terms could not be changed. It could be eliminated later, but never changed—remember, it was conditional. The unconditional new covenant makes the conditional old covenant inoperative in the life of a believer. From what we have studied thus far, why does the new covenant make the old covenant obsolete? In answering the previous question, consider which type of blood sealed each covenant and what the two types of blood accomplished.

5. What does Leviticus 17:11 say about *"blood"*? Could we therefore conclude that the shed blood only symbolizes that a death has occurred? If blood alone had atoned for (covered) sin under the old covenant, could not the animals have been partially bled instead of killed? Had blood alone been necessary for forgiveness under the new covenant, could not a portion of Christ's blood have been applied to the cross and the Father's justice been satisfied? According to Hebrews 9:15-17, how does Christ's death relate to the *"new covenant"*? Does this help you better understand what occurred on the cross? If so, why?

Fifth Day

1. Read Hebrews 9. From verse 23, how was the heavenly tabernacle *"cleansed"*? Why would the heavenly tabernacle need cleansing? (The answer is included in this week's lesson, but don't go there until you have exhausted all other resources.) According to the last phrase of verse 24, what is Jesus doing now that He is in heaven? What encouragement do you draw from this?

2. What do verses 25 and 26 communicate regarding the supremacy of Christ's sacrifice? What would need to occur on an ongoing basis should Jesus' death on the cross have been a partial work (vv.25-26)? Is it possible for Jesus to be crucified multiple times (Hebrews 9:12; Hebrews 9:25-26)? From the last phrase of verse 26, what did Jesus' sacrifice accomplish in regard to the sins of the Old Testament believers?

3. How does verse 27 relate to what we are studying in this chapter? Is verse 27 saying that every man who has lived, or will live, will *"die once"*? Be careful with your answer. The writer also states that after a person experiences physical death he/she will face *"judgment."* What type of *"judgment"* will an unbeliever face (Revelation 20:11-15)? What judgment will we as New Testament believers face (Romans 8:1; 2Corinthians 5:10; 1Corinthians 3:10-15)?

4. According to verse 28, how many times will Christ die for the sin of man? How does this relate to what we studied in verses 25 and 26? Should you experience physical death, or the Rapture occur, how many of your sins will God mention when you see Him (v.28)? Does He have a list of your sins? Why should this truth allow you to better appreciate the cross?

Sixth Day

1. Read Hebrews 9. Read all of this week's lesson and record any new insights below. The lesson is somewhat lengthy, but take ample time to read every word. It emphasizes points relating to Hebrews 9 that could not be covered in this week's questions.

Hebrews 9 Lesson

We must understand a weighty truth if we are to view this chapter properly. Just because the new covenant replaced the old covenant does not mean that the old covenant had no value. The old covenant was a "picture" of what Christ did for us as Savior, and what He is now doing for us as high priest. Thus, it had great value. The unbelieving Jews, however, worshipped the "system" rather than the Savior and high priest to which it pointed. We too must be careful not to worship man, programs, Christian organizations, and yes, even the church. We must *"worship God"* and God alone (Revelation 22:9).

No doubt, *"the first covenant had regulations of divine worship* [offerings and sacrifices] *and the earthly sanctuary"* (Hebrews 9:1). The words *"earthly sanctuary"* (v.1) refer to the earthly *"tabernacle"* (v.2) rather than King Solomon's temple or King Herod's temple, both of which were constructed <u>after</u> Israel returned to Canaan from Egypt. More information about the *"earthly"* tabernacle, as well as the *"regulations of divine worship"* associated with this amazing structure (v.1), can be found in Exodus 25-31 and Exodus 35-40. If you haven't read these chapters recently, I highly recommend that you do so at your earliest convenience. You should take time now to review the diagram titled "The Earthly Tabernacle" located in the Reference Section.

The outer court of the tabernacle was 150 feet long and 75 feet wide (Exodus 27:18)—a cubit being equivalent to approximately a foot and a half. Inside the court were the *"bronze...altar"* (Exodus 27:1-8; Exodus 40:29), the *"laver"* (Exodus 30:17-21; Exodus 40:30-32), and a 45 foot by 15 foot area which housed the holy place and the Holy of Holies (Exodus 26:15-22). The *"holy place"* measured 30 feet by 15 feet, and is referred to as the *"outer"* *"tabernacle"* in Hebrews 9:2. Within this outer tabernacle (*"holy place"*) stood the *"lampstand"* (the golden *"lampstand"*— Exodus 25:31-40) and the *"table"* on which the sacred *"bread"* was placed (Exodus 25:23-30)— one loaf for each of the twelve tribes of Israel (Leviticus 24:5-9). The *"lampstand"* was positioned *"on the south side of the"* holy place (Exodus 40:24) with the *"table"* to its *"north,"* on the opposite side of the room (Exodus 40:22).

"The veil," referred to as *"the second veil"* in Hebrews 9:3, separated the holy place from the Holy of Holies. *"The veil"* is described more specifically in Exodus 26:31-33. Evidently, the Holy of Holies was a perfect cube, 15 feet long, 15 feet wide, and 15 feet high. Within this 15 foot cubical area sat *"the ark of the covenant covered on all sides with gold"* (Hebrews 9:4; Exodus 25:10-15). Inside the ark *"was a golden jar holding the manna"* (Hebrews 9:4; Exodus 16:31-34), *"Aaron's rod which budded"* (Hebrews 9:4; Numbers 17:10), *"and the tables of the covenant"* (Hebrews 9:4; Exodus 25:16; 31:18; Deuteronomy 9:9). Each of these three articles represent Israel's rebellion. For example, Israel complained about a lack of food, and God sent *"manna"* (Exodus 16:1-31). The people questioned Aaron's leadership (Numbers 16:1-50), and God responded by causing Aaron's *"rod"* to *"sprout"* and bear *"almonds"* (Numbers 17:1-11). Lastly, the people rebelled while Moses received the Ten Commandments (*"the tables of the covenant"*—Hebrews 9:4) on Mount Sinai (Exodus 32:1-20). *"The mercy seat"* with the two *"cherubim,"* however, was positioned *"above"* the ark (Hebrews 9:5)—the very place where God met with Israel (Exodus 25:22). What a magnificent picture of God's grace and mercy! In fact, His mercy allows Him to remove all our sin (Hebrews 8:12). Absolutely nothing should be allowed to take this truth from us!

God's mercy allows Him to remove all our sin. Absolutely nothing should be allowed to take this truth from us!

We must be careful while researching the details of the tabernacle. Why? The priesthood and offerings, and even the manner in which the tabernacle was constructed, point to Christ in graphic and meaningful ways. Yet, the writer states that certain aspects of the tabernacle cannot, at the present time, be spoken of *"in detail"* (Hebrews 9:5). Therefore, let's hold to the things that obviously point to Christ, appreciate and enjoy them, but refrain from going overboard when attempting to comprehend the intricacies of this intriguing structure.

We need to backtrack for a moment and return to the beginning of Hebrews 9:4. There the writer speaks of the *"golden altar of incense,"* described in more detail in Exodus 30:1-10 and Exodus 37:25-29. Hebrews 9:3-4 <u>seems</u> to indicate that the *"altar of incense"* was positioned inside the Holy of Holies. If it was placed there, however, the writer of Hebrews contradicts Exodus 40:26—where we find that the *"altar"* of incense was located in the holy place (the outer tabernacle). What could possibly solve our dilemma? The solution is simple—for both references are correct. Although the golden altar of incense was positioned inside the holy place, just outside the veil, the aroma that proceeded from the smoldering incense passed through the veil into the Holy of Holies (a subject addressed earlier in the Second Day's questions). Thus, its ministry was inside the Holy of Holies (in the presence of God) although it was physically situated in the holy place. Again we discover that God's Word is contradiction free!

Verses 6 and 7 of Hebrews 9 speak of the responsibilities of the *"priests"* who ministered in the *"tabernacle."* The regular *"priests"* could minister in the holy place (v.6; Exodus 28:43; 35:19) but were not allowed to enter the Holy of Holies (Leviticus 16:2). They were *"continually"* going in and out of the holy place performing their priestly duties (Hebrews 9:6). But the high priest had responsibilities in both the holy place (Exodus 30:7-8; Leviticus 24:1-8) and the Holy of Holies (Hebrews 9:7):

> *but into the second only the high priest enters, once a year, not without taking blood, which he offers for himself and for the sins of the people committed in ignorance.* (Hebrews 9:7)

One day each year—on the day of *"atonement"* (Leviticus 16:29-34)—the high priest would enter the Holy of Holies, first, with *"blood...for himself,"* and a second time with *"blood...for the sins of the people committed in ignorance"* (Hebrews 9:7).

The last phrase of verse 7, *"for the sins of the people committed in ignorance,"* is highly significant. When a Jew knowingly disobeyed, he could present an animal to the priest and his sin was atoned for (covered). This privilege was available to him throughout the year. (Notice that these sins were atoned for, or covered—not forgiven. As to <u>when</u> Old Testament believers' sins were forgiven will be addressed later. Also, these daily sacrifices were required to be offered in faith or no atonement resulted.) But sins might exist that had been committed in ignorance, hidden sins, or even sins that had been forgotten. Such sins were <u>covered</u> on *"the day of atonement"* (Leviticus 16; 23:27-28; 25:9). As a result, only one day of the year could a Jew know that all his/her sins were covered. No wonder the Law is inferior to what Christ offers through grace!

A vital issue needs to be considered before continuing. So long as the first tabernacle stood (the tabernacle built in the wilderness), the way into the holy place (Holy of Holies on the diagram) was accessible only to the high priest—no common person could enter. Only one person out of the entire nation could enter the Holy of Holies, just one day of the year. The common Jew could get no closer to the Holy of Holies than the outer court! These restrictions meant that access to God was limited so long as the first *"tabernacle"* was *"still standing,"* a truth validated by *"The Holy Spirit"* (Hebrews 9:8). Such a situation existed because the sins of the Old Testament believers were only covered through the sacrificial system; they were not forgiven. Due to the inability of these sacrifices to remove sin, the Old Testament believers were limited in their access to God.

The first phrase of Hebrews 9:9 describes the earthly tabernacle as *"a symbol for the present time."* The word *"symbol"* means "parable"—which communicates that the earthly tabernacle was only a picture of the real thing. We will deal with the "real thing" shortly. Know, therefore, that the earthly tabernacle was a copy rather than the original.

One of the most significant truths to understand regarding the old covenant is that not even a sacrifice on the Day of Atonement could clear the worshipper's *"conscience"* (Hebrews 9:9). After all, what if the *"scapegoat"* returned (read Leviticus 16:7-10, 21-22)? The old covenant most definitely was limited. In fact, it related *"only to food and drink and various washings, regulations for the body imposed until a time of reformation"* (Hebrews 9:10). Addressing externals alone, it could not remedy the turmoil that flourished within.

*N*ot even a sacrifice on the Day of Atonement could clear the worshipper's conscience.

Let's take a moment to examine the phrase, *"a time of reformation"* (v.10). The word *"reformation"* means *"a process of making straight or right,"* a correction in other words. The old system was not designed to exist forever, for it was incapable of making things right between God and man. It took effect under Moses and was, thus, removed through the cross. (Do you realize that approximately 2,000 years have passed since a sacrifice was offered in the temple?) The old covenant was temporary and continued only *"until a time of reformation"* (v.10). An amazing transformation accompanied this *"reformation"*: The Old Testament believers' sins, previously covered (atoned for), were forgiven. (This truth will be confirmed to a greater degree later in the study.) In fact, only <u>after</u> the cross were Old Testament believers allowed to enter heaven. Before, they had inhabited *"Abraham's bosom"* (Luke 16:22).

Hebrews 9:11 makes an astounding statement:

> *But when Christ appeared as a high priest of the good things to come, He entered through the greater and more perfect tabernacle, not made with hands, that is to say, not of this creation;*
> (Hebrews 9:11)

Beginning with this passage, the writer validates the surpassing value of Christ's priesthood by proving that the new spiritual, internal, and eternal covenant associated with grace supersedes the old physical, external, and temporary covenant associated with the Law. This section of Scripture is truly wonderful, so enjoy yourself as we feast on the meat of the Word!

Based on the first phrase of verse 11, Christ is *"a high priest."* In fact, He is *"a high priest of the good things to come."* This truth proves that the *"things"* following Christ's death, burial, and resurrection are *"good things."* Thus, the gospel is good news and *"glorious"* (1Timothy 1:11). *"Good things"* follow because *"He entered through the greater and more perfect tabernacle, not made with hands, that is to say, not of this creation"* (Hebrews 9:11). In other words, the *"tabernacle"* that Christ *"entered"* is *"perfect,"* not having been built by man. Nor is it like the temples erected by King Solomon and King Herod, both of which were destroyed. It was and is an eternal tabernacle, made of heavenly resources, and built by Jehovah alone (Acts 7:48-50; 17:24).

Have you considered the ramifications of what the writer is communicating here, especially when coupled with other portions of God's Word? Paul states that all New Testament believers are *"in Christ"* (2Corinthians 5:17). He can make this statement because we have been *"raised...up with Him, and seated...with Him in the heavenly places, in Christ Jesus"* (Ephesians 2:6). Because Jesus is in heaven, dwelling in the heavenly tabernacle (since He is high priest), we are there as well! As a result, we can speak with God any time we like! Also consider that the veil in King Herod's temple, which separated the holy place from the Holy of Holies, was torn in half when Jesus died (Matthew 27:50-51). Consequently, after Jesus' death, nothing separated the holy place from the Holy of Holies. Hence, as priests (1Peter 2:9), we can speak with God on a moment-by-moment basis (Hebrews 4:16; Hebrews 6:19; 10:19-20). Doesn't this truth motivate you to know Christ's heart to the greatest degree possible?

*H*e grants eternal redemption to all who repent and believe while depraved.

Only one day of the year (on the Day of Atonement), the high priest entered the Holy of Holies with the blood of a *"bull...for himself"* (Leviticus 16:11) and the *"blood"* of a *"goat...for the people"* (Leviticus 16:15). Not so with Jesus: According to Hebrews 9:12, He entered the heavenly tabernacle, not with *"the blood of goats and calves"* (bulls), but with *"His own blood."* Jesus also *"entered...once for all"* sin (v.12), since He bore all the sin of all mankind on the cross. Therefore, He grants *"eternal redemption"*—not temporary or perishable—to all who repent and believe while depraved (v.12). (Note: Jesus entered the heavenly tabernacle *"once"* because He, unlike the Levitical priests, was not required to first offer blood for His own sins—since He is sinless). Isn't it comforting to know that the redemption (salvation) obtained through Christ is eternal (once we repent and believe while depraved), and that we are secure in Him?

The Old Testament sacrifices were limited to outward *"cleansing"* only (v.13). They could cleanse the flesh—but never the heart. (Numbers 19 helps clarify the writer's message here, so a quick read of those passages would be beneficial.) Christ's sacrifice, however, brings inward cleansing (forgiveness), which results in a purified *"conscience"*:

> *how much more will the blood of Christ, who through the eternal Spirit offered Himself without blemish to God, cleanse your conscience from dead works to serve the living God?* (Hebrews 9:14)

Also consider that God eradicated our Adamic nature (old man, old self, sinful nature, etc.—all synonymous) when we exercised repentance and faith while depraved (Romans 6:6; Ephesians 4:22; Colossians 3:9). Thus, we have become *"new"* creations (2Corinthians 5:17), even saints—saints who sometimes sin, not lowly sinners saved by grace. The knowledge of this truth brings joy and peace, which results in effective service (last phrase of Hebrews 9:14)—not dead works produced from a lifestyle of fruitless activity.

Notice that Jesus *"offered Himself...to God"* through the avenue of *"the eternal Spirit"* (v.14). Yes, the *"Spirit"* empowered Jesus as He submitted to the cross. We too can be empowered if we will but yield to His (the Spirit's) leading.

The writer, in verse 15, records truth regarding the cross that is essential to understand:

> *And for this reason He is the mediator of a new covenant, in order that since a death has taken place for the redemption of the transgressions that were committed under the first covenant, those who have been called may receive the promise of the eternal inheritance.* (Hebrews 9:15)

The first phrase of verse 15, *"And for this reason,"* confirms that we are to consider the previous teachings before interpreting what follows. No doubt, the supremacy of Christ's sacrifice allowed Him to be *"the mediator of a new covenant"* (v.15). A *"mediator"* is one who intervenes between two parties to ratify a covenant, establish peace, or both. Jesus' death on the cross allowed the Father to establish peace between Himself and those who choose (while depraved) to receive His Son as Savior. In this way, Jesus became *"the mediator of a new covenant."*

We discovered earlier that the old covenant (the Law) could convict man of sin but never empower him to do right. We also learned that the sacrifices offered under the old covenant only covered (atoned for) sins—never removing them. (We will address these subjects in more detail in Hebrews 10). Thus, a new covenant was the only solution to man's dilemma. In Jeremiah 31:31-34, along with the book of Ezekiel, we find a description of this *"new covenant."* It not only makes provision for the forgiveness of sin (Jeremiah 31:34), but also provides the power for believers to walk in obedience once they choose to obey (Jeremiah 31:33; Ezekiel

11:19-20; 36:26-27). Even Jesus spoke of the *"new covenant"* in Luke 22:20, saying:

> ... *"This cup which is poured out for you is the new covenant in My blood."* (Luke 22:20)

All New Testament believers live under this *"new covenant."* It would be totally unwise, therefore, for these Hebrew Christians to return to the sacrificial system in Jerusalem?

A question that I often hear is, "What did God require of individuals who lived during Old Testament times before declaring them righteous?" The answer is quite simple. They were to look forward (in faith) to the coming of Christ just as we look back (in faith) to the fact that He came. After all, He is the *"seed"* of Genesis 3:15 based on Galatians 3:16—so they would have known of His coming as early as Genesis 3. (Their faith was exercised in their depravity, faith not being a work based on passages such as Romans 3:27-28.) Consequently, Old Testament believers were saved by grace through faith. Yet, they were saved on credit, for their sins were not forgiven until the cross. No wonder Hebrews 9:15 states: *"in order that since a death has taken place for the redemption of the transgressions that were committed under the first covenant."*

Old Testament believers were saved on credit.

Unquestionably, Christ's death (blood) <u>removed</u> the sins of the Old Testament believers that the sacrifices under the *"first covenant"* only <u>covered</u>. As a result of Jesus' death, burial, and resurrection, Old Testament believers were also *"made perfect"* (Hebrews 12:23) in their souls and spirits. Previously, they were only <u>declared</u> perfect in their souls and spirits. What did they receive as a result of this wonderful act? They received *"the eternal inheritance"* (v.15). For starters, they were moved to heaven from *"Abraham's bosom,"* where Old Testament believers resided (Luke 16) until Jesus' ascension. One day they will also receive resurrected bodies and enjoy the benefits of Christ's one thousand year reign on earth. Afterwards, they will reside for all eternity in the eternal order. What a wonderful *"inheritance"*!

You and I, unlike believers before the cross, were forgiven and made perfect (in our souls and spirits) the moment we exercised personal repentance and faith while depraved (Hebrews 10:14). We will begin reaping our *"eternal inheritance"* (Hebrews 9:15; 1Peter 1:4) when our bodies cease operating and our souls and spirits enter heaven (2Corinthians 5:8).

> To obtain an inheritance which is imperishable and undefiled and will not fade away, reserved in heaven for you, (1Peter 1:4)

> we are of good courage, I say, and prefer rather to be absent from the body and to be at home with the Lord. (2Corinthians 5:8)

If these last few statements seem confusing, I highly recommend that you obtain a copy of the *Romans 1-8* study distributed by this ministry.

In Hebrews 9:16-17, the writer changes his subject matter from covenants, as such, to wills. (The word *"covenant"* can actually be translated "will" in these two passages). The writer desires to communicate how wills are initiated and why they are binding. He does so to confirm what Christ's death accomplished for believers. So long as the initiator of the will is alive, he can change the will in any manner he chooses. But once he dies, the will is binding, unalterable, and irrevocable. These facts confirm that the new covenant, with all of its blessings, is binding, unalterable, and irrevocable due to Christ's death. Doesn't this portion of Hebrews cause you to appreciate, to even a greater degree, all that the cross accomplished?

Through the old covenant, God made a pact between Himself and man. God *"inaugurated"* (established) the *"covenant"* with *"blood"* (v.18), even though it was *"the blood"* of animals (vv.19-21). In this case, therefore, the One Who made the covenant did not die. Animals died instead, for Moses *"took the blood of...calves and...goats...and sprinkled...the book"* as well as *"all the people"* (v.19; Exodus 24:6-8).

Clearly, the blood of animals sealed the old covenant. Why blood? According to Leviticus 17:11, *"the life of the flesh is in the blood"*—proving that blood is a symbol of death. Thus, the old covenant was sealed through *"the blood of"* animals (Hebrews 9:19), just as the new covenant was sealed through the *"blood"* of Christ (Matthew 26:28). Hence, *"without shedding of blood there is no forgiveness"* (Hebrews 9:22). The writer's intention was for his readers to recognize Moses' actions as pointing to the greater and more perfect sacrifice, the blood and death of the Messiah. Only Jesus' sacrifice could make forgiveness available to all mankind. We know, however, that only those who (while depraved) recognize their need for a Savior, repent of their sin, and accept Christ through faith, can be saved through Christ's finished work on the cross.

Once the old covenant was sealed with blood, its terms could not be changed. It could later be removed, but never altered. The new covenant renders the old covenant inoperative in a New Testament believer. Why? Because the new covenant is superior, sealed with better blood—the blood of Jesus.

We must never forget that *"the life of the flesh is in the blood"*:

> *'For the life of the flesh is in the blood, and I have given it to you on the altar to make atonement for your souls; for it is the blood by reason of the life that makes atonement.'*
> (Leviticus 17:11)

The shedding of blood (under the old covenant) only symbolized that a death had occurred. If the blood of animals (by itself) had atoned for (covered) sin, the animals could have been partially bled rather than killed. Consider also that bloodless offerings, under certain conditions, were permitted to atone for sin (Leviticus 5:11). Why? They symbolized the blood sacrifices of the animals, just as the animal sacrifices symbolized Christ's future sacrifice. Christ's shed blood confirmed that He had died. Consequently, His death was the means through which forgiveness was ultimately provided. Simply applying a portion of Christ's blood to the cross would have failed to meet the requirements. Only Jesus' *"death"* would suffice (Hebrews 9:15-17).

Jesus had to die to be Savior, for *"the wages of sin is death"* (Romans 6:23), and *"the soul who sins will die"* (Ezekiel 18:4). It took the death of the perfect God-man to remove the sin of imperfect man. Thank you Jesus for your indescribable gift (John 3:16)!

The writer has already verified that the earthly tabernacle was a copy of the *"heavenly"* one, and he mentions this fact again in Hebrews 9:23:

> *Therefore it was necessary for the copies of the things in the heavens to be cleansed with these, but the heavenly things themselves with better sacrifices than these.* (Hebrews 9:23)

The copy was cleansed with animal sacrifices, but the *"heavenly"* tabernacle was cleansed *"with better sacrifices than these"* (v.23). The *"better"* sacrifice was the blood (and body) of the Holy Son of God, Jesus Christ. Why would the *"heavenly"* tabernacle need cleansing? Ezekiel's description of Satan's activities provides the answer:

> *Your heart was proud and lifted up because of your beauty; you corrupted your wisdom for the sake of your splendor. I cast you to the ground; I lay you before kings, that they might gaze at you. You have profaned your sanctuaries by the multitude of your iniquities and the enormity of your guilt, by the unrighteousness of your trade...* (Ezekiel 28:17-18 AMP—emphasis added)

The word *"sanctuaries"* (Ezekiel 28:18) means "holy places." Thus the words, *"your sanctuaries"* (Ezekiel 28:18), verify that Satan had some type of priestly function in heaven before his fall. The word *"sanctuaries,"* being plural, also confirm that Satan served in both the holy place and

Holy of Holies in the heavenly tabernacle. Satan's sin, therefore, corrupted the holy place and Holy of Holies in heaven. For certain, the heavenly tabernacle needed cleansing!

It was the high priest's responsibility under the old covenant to appear in the presence of God on behalf of the people. For this reason, the writer records:

> *For Christ did not enter a holy place made with hands, a mere copy of the true one, but into heaven itself, now to appear in the presence of God for us;* (Hebrews 9:24)

Our high priest *"did not enter"* the earthly tabernacle, but *"into heaven itself…to appear in the presence of God for us"* (Hebrews 9:24). How comforting to know that Jesus entered heaven *"to make propitiation for"* our *"sins"* (Hebrews 2:17). Yes, He removed our sin and allowed us to become friends with the Father. He is also available to assist us in time of need (Hebrews 2:18).

Jesus entered heaven once, signifying that His blood was not only sufficient, but the final blood offering:

> *nor was it that He should offer Himself often, as the high priest enters the holy place year by year with blood not his own.* (Hebrews 9:25)

The earthly priests *"often"* entered the earthly tabernacle (v.25), indicating that their work was insufficient and ongoing. Why? Their offering consisted of animal blood, which can never remove sin (Hebrews 10:4).

It is impossible to read Hebrews 9:26 and miss the finality and magnificence of what the cross accomplished in regard to sin:

> *Otherwise, He would have needed to suffer often since the foundation of the world; but now once at the consummation of the ages He has been manifested to put away sin by the sacrifice of Himself.* (Hebrews 9:26)

Had Christ's work been incomplete, *"He would have needed to suffer often since the foundation of the world"* (Hebrews 9:26). In fact, He would have needed to die continually. However, *"once at the consummation of the ages He has been manifested to put away sin by the sacrifice of Himself"* (v.26). *"Once"*— not twice, not three times, not every time we sin—*"once at the consummation of the ages"* Christ died. Yes, His crucifixion took place *"at the consummation of the ages."* Even the apostle Peter wrote, *"The end of all things are at hand"* (1Peter 4:7). The apostle John also penned, *"Children, it is the last hour"* (1John 2:18). All the apostles believed the end was near. Why? Jesus on the cross was *"the consummation of the ages."* His sacrifice *"put away sin"* (Hebrews 9:26).

Have you realized that Jesus' sacrifice took away your past, present, and future sins—not just your past sins? Hence, His one sacrifice abolished sin—took away every sin we have committed in the past or will commit in the future. Otherwise, Jesus would need to be crucified each time we sin. Multiple crucifixions, however, are a total impossibility! He died *"once,"* never to die again (vv.12 and 26).

We must be careful with Hebrews 9:27:

> *And inasmuch as it is appointed for men to die once and after this comes judgment,*
> (Hebrews 9:27)

The phrase, *"And inasmuch as it is appointed for men to die once,"* is a general statement that must be handled with care. For instance, Lazarus died twice—once before Jesus raised him back to natural life (John 11:14, 43-44) and later as well. The same was true for others who were raised back to natural life during biblical times. Also, Enoch and Elijah never died. Neither will those who are raptured. Verse 27 is, therefore, a general statement that is not applicable to all. Its message is that once Jesus died, He could never die again. This will become evident as we transition into verse 28.

"Judgment" follows physical death (v.27). All the unredeemed will face the *"great white throne"* judgment of Revelation 20:11-15, a judgment of condemnation. The church, on the other hand, will face *"the judgment seat of Christ"* (2Corinthians 5:10), a judgment for rewards (1Corinthians 3:10-15). After all, *"There is...no condemnation for those who are in Christ Jesus"* (Romans 8:1). When we combine this truth with Hebrews 9:28, we will not be surprised to find that Christ's death (and subsequent resurrection) prevents us from facing God's condemnation. In fact, not a single misdeed will be mentioned when we see Jesus face to face:

> so Christ also, having been offered once to bear the sins of many, shall appear a second time for salvation without reference to sin, to those who eagerly await Him. (Hebrews 9:28)

Do you know what this means? It means that we live in a constant state of forgiveness. Yes, we must confess sin and repent of sin when we disobey. We do so, however, not to receive forgiveness, but to have fellowship restored with the Father. Why should we seek forgiveness for that which has already been forgiven? If you have a copy of the *Romans 1-8* course distributed by this ministry, it would be profitable to read the section associated with Romans 6:7. The subject of forgiveness is addressed in much detail there.

The New Testament believer lives in a constant state of forgiveness.

One final thought and we will progress to Hebrews 10. On the Day of Atonement, the high priest appeared to the people after entering God's presence. He did so to ensure the nation that everything had gone as planned and that his offering had been accepted. In the same way, Jesus' return will confirm that His offering was well pleasing to the Father.

We will take what we have studied and apply it to next week's material. Because Hebrews 10 is necessary input for victorious living, it will be examined in as much depth as possible. Warning: Don't become overly concerned if you fail to grasp everything the first time through. To digest the depths of what is recorded in this fascinating chapter (chapter 10) will require a lifetime and more.

Have a great day, and know that God is well pleased with your progress!

Hebrews 10 Questions

First Day

More "meaty" material will be covered this week than in any of the previous weeks. In fact, chapter 10 may be the most important chapter in this entire epistle. Be sure to work through all the questions and read the entire lesson before progressing to Hebrews 11. You will be glad you did, even though it will take more time and a greater commitment than in prior chapters.

1. Read Hebrews 10. If *"the Law…has only a shadow of the good things to come and not the very form of things"* (v.1), what is the real thing? Consult Colossians 2:16-17 for assistance. What was the Law incapable of accomplishing (Hebrews 10:1)? Note: The word *"perfect"* means, "to have reached an end, to be finished or complete." In this context, therefore, it means to be <u>made</u> *"perfect"* and totally forgiven before the Father—and granted access into His presence.

2. How does verse 2 tie in with what you gleaned from verse 1? How did the *"sacrifices"* offered under the old covenant negatively impact the worshipper (v.3)?

3. Did the animals offered under the old covenant remove *"sin"* (v.4)? What purpose did these offerings serve? (We dealt with the answer in last week's lesson.) Was faith required on the part of the person presenting the offering, or did God accept these offerings regardless of the condition of the heart (Isaiah 1:11-15; Jeremiah 6:20; 7:22-23; Amos 5:22-24; Micah 6:6-8)?

4. What do verses 5-9 teach regarding the ineffectiveness of the sacrifices offered under the Law? What did God *"prepare"* (v.5), and Who lived in it (vv.5, 7, and 9)? To what do the words *"first"* and *"second"* in the last phrase of verse 9 refer? Considering the historical setting of this book, what would you have been thinking by now had you been one of the Hebrew Christians addressed in this epistle? What are you doing to make sure that you are laying aside all forms of legalism and latching on to Christ's *"freedom"* (Galatians 5:1)?

5. To be *"sanctified"* in this application (v.10) means to be <u>made</u> holy, set apart, <u>made</u> into a saint. Thus, if you are a believer, have you been *"sanctified"* (v.10) in your soul and spirit—made a saint? Why is it important to know that you have been <u>made</u> holy and not just <u>declared</u> holy? Through what avenue were you made holy (v.10)?

6. According to verse 10, how many times can Jesus die? Challenge question: If you are a believer, did you die with Christ (v.10)? How does this relate to Romans 6:6 and Romans 7:4?

Second Day

1. Read Hebrews 10. Don't forget to pray. How often did the Levitical priests offer *"sacrifices"* for sin (v.11)? What does this communicate about the ineffectiveness of these sacrifices? Did the priests stand or sit while offering these sacrifices (v.11)? Did these sacrifices *"take away"* sin (v.11)? Again, what did these sacrifices accomplish in the life of the offender?

2. How many sacrifices did Jesus offer for sin (v.12)? How many sins were placed on Christ (v.12)? What does this communicate concerning the effectiveness of His sacrifice? Does this superior effectiveness mean that the New Testament believer is totally forgiven and no longer required to seek forgiveness for sin? What did Jesus do (what posture did He assume) after offering His sacrifice (v.12; Hebrews 1:3)? What is He doing today (Romans 8:34; Hebrews 7:25)?

3.   For what is Jesus *"waiting"* (v.13)? What occurred with Christ's enemies as a result of the cross (reference Hebrews 2:14 and Colossians 2:14-15 for assistance)?   Will His enemies eventually *"bow"* to Him (Philippians 2:10-11; Revelation 19:11-16)?

4.   The New International Version translates Hebrews 10:14 as, *"because by one sacrifice he has made perfect forever those who are being made holy."* How could a person who has been *"made perfect"* be in the process of *"being made holy"*? Think long and hard before answering, for this is one of the most important questions we will address. If you have been *"perfected for all time"* (v.14 NASB), is it possible for you to become imperfect and lose your righteousness? How does Philippians 1:6 tie in here?

5.   Verses 15-18 deal with the new *"covenant."* How does verse 15 confirm that Jeremiah's statements in Jeremiah 31:33-34 (quoted in Hebrews 10:16-17) were spoken through the avenue of the *"Spirit"* of God? No doubt, the Word of God is totally inspired—God breathed. Does God have a list of the *"sins"* committed by those who have entered into the new covenant (Hebrews 10:17)? After Jesus was crucified, could any future *"offering"* remove man's sin (Hebrews 10:18)? If not, why not?

Third Day

1.   Read Hebrews 10. Why does verse 19 confirm that this epistle was written to believers? If the words *"holy place"* (v.19) refer to the Holy of Holies, what were these believers permitted to do that was prohibited under the Law? What allowed them to do so (v.19)? To what does the phrase, *"by a new and living way"* (v.20), make reference?

2.   Prior to Jesus' crucifixion, His *"flesh"* was the barrier between God and man (v.20)—much the same as the veil in the temple served as a barrier between God and man. What occurred in the earthly *"temple"* when Jesus died (Matthew 27:50-51)? Under the old covenant, and before Jesus was crucified, could a priest enter the presence of God anytime he liked? Can New Testament believers, as priests (1Peter 2:9), enter God's presence whenever they desire? What then does the writer mean by the phrase, *"the veil, that is, His flesh"* (Hebrews 10:20)? Could we approach *"the throne of grace"* (Hebrews 4:16) had Jesus not died physically?

3.   How is Jesus described in verse 21? What does His high priesthood allow us to do as New Testament believers (v.22)? What does the phrase, *"having our hearts sprinkled clean from an evil conscience and our bodies washed with pure water"* (v.22), communicate to you? This week's lesson has much to say regarding this phrase, but don't go there until you have spent ample time attempting to answer the question on your own. You might read Leviticus 8:30 and Exodus 29:21, along with Leviticus 8:6, for assistance. Does Hebrews 10:22 teach that water baptism is required for spiritual regeneration?

4.   Did the writer pen verse 23 for the purpose of encouraging these believers to *"hold fast"* to their salvation? If not, to what were they to *"hold fast"*? What statement in this verse should have motivated them to do so? Do you always view Christ as verse 23 describes Him? If not, why not?

5.   What were these readers encouraged to do in verse 24? How does verse 25 confirm that these believers had feared *"assembling together"*? A certain *"day"* was *"drawing near"* (v.25). To what *"day"* is the writer making reference? Read Matthew 24:2, Luke 21:6, and Luke 21:20-24 for assistance.

Fourth Day

1. Read Hebrews 10. It is impossible to properly interpret verses 26-31 without considering the historical background of this epistle. Willful sin (v.26) is premeditated sin, sin we commit understanding its wrongness from the beginning. Different from sins committed in ignorance, willful sin applies to the book of Hebrews as follows: After receiving Christ, to continue offering animal sacrifices out of a lack of understanding was one thing. To offer them after knowing better was another. Thus, willful sin would have resulted had these Hebrew Christians offered animal sacrifices at the temple. Why so? They had been warned against such actions through the writer's instruction. Does verse 26 teach that these believers would have lost their salvation had they willfully disobeyed, or does it teach that no sacrifice atoned for sin now that Jesus has died? Also, had they been capable of losing their salvation through willful sin, could they have regained it later (Hebrews 6:6)? Could it be that the writer desired his readers to understand that sacrifices after the cross failed to atone for sin? Therefore the phrase, *"there no longer remains a sacrifice for sins"* (Hebrews 10:26).

2. After answering the following questions, verse 26 should come alive. Was it proper to offer sacrifices on the Monday before Jesus was crucified on Friday? What about the day before He died? Let's jump to the Monday after the resurrection. Was it still proper to offer sacrifices? If not, why not? Do you better understand the phrase, *"there no longer remains a sacrifice for sins"* (v.26)? If so, why? How does this relate to what we studied in Hebrews 10:18?

3. What resulted when willful sin was committed in Old Testament times (Numbers 15:30; Exodus 21:14)? Would these Hebrew Christians have been familiar with this teaching? What happened in Corinth (in the New Testament) when willful sin was committed (1Corinthians 11:27-30)? Considering the historical background of Hebrews and the coming of A.D. 70 (when the *"judgment"* of *"fire"* would destroy Jerusalem and the unbelieving Jews, God's *"adversaries"*), what would Hebrews 10:27 have communicated to these readers? Can you now see why verses 26 and 27 are <u>not</u> dealing with believers losing their salvation? Explain.

4. Verse 28 is based on Deuteronomy 17:2-6. What happened to those who sinned willfully under *"the Law of Moses"* (Deuteronomy 17:2-6)? How does this confirm our earlier findings regarding willful sin? Had the Hebrew Christians addressed in this epistle sinned willfully, what would they have experienced (Hebrews 10:29)? Were they already *"sanctified"* in their souls and spirits (v.29)? Can believers (who are *"sanctified"* in their souls and spirits) sometimes exhibit the behavior described in verse 29? Do they lose their salvation when they respond as such? If salvation could be lost, could it be regained at a later date (Hebrews 6:6)? If these questions seem confusing, the *Romans 1-8* course (distributed by this ministry) can add much assistance.

5. Considering that Hebrews 10:30 is based on Deuteronomy 32:35-36, Hebrews 10:30-31 addresses the chastening, or correction, these believers would receive should they return to Judaism. We will discover in Hebrews 12 that God *"disciplines"* believers for the purpose of correcting their behavior (this differs from the wrath that He displays toward unbelievers). How do 1Corinthians 5:5 and Acts 5:1-6 confirm that God sometimes takes believers out of the world (due to His love for them) rather than allow them to continue wallowing in sin?

6. How do verses 32-34 prove that the recipients of this epistle were believers? From the last phrase of verse 34, what did they know that allowed them to respond so righteously prior to their present state of weakness? Does this perspective characterize your life? If not, why not? How does the fact that these believers once walked in the authority of God, and then became *"dull of hearing"* (Hebrews 5:11-14), encourage you to *"pay...closer attention to what we have heard"* (Hebrews 2:1)?

Fifth Day

1. Read Hebrews 10. Does verse 35 teach that these believers were not to *"throw away"* their salvation? If not, what is it communicating? Why was it important for the readers to possess *"confidence"*? How do you retain your *"confidence"*? How does the last phrase of verse 35 tie in with the following passages: 1Corinthians 3:11-15; 2Corinthians 5:10; 2Timothy 4:7-8; James 1:12; 1Peter 5:1-4; Revelation 2:10. Not once does the author threaten his readers with a loss of salvation. His concern is their loss of rewards at the judgment seat of Christ along with the impending danger of A.D. 70.

2. What did these believers *"need"* (v.36)? How is *"endurance"* obtained (2Corinthians 12:9; Hebrews 4:16)? What would the readers receive after doing *"the will of God"* (Hebrews 10:36)? How does this relate to Hebrews 10:35?

3. Verses 37-38 quote Habakkuk 2:3-4. God had revealed to Habakkuk that certain events would transpire among his people, but Habakkuk was to wait in patient endurance for their fulfillment (Habakkuk 2:3). He was also to wait in *"faith"* (Habakkuk 2:4). Why would the writer of Hebrews desire that his readers consider this segment of Habakkuk's life?

4. How does verse 39 confirm that believers are secure in their relationship with Christ?

Sixth Day

1. Read Hebrews 10. Read this week's lesson and record any new insights. This lesson is very long, but one you should read and thoroughly digest. I can't stress enough the importance of learning the details of Hebrews 10. Have fun, but don't feel pressed to finish the lesson in one day—or maybe even two or three days!

Hebrews 10 Lesson

This chapter contains an abundance of "meat," so prepare for a feast. We will first deal with the ineffectiveness of the sacrifices offered under the old covenant (vv.1-4), move next to the superiority of Christ's sacrifice (vv.5-18), and conclude by studying some of the most thought-provoking and, many times, misinterpreted passages in the entire Word of God (vv.19-39).

The writer begins this chapter with an amazing truth:

> *For the Law, since it has only a shadow of the good things to come and not the very form of things, can never by the same sacrifices year by year, which they offer continually, make perfect those who draw near.* (Hebrews 10:1)

Because the Law is *"a shadow of the good things to come"* (v.1), the sacrifices associated with the old covenant only pointed to the real thing—for *"a shadow"* validates that an object exists. The real thing was (and is) Jesus Christ. Note how Colossians 2:16-17 confirms this truth:

> *Therefore let no one act as your judge in regard to food or drink or in respect to a festival or a new moon or a Sabbath day — things which are a mere shadow of what is to come; but the substance belongs to Christ.* (Colossians 2:16-17)

The Law is *"a shadow...and not the very form of things"* (Hebrews 10:1) because Christ is the substance to which the Law points. Consequently, the phrase, *"the good things to come"* (Hebrews 10:1), refers to the finished work of Jesus Christ (His life, death, resurrection, ascension, etc.) and all that results from those miraculous events—of which the Law is only *"a shadow."*

Under the old covenant, the *"sacrifices"* were offered *"continually,"* *"year by year"* (v.1). Yet, they could never *"make"* the worshipper *"perfect"* (v.1). The word *"perfect"* means, "to have reached an end, to be finished or complete." In this context it means to be made totally *"perfect"* in your person—in your soul and spirit. Only through Jesus' death, burial, and resurrection can such a transformation be realized. Thus, through the finished work of Jesus, who you were before you became new (the Adamic nature, old man, old self, sinful nature, dead spirit—all synonymous) has been eradicated (Romans 6:6; 7:4; Galatians 2:20). You have also been forgiven (Ephesians 4:32; Colossians 2:13; 1John 2:12), and you are *"in Christ"* at the right hand of the Father in heaven (Ephesians 2:6). You, therefore, are <u>perfect</u> before the Father in your person—as will be verified again in Hebrews 10:14. Yet, the Law and its sacrificial system could never bring the Jewish nation into God's presence. Before the cross, only one man from one tribe (and from one nation) could approach Him one day of the year—with blood for himself and for the people. Undeniably, the Law made no one *"perfect."*

Had the animal sacrifices under the old covenant produced perfection, they would *"have ceased to be offered"* (v.2). The *"worshippers"* would have been totally *"cleansed"* and relieved of any *"consciousness of sins"*:

> *Otherwise, would they not have ceased to be offered, because the worshipers, having once been cleansed, would no longer have had consciousness of sins?* (Hebrews 10:2)

Instead of easing the worshipper's conscience, the *"sacrifices"* served as *"a reminder"* that sins had not yet been removed:

> *But in those sacrifices there is a reminder of sins year by year.* (Hebrews 10:3)

No matter how many animals were offered, the awareness of sin remained. Why? Sins were not removed through the offerings presented under the Law. They were only covered (Romans

3:25; Acts 17:30), atoned for:

> *For it is impossible for the blood of bulls and goats to take away sins.* (Hebrews 10:4)

Under the new covenant, on the other hand, God remembers our sins *"no more"* (Jeremiah 31:33-34). Thank you Jesus!

Note that only *"bulls and goats"* are mentioned in the last portion of verse 4? *"For it is impossible for the blood of bulls and goats to take away sins."* The writer is emphasizing the sacrifices offered on the Day of Atonement, even though other sacrifices were offered daily, weekly, and monthly throughout the year. On this special day, the high priest would first enter the Holy of Holies with blood for his own sins (the blood of a *"bull"*—Leviticus 16:11-14), leave the Holy of Holies and return with blood for the sins of the people (the *"blood"* of a *"goat"*—Leviticus 16:15). Consequently, although the writer emphasizes the Day of Atonement, we must see that neither the blood of animals nor any sacrifice sanctioned by the old covenant could take away sin. The sacrifices offered under the Law only covered (atoned for) sin until Christ's death on the cross. After Christ's crucifixion, no sacrifice or offering any longer covered (atoned for) sin.

Let's make sure that we understand the significance of the sacrifices offered under the old covenant. We have learned that they were but a shadow of the real thing—of what Christ would accomplish on the cross. They did not provide forgiveness, but rather covered sin (made atonement for sin) until Christ could die. You may ask, "Did they, in every case, serve as a covering for sin?" No! Only sacrifices offered in faith were capable of doing so. You may then ask, "What was required for a sacrifice to be offered in faith?" Beyond complying with the ceremonial Law, the person bringing the offering had to view it as pointing to the greater, more perfect sacrifice of the Messiah, Jesus Christ. To merely offer a sacrifice, even if it complied with the ceremonial Law, brought no atonement. Faith in the *"seed"* of Genesis 3:15, Who is *"Christ"* (Galatians 3:16), has always been the difference maker—regardless of whether a person lived before or after the issuing of the Law (Romans 4:13-16). We will address the subject of faith more fully in Hebrews 11.

The sacrifices offered under the Law could never remedy man's core problem. Mankind had inherited a sin nature from Adam, a nature that loves and enjoys sin. This sin nature is also known in theological circles as the Adamic nature, old self, old man, or dead spirit. Animal sacrifices could only cleanse outwardly. (Read Hebrews 9:13-14 and Numbers 19 for verification.) Man was in need of a sacrifice that could transform inwardly—rectify the issues of the heart, the core of man. Jesus Christ was and is the only remedy!

Jesus Christ was and is the only remedy.

Have you considered that the animals selected as an offering for sin had no choice in the matter? They could not refuse to be sacrificed. Jesus, however, had a choice. Thus, His decision to die was based on faith. His very spirit and soul were involved when He submitted to the cross. Only sacrifices offered in faith pleased God (read Isaiah 1:11-15; Jeremiah 6:20; 7:22-23; Amos 5:22-24; Micah 6:6-8). Hence, Jesus' offering was exceedingly more pleasing to the Father than the animal offerings associated with the Law.

Because Jesus is the Son of the Father, and not the son of Joseph, He was born void of a sin nature. Having been born void of a sin nature, along with the fact that He lived a sinless life, is why He was the perfect sacrifice. It is also why a believer's inward being benefits from His sacrifice. In fact, in Romans 6:6 we find that our *"old self"* (the sin nature, Adamic nature, old man, or dead spirit that we inherited from Adam) *"was crucified"* on the cross *"with"* Christ. (The *Romans 1-8* study distributed by this ministry addresses this subject in much depth.) Also, 2Corinthians 5:17 states that all New Testament believers have been placed *"in Christ"* and made *"new."* As a result, we want to serve Christ with all that is within us, even though we, at times, commit acts of sin. In light of these truths, why New Testament believers' hearts are so radically altered through faith in God's selfless Son is easily understood.

Hebrews 10:5-9, which quotes portions of Psalm 40:6-8 along with additional truths, fits perfectly with what we have recently studied. The animal sacrifices, even though covering sin when properly offered, could not remove sin. Thus, in this sense, God took *"no pleasure"* in them (Hebrews 10:5, 6, and 8). Only a perfect sacrifice, one in which a sinless God-man would choose (through faith) to die for sinful man, could remove man's sin. God, as a result, *"prepared"* *"a body"* for His Son:

> *Therefore, when He comes into the world, He says, "SACRIFICE AND OFFERING THOU*
> *HAST NOT DESIRED, BUT A BODY THOU HAST PREPARED FOR ME;* (Hebrews 10:5)

His Son lived in that *"body"* (v.5), chose through faith to do the Father's *"will"* (vv.7 and 9), and died so a repentant sinner might be made new.

The writer makes a statement in the latter portion of verse 9 that deserves special attention:

> *then He said, "BEHOLD, I HAVE COME TO DO THY WILL." He takes away the first in*
> *order to establish the second.* (Hebrews 10:9)

Note the words, *"He takes away the first in order to establish the second."* The *"first"* refers to the old covenant and its accompanying animal sacrifices, while the *"second"* points to Christ's sacrifice and the ushering in of a totally new covenant. Yes, the old covenant is null and void, totally eclipsed by the new.

Let's take what we have gleaned and plug it into the events of 64-66 A.D. The unbelieving Jews controlled Jerusalem and desired that all Jews (even those who had accepted Christ) offer sacrifices at the temple. These unbelieving Jews mistakenly presumed that righteousness could be attained through the ritualistic observance of the ceremonial law—through merely offering the sacrifices. But why would the Jews who had accepted Christ choose to live under such an obsolete system? Because it would be foolish for them to do so, the writer is encouraging his readers to accept the persecution from the unbelieving Jews, remove themselves (or remain separated) from the temple sacrifices, and walk in faith. No doubt, the writer has made his point and made it well.

Are you seeing the importance of laying aside all forms of legalism and latching on to Christ's *"freedom"* (Galatians 5:1)? We must *"be diligent to enter"* the *"rest"* available through Jesus alone (Hebrews 4:9-11).

Verses 10-14 of Hebrews 10 contain some of the most exciting truths in the entire Word of God. In verse 10 we find that the New Testament believer has *"been sanctified"*:

> *By this will we have been sanctified through the offering of the body of Jesus Christ once for all.*
> *(Hebrews* 10:10)

To be *"sanctified"* means to be <u>made</u> holy, set apart, <u>made</u> a saint. Notice that we are not <u>declared</u> holy, or <u>declared</u> saints, but rather are <u>made</u> holy, <u>made</u> saints. This truth is not "Positional Truth," as some claim. "Positional Truth" suggests that God somehow <u>declares</u> us to be *"sanctified,"* holy, and a saint, yet <u>perceives</u> us as nothing more than lowly sinners saved by grace. Consequently, according to this view, we are both holy and unholy at the same time. Let's (from a Scriptural basis) prove this invalid.

The New Testament believer is not <u>declared</u> holy when he accepts Christ as Savior, but rather is <u>made</u> holy. We can be dogmatic here because the word *"sanctified"* (v.10) is in the perfect tense. (It is a perfect, passive, participle for you Greek students.) The perfect tense communicates past, completed action, with a resulting state of being. Therefore, we need not worry

The New Testament believer is not declared holy, but rather is made holy.

about losing our saintly status (losing our salvation), for we have forever been *"sanctified"* (made holy) in our person (in our souls and spirits). Actually, our person (who we were made into at the point of justification) will be no more holy or saintly when we see Jesus than when we were saved (*"justified"*—Romans 5:1). We will <u>behave</u> in a more saintly manner the more we mature in Christ (because we love righteousness and hate sin), but our identity (who God made us into subsequent to our repenting and believing while depraved) does not depend on how well we behave. As was emphasized earlier in our study, what we do is not who we are, even though who we are has a tremendous impact on what we do. If you know Jesus, you are a saint who sometimes sins, not a lowly sinner saved by grace. If you should tell a lie, you are a saint who has told a lie—not a filthy, no-good liar. Think about what has been stated here, ponder this amazing truth, and digest as much as you can. We will cover this subject in more depth when we arrive at Hebrews 10:14. (The *Romans 1-8* study deals with this subject in great depth as well.)

The reason you have been *"sanctified"* (made holy, made a saint) in your person (soul and spirit) is that Jesus was offered *"once for all"* (Hebrews 10:10). In other words, He died one time *"for all"* sin and, therefore, for all people—so those who repent and believe (while depraved) can be spiritually regenerated—be made new. Once your Adamic nature was eradicated (Romans 6:6; Romans 7:4; Galatians 2:20), it was replaced by the *"new"* man (2Corinthians 5:17) who is *"holy"* (Ephesians 1:4) and *"perfect"* (Hebrews 10:14). (The *Romans 1-8* study can be referenced for additional input should you possess a copy.)

The priests under the old covenant offered *"the same sacrifices"* *"time after time,"* *"sacrifices"* which could *"never take away sins"* (Hebrews 10:11:

> *And every priest stands daily ministering and offering time after time the same sacrifices, which can never take away sins;* (Hebrews 10:11)

The priests' work was never done; thus they <u>stood</u> daily (v.11). Not so with Jesus. He *"sat down"* (Hebrews 1:3) when He offered His *"blood"* in the heavenly tabernacle (Hebrews 9:12), confirming that His work in regard to forgiveness is complete. His responsibilities today lie in the area of intercession for the saints (Romans 8:34; Hebrews 7:25), for He has dealt with sin once and for all.

Hebrews 10:12 confirms these truths:

> *but He, having offered one sacrifice for sins for all time, SAT DOWN AT THE RIGHT HAND OF GOD,* (Hebrews 10:12)

Jesus *"offered one sacrifice for sins for all time."* He then *"sat down at the right hand of God."* Conclusion: We are a forgiven people—we live in a state of forgiveness. Consequently, when we repent and confess sins as New Testament believers, we do so to restore fellowship with the Father—not to receive forgiveness. We will confess and repent so long as we live in earthly bodies. But to ask for forgiveness, something we already possess, is an unscriptural prayer. Why? Jesus' blood removed *"sins for all time"* (v.12)—*"all"* our past, present, and future *"sins."* Note: Jesus died for the sins of all mankind, not just the sins of believers (Hebrews 10:12; John 3:16). Only through personal repentance

Jesus died for the sins of all mankind, not just the sins of believers.

and faith (exercised while depraved), however, does God bestow forgiveness to the New Testament believer. For more input, read what the *Romans 1-8* study (distributed by this ministry) states regarding Romans 6:7.

Jesus is waiting for the day when His *"enemies"* will *"be made a footstool for His feet"* (Hebrews 10:13; Psalm 110:1). This "event" will occur in conjunction with His Second Coming, at which time He will return to war against His foes (Revelation 19:11-16). His enemies were actually conquered at the cross (Hebrews 2:14; Colossians 2:14-15), but they will not bow at His feet (Philippians 2:10-11) until after He returns.

We must be careful with Hebrews 10:14 or some wonderful truths will be overlooked. The verse states:

> *For by one offering He has perfected for all time those who are sanctified.* (Hebrews 10:14 NASB)

The word *"perfected"* is in the perfect tense, making it past, completed action, with a resulting state of being. The word *"sanctified,"* on the other hand, is in the present tense, indicating an ongoing process. For this reason, the words, *"being sanctified,"* are found in the margins of some New American Standard Bibles. This distinction also explains why the New International Version translates Hebrews 10:14 as:

> *"because by one sacrifice he has made perfect forever those who are <u>being made holy</u>."*
> (Hebrews 10:14 NIV—emphasis added)

What an amazing thought!

Have you realized that God can make New Testament believers (their spirits and souls) perfect (holy) before their behavior has been perfected and made holy—before their actions line up with who they are in their spirits and souls? Again, what you do is not who you are, even though who you are has a tremendous impact on what you do. Thus, God's acceptance of you is not performance-based. His acceptance of you is Jesus-based! Note: The words, *"being made holy"* (NIV), or *"are sanctified,"* or *"being sanctified"* (NASB), are in the passive voice, verifying that God is the One Who sanctifies our behavior as we mature in the faith. Our responsibility, therefore, is to exercise our free will and choose to pursue His heart. As we do so, we find that our choices line up with His will on an ever-increasing basis. Consequently, God doesn't remove our freedom of choice as He sanctifies our behavior—as some have incorrectly assumed. Rather, He honors our choices to know Him intimately by revealing His Person—which automatically affects the decisions we make (by means of our own wills) as sons. This progression fits perfectly with what Paul teaches in 2Corinthians 3:18:

> *But we all, with unveiled face beholding as in a mirror the glory of the Lord, are being transformed into the same image from glory to glory, just as from the Lord, the Spirit.*
> (2Corinthians 3:18)

Because we were *"made perfect forever"* (Hebrews 10:14 NIV), or *"for all time"* (Hebrews 10:14 NASB) when we were saved (made new), we cannot, under any circumstance, become imperfect or lose our righteousness. This security should be comforting news for all who have wondered if they would finish the race. One fact is certain: God's grace will carry us to the end (Philippians 1:6). So rest, dear friend, in God's ability to fulfill what He has promised!

Rest, dear friend, in God's ability to fulfill what He has promised!

Hebrews 10:15-18 emphasizes the advantages of the new *"covenant."* The fact that those who worshiped under the old covenant would one day be perfected and forgiven is recorded in Old Testament Scripture (read Jeremiah 31:33-34) and quoted in

Hebrews 10:16-17. Notice that *"the Holy Spirit"* receives credit for speaking through Jeremiah (Hebrews 10:15). Thus, *"the Holy Spirit"* (v.15) verified that God would *"write"* His *"laws upon"* the hearts of men (v.16) at some point in the future—and believers would receive new hearts (Hebrews 10:16; Jeremiah 31:33; Ezekiel 11:19-20; 36:26-27) due to the eradication of the Adamic nature (Romans 6:6) and birth of the *"new"* man (2Corinthians 5:17). God would also forget (and forgive) their *"sins"* (Hebrews 10:17; Jeremiah 31:34). No doubt, when sins are forgiven, *"there is no longer any offering for sin"* (Hebrews 10:18). As a result, Christ's selfless and sinless *"offering"* not only frees God to perfect and forgive repentant sinners, but to render all other offerings obsolete. Remember this truth when we address Hebrews 10:26.

The writer has proven that the sacrifices associated with the old covenant could never remove sin. He has also established that all offerings subsequent to the cross are ineffective. His goal of convincing his readers to denounce the temple sacrifices and go on to spiritual maturity would come to full fruition. They followed his instruction, and not one of them died in the destruction of 70 A.D. Yes, truth always sets us free!

Unquestionably, the most intense theology addressed in Hebrews is behind us. Beginning with verse 19 and continuing to the end of the book, we will study how New Testament believers are to apply these truths in their daily experience.

The word *"therefore"* in verse 19 substantiates our need to consider what we have studied previously:

> *Since therefore, brethren, we have confidence to enter the holy place by the blood of Jesus,*
> (Hebrews 10:19)

Notice that the writer is addressing Jewish believers (*"brethren"*—v.19). Due to Jesus' perfect offering, these Hebrew Christians could *"have confidence to enter the holy place."* Can you imagine how these words affected their perception of God? Remember, the writer is addressing Jews—Jews who all of their lives understood that only the high priest entered God's presence one day of the year. They were now being told to *"enter the holy place"* anytime they desired. (When the writer uses *"holy place"* he is referring to the Holy of Holies, where God's presence dwelt.) And why could they enter? Jesus' *"blood"* had been shed (v.19), and Jesus' *"flesh"* (body) had been offered (v.20):

> *by a new and living way which He inaugurated for us through the veil, that is, His flesh,*
> (Hebrews 10:20)

These readers could enter God's presence because *"a new and living way"* (v.20) had been *"inaugurated"* through Christ's offering. The *"way"* was *"new"* because Christ's *"blood"* had just been shed and His body *("flesh")* had just been offered. It was *"living"* because the Sacrifice Who had provided forgiveness and new life was alive and well at the right hand of the Father.

In light of what we have gleaned, let's draw some solid conclusions. Obviously, more took place on the cross than Jesus shedding His blood. He also died! Did He die alone? No, because *"our old self"* died *"with Him"* (Romans 6:6). Consequently, had a major portion of His blood been shed without His accompanying death, we would still be shackled in sin. Why? Two things had to transpire before we could become members of God's family: (1) Our *"old self"* was required to be eradicated (2) Our acts of sin had to be forgiven. Now consider this: Our sins were forgiven through Christ's shed *"blood"* (Hebrews 9:24-26; Revelation 1:5), which symbolized the fact that He had died. On the other hand, our *"old self"*—our Adamic nature, or old man, who we were prior to salvation—was eradicated through Christ's *"body"* (Romans 6:6; Romans 7:4). The *"old self"* was then replaced by the *"new"* man, or the *"new"* creation (2Corinthians 5:17). For specific information regarding the *"new"* man, and the eradication of the *"old self,"* reference the *Romans 1-8* study (should you have a copy).

Salvation includes much more than receiving forgiveness for sin.

Salvation (justification) includes much more than receiving forgiveness for sin. Our old self (old man, sinful nature, dead spirit, or Adamic nature—all synonymous) had to also be removed. Why? Ephesians 2:3 speaks of our condition before we were justified (saved) and made new. We were *"children of wrath"* because of our in-born identity, the nature we had inherited from Adam. Thus, our acts of sin would not have condemned us to hell but who we were in our *"nature"* (Ephesians 2:3). This noteworthy distinction doesn't mean, however, that in our lost (depraved) state we were incapable of recognizing our sin and, in turn, accepting Christ as Savior. After all, Adam and Eve *"knew that they were naked"* subsequent to sinning and becoming depraved (Genesis 3:7). Understanding this truth in the midst of their depravity confirms that they were anything but spiritual corpses. (The *God's Heart* series distributed by this ministry covers this subject in much greater depth.)

Let's now examine the statement, *"the veil, that is, His flesh"* (Hebrews 10:20). Before Jesus was crucified, His *"flesh"* was the barrier between God and man—much the same as the veil in the temple served as a barrier between God and man. Therefore, had Christ not died, our access to God would have forever been prohibited. As a result, the veil in the temple, as a symbol of His *"flesh,"* *"was torn in two"* at the point of His physical death (Matthew 27:50-51). In fact, after the veil was split, nothing separated the holy place from the Holy of Holies (as was addressed earlier in the study). This removal of the veil symbolized that these believers, as priests (1Peter 2:9), could speak with God as often as they liked (Hebrews 4:16; 6:19; 10:19-20). And so can we!! Isn't this terrific news?

Note that Jesus is *"a great priest"* (Hebrews 10:21), a fitting description due to His crucifixion, burial, and resurrection. He is also <u>our</u> priest, for we read, *"we have a great priest"* (v.21). Isn't it encouraging to know that our high priest is the holy Son of God, the perfect sacrifice through Whom we have access to the Father? Jesus is also *"over the house of God"* (v.21), and we live *"in"* Him (Ephesians 2:6). Wow!

While on the subject of priests, the writer's wording of verse 22 draws attention to the Old Testament rites of priestly purification:

> *let us draw near with a sincere heart in full assurance of faith, having our hearts sprinkled clean from an evil conscience and our bodies washed with pure water.* (Hebrews 10:22)

Notice the phrase, *"having our hearts sprinkled clean from an evil conscience and our bodies washed with pure water"* (v.22). Moses was required to sprinkle Aaron and his sons with the *"blood"* of an animal, along with *"some of the anointing oil"* (Leviticus 8:30; Exodus 29:21), before they could function as priests. He was also required to wash them *"with water"* (Leviticus 8:6). Thus, the sins of the priests (covered through the blood of an animal), along with the cleansing of their bodies with water, had to be addressed before they could function in their priestly office. Let's examine these two rites of purification, link them to what we have discovered, and discuss how they relate to the New Testament believer's relationship with Christ.

As has already been stated, Moses was required to sprinkle Aaron and his sons with *"blood"* and *"anointing oil"* (Leviticus 8:30; Exodus 29:21). Because the *"blood"* of animals only covered (atoned for) sins (Hebrews 10:4), the priests lived with a *"consciousness of sins"* (Hebrews 9:9; 10:2). The blood of Jesus, however, *"put away sin"* (Hebrews 9:26) and therefore removes sin's accompanying guilt. Consequently, New Testament believers, as priests (1Peter 2:9), can approach God with a clear *"conscience"* (Hebrews 10:22), knowing their sins have been erased. These truths explain why the phrase, *"having our hearts sprinkled clean from an evil conscience"* (v.22), is in the perfect tense—signifying past, completed action, with a resulting state of being. New Testament believers are capable of living with a perfectly clear conscience, for we dwell in a state of perpetual forgiveness (1John 2:12). We must *"confess"* (1John 1:9) and repent (2Corinthians

7:9-10) of the sins committed after new birth, but not for the purpose of receiving forgiveness. Why should we ask for something we already possess? (Again, the *Romans 1-8* study addresses this subject more thoroughly.)

Moses also *"washed" "Aaron and his sons"* with *"water"* (Leviticus 8:6), cleansing their outer bodies. Through Jesus, on the other hand, New Testament believers are cleansed inwardly. In fact, they become new on the inside. As far back as Jeremiah 31:31-33, God spoke of a day when He would change man's *"heart."* After the cross, this change became a reality in the truest sense of the word—which explains Paul's declaration in 2Corinthians 5:17 that Christians have become *"new"* creatures. This new creature (new man) has *"been sanctified"* (Hebrews 10:10), made *"holy"* (Ephesians 1:4), and *"perfected"* (Hebrews 10:14). Sanctification points to being set apart for a special purpose—made holy in other words. Because the phrase, *"and our bodies washed with pure water"* (Hebrews 10:22), is in the perfect tense (again signifying past, completed action, with a resulting state of being), and because the outward washing of the priests pointed to the day when man would be made new inwardly, the New Testament believer's soul and spirit are forever sanctified—forever made holy. This sanctification is why the writer references the *"water"* as *"pure,"* the only place in the entire Bible where *"water"* is described as such. He is using a play on words, illustrating that unlike the outer cleansing of the priests who served under the Levitical system, Jesus makes the New Testament believer pure from within. This purification fits perfectly with what we studied in Hebrews 10:10 and Hebrews 10:14, which teach that our person (the new man) has *"been sanctified"* and *"perfected"* to the fullest degree possible. The *"old self,"* who we were before we were made new, has been *"crucified"* (Romans 6:6)—eradicated. Yet, the *"new"* man—the holy, blameless, redeemed, justified, sanctified, and glorified person we are now—lives on (2Corinthians 5:17).

It should be apparent at this juncture that Jesus' *"blood,"* which pointed to His death, *"released us from our sins"* (Revelation 1:5). It should also be apparent that through His *"body"* the *"old self"* was eradicated (Romans 6:6; 7:4), allowing the *"new"* man to be born (2Corinthians 5:17). As a result, these Hebrew Christians could draw near to God *"with a sincere heart in full assurance of faith"* (Hebrews 10:22) without a guilty conscience. Unlike the Old Testament priests, they had been *"sprinkled"* (past tense) with Christ's blood—which allowed their sins to be totally forgiven. This forgiveness occurred when they were spiritually regenerated (subsequent to exercising personal repentance and faith while depraved) and became priests (1Peter 2:9). The Old Testament priests' sins, on the other hand, were only covered through the purification rites associated with the Law. Also, these readers (their person—their inward identity) had been made totally new, unlike the Old Testament priests who had been washed in the outward sense only. (Remember that the outward washing of the priests pointed to the day when repentant sinners would be forgiven and made new inwardly through Jesus Christ.)

Old Testament believers were neither forgiven (Hebrews 10:12) nor *"made perfect"* until the cross (Hebrews 12:23—notice the phrase, *"the spirits of righteous men made perfect"*). The Old Testament believers, therefore, were saved "on credit" (Acts 17:30; Romans 3:25). We will discuss this subject in more detail later in the course.

> *Old Testament believers were neither forgiven nor made perfect until the cross.*

Some individuals have used the phrase, *"and our bodies washed with pure water"* (Hebrews 10:22), to attempt to prove that water baptism is required for spiritual regeneration. This idea is far from what is being communicated.

In Hebrews 10:23 we find the words, *"hold fast the confession of our hope without wavering."* Note that the readers were <u>not</u> encouraged to *"hold fast"* their salvation. Their salvation (their righteous standing before God) was secure. What were they to *"hold fast"*? They were to *"hold fast...without wavering"* their *"confession"* that Jesus is Messiah, the final sin offering. The Object of their *"hope,"* being *"faithful,"* and having *"promised,"* would sustain them to the end (v.23).

The writer encourages his readers *"to stimulate"* fellow believers *"to love and good deeds"* (v.24). Note that *"love"* is mentioned prior to *"good deeds."* The writer knew well that *"good deeds"* which impact lives flow from hearts inundated with God's *"love."* Consequently, if we desire to be used by the Lord, truly used by Him, we must first fall deeply in love with the God of love and *"good deeds"* will naturally follow. Other believers will be stimulated in the process. In fact, as they observe our lives, they will be invigorated to respond in a similar manner. Therefore, an exciting adventure awaits those who spend more time being a friend to Christ than a friend to others.

The readers are next urged to assemble for worship (Hebrews 10:25):

> *not forsaking our own assembling together, as is the habit of some, but encouraging one another;*
> *and all the more, as you see the day drawing near.* (Hebrews 10:25)

Evidently, *"some"* of these believers had feared *"assembling together"* (notice the phrase, *"as is the habit of some"*) because of persecution from the unbelieving Jews. Thus, the writer exhorts them to meet *"all the more"* as they *"see the day drawing near."* The *"day drawing near"* was the *"day"* addressed by Jesus in Matthew 24:2 and Luke 21:6, 20-24—the destruction of Jerusalem in A.D. 70.

One of the most debated verses in all the Scriptures is Hebrews 10:26:

> *For if we go on sinning willfully after receiving the knowledge of the truth, there no longer*
> *remains a sacrifice for sins.* (Hebrews 10:26)

As has already been established, willful sin (v.26) is premeditated sin, sin we commit knowing that it is wrong from the beginning. Different from sins committed in ignorance, willful sin applied to these Hebrew Christians as follows: To offer animal sacrifices (due to a lack of understanding) was one thing, but to offer them after knowing better was another. In fact, should they return to temple worship after having read Hebrews 1:1-10:25, they would be guilty of willful sin.

Some believers perceive Hebrews 10:26 as teaching that willful sin results in a loss of salvation. If this view were correct, one willful act of sin would bring eternal condemnation with no hope of restoration. I don't know about you, but I find it hard to believe that this mindset is in agreement with the gospel for which the apostles died. After all, Hebrews 6:6 verifies that if we could lose our salvation we could never gain it back—*"and then have fallen away, it is impossible to renew them again to repentance."* Surely, such an assessment of Hebrews 10:26 is improper.

To interpret verse 26 correctly, we must consider the historical events surrounding the passage. What follows will be somewhat of a review, but much needed input for proper analysis.

Jesus had been crucified some 34 to 36 years earlier, but many of these Hebrew Christians misunderstood the depth of the positive ramifications of His sacrifice. They evidently realized that sins were covered (atoned for) through the animals offered before the cross. They misunderstood, however, the worthlessness of the animal sacrifices subsequent to Jesus' death. Did these sacrifices continue to cover sin, or did Jesus' blood render them null and void? The best way to answer this question is to ask some questions—in fact, ask some of the same questions addressed earlier in the course.

Was it proper to offer sacrifices on the Monday before Jesus was crucified on Friday? Yes, if they were offered in anticipation of Christ's future sacrifice for sins! What about the day before He died? Of course they were proper! Let's jump to the Monday after the resurrection. Did it remain proper to offer animal sacrifices at this time? No way! The sacrifice for all sin, *"for all time,"* had just been offered (Hebrews 10:12). No other sacrifice could ever, under any circumstance, cover or remove sin. Thus the phrase, *"there no longer remains a sacrifice for sins"* (Hebrews 10:26). This truth fits perfectly with what was addressed in Hebrews 10:18 (you might want to review those notes).

Notice that the writer uses the term *"we"* (v.26). Should he or any of his readers sin willfully by returning to the obsolete sacrificial system associated with the Law, their sacrifices would mean nothing. There *"no longer"* remained *"a sacrifice for sins,"* for any and all additional sacrifices were now unacceptable. In the Old Testament, willful sin carried the sentence of physical death (Numbers 15:30; Exodus 21:14), a teaching familiar to these readers. A perfect New Testament example is 1Corinthians 11:30, where believers who refused to change their sinful ways experienced sickness and even death. If these Hebrew Christians returned to the temple sacrifices, they would be trapped in Jerusalem when the Romans arrived in A.D. 70. Entangled in the judgment directed toward the unbelieving Jews, they would lose their physical lives. This backdrop is basically to what Hebrews 10:27 is making reference:

> *but a certain terrifying expectation of judgment, and the fury of a fire which will consume the adversaries.* (Hebrews 10:27)

Note that the *"judgment"* would come against *"the adversaries."* We must never forget that the *"judgment"* of A.D. 70 was directed toward the unbelieving Jewish community, and that the *"fire"* consumed the city of Jerusalem along with hoards of unredeemed Jews. God did not allow the destruction for the purpose of judging Hebrew Christians who might be in Jerusalem unwisely submitting to the Law. They would, never the less, suffer the consequence of physical death should they be present when the Romans arrived. This discipline (or chastening) is not the same as judgment for the purpose of eternal condemnation, for *"There is…now no condemnation for those who are in Christ Jesus"* (Romans 8:1). The *"discipline"* does serve, however, as a means through which God corrects His erring children (Hebrews 12:8-11). The encouraging news is that, as a result of this epistle (along with passages such as Luke 21:20-24), no Hebrew Christian died in the judgment of A.D. 70. They had all fled before the Romans arrived.

In Hebrews 10:28-31, the writer contrasts willful sin during Old Testament times with willful sin in his day. In verse 28, he pens:

> *Anyone who has set aside the Law of Moses dies without mercy on the testimony of two or three witnesses."* (Hebrews 10:28)

This teaching is in agreement with earlier findings regarding willful sin under the old covenant (read Deuteronomy 17:2-6.) No doubt, these Hebrew Christians, living under the new covenant, were contemplating committing willful sin by reattaching themselves to the temple sacrifices. By doing so, they would experience *"much severer punishment"* (Hebrews 10:29), a more severe physical death in A.D. 70 than they could have imagined:

> *How much severer punishment do you think he will deserve who has trampled under foot the Son of God, and has regarded as unclean the blood of the covenant by which he was sanctified, and has insulted the Spirit of grace?* (Hebrews 10:29)

For some intriguing insights, read Josephus' account of the destruction of Jerusalem in 70 A.D. (his writings can be found online or ordered through most Christian bookstores). What Josephus records is amazingly gruesome, so make sure your meal is well digested before embarking on this endeavor!!

By going back under the Law, a Hebrew Christian male would disobey in the following manner: (1) He would trample *"under foot the Son of God"* (v.29), meaning that he would treat Christ with dishonor (2) He would regard *"as unclean the blood of the covenant by which he was sanctified"* (v.29), for his actions would indicate that Christ's blood was an insufficient offering—maybe even unholy (3) He would insult *"the Spirit of grace"* (v.29). After all, he had been *"born…of the Spirit"* (John 3:6, 8) *"by"* God's *"grace through"* the personal *"faith"* (Ephesians 2:8-9) exercised prior to spiritual regeneration. Should he return to the sacrificial system in Jerusalem, he would also be identifying himself with the generation of Jews guilty of the *"blasphemy"* of the Holy *"Spirit"* (Matthew 12:31)—the generation that rejected Christ's Messiahship, the generation that would receive God's indignation in A.D. 70. By such actions *"the Spirit of grace"* would be *"insulted"* (Hebrews 10:29).

> *Should these Hebrew Christians return to Judaism, they would dishonor Christ's sacrifice.*

Simply put, should these Hebrew Christians (who were *"sanctified"*—v.29) return to Judaism, they would dishonor Christ's sacrifice. God's *"punishment"* (or chastening) would follow (first phrase of verse 29), not for the purpose of condemning them to eternal damnation, but for the purpose of correcting their wayward behavior. This input allows us to properly interpret verses 30-31, especially verse 30's partial quote of Deuteronomy 32:35-36—*"Vengeance is Mine, I will repay,"* and *"The Lord will judge His people."* The writer in this instance takes an Old Testament principle and applies it to his day. Under the old covenant, willful disobedience (sin) resulted in physical death. These Hebrew Christians would reap the same consequence should they refuse to abandon the notion of returning to the temple sacrifices, such action being classified as willful sin.

God many times takes believers out of the world rather than allow them to continue in sin. 1Corinthians 5:5 verifies this fact, for Paul instructs the Corinthians *"to deliver"* the erring *"one to Satan"* to destroy *"his flesh."* This man repented and was restored to fellowship in 2Corinthians 2:6-8. Had he not done so, God may very well have taken him home (as was the case with Ananias and Sapphira in Acts 5:1-6). We must realize, however, that even when New Testament believers' sins result in physical death, *"condemnation"* in no way awaits them (Romans 8:1).

Truly:

> *It is a terrifying thing to fall into the hands of the living God.* (Hebrews 10:31)

Even when I fell into the hands of my earthly father (for the purpose of one of those old fashioned "whippings") it was one of the most terrifying moments of my childhood (I am thankful that he loved me enough to respond in this manner). But those times of discipline never caused me to lose my sonship. Our relationship with our heavenly Father is the same.

Verses 32-34 validate, beyond doubt, that this epistle was written to believers. In *"the former days,"* *"after being enlightened,"* they had *"endured a great conflict of sufferings"* (v.32). They had been *"made a public spectacle"* (v.33), which in the Greek means being exposed as in a theater, made a gazing-stock, an object of scorn, *"through reproaches and tribulations."* They had also suffered at the hands of unbelievers because of their association with fellow believers (v.33). They had shown *"sympathy"* toward God's people who were imprisoned (v.34) as well as *"accepted joyfully the seizure of"* their *"property"* (v.34). We must not overlook how they had endured. They had endured by appropriating the fact that *"a better possession and an abiding one"* awaited them in heaven (v.34).

Do you live as these Hebrew Christians once lived—prior to their compromise and resulting sin? Do you *"set your mind on the things above,"* on the heavenly things, rather than *"the things that are on earth"* (Hebrews 10:34; Colossians 3:2; 2Corinthians 4:18)? Jesus said that He was going *"to prepare a place for"* us (John 14:2-3), while Peter stated that we have an *"inheritance...reserved in heaven"* (1Peter 1:4). These phrases confirm what we will be studying in Hebrews 11:16 and Hebrews 13:14, passages that address our eternal home. Pure treasure awaits us there—*"a better possession and an abiding one"* (Hebrews 10:34). Therefore, we must allow the joy of this heavenly *"possession"* to free us from the trappings of the *"things of the world"* (first phrase of 1John 2:15).

Despite bearing much fruit earlier on, these believers failed to go on to spiritual maturity and had *"become dull of hearing"* (Hebrews 5:11-14). The same can happen to us unless we remain alert. Consequently, they were exhorted to *"pay much closer attention to what"* they had *"heard"* (Hebrews 2:1). Through doing so they would *"not throw away"* their *"<u>confidence, which has a great reward</u>"* (Hebrews 10:35):

Therefore, do not throw away your <u>confidence</u>, which has a great <u>reward</u>. (Hebrews 10:35—emphasis added)

This passage in no way teaches that salvation can be cast aside. We have validated on a variety of occasions the impossibility of such a development. Neither does this *"confidence"* have to do with an ability to somehow keep ourselves saved. Rather, it points to the *"confidence"* we should maintain in our faithful high priest as He saves us *"forever"* (Hebrews 7:25).

Clearly, Hebrews 10:35 is not dealing with these believers losing their salvation! Rather, it addresses their loss of rewards at the judgment seat of Christ should they *"throw away"* their *"confidence"* in choosing to disobey. All New Testament believers will be rewarded at *"the judgment seat of Christ"* for *"deeds"* done in faith (1Corinthians 3:11-15; 2Corinthians 5:10). Therefore, the <u>quality</u> of the work done through our lives will be judged—not <u>quantity</u>. In other words, if we have trusted Christ to do a particular work through us, we will receive a reward regardless of the outcome—even if the work "appears" to have been unfruitful. On the other hand, if we have performed a work in our own strength, no reward will be received—even if the work "appears" to have been fruitful. Different types of *stephanos* crowns (the crowns of an overcomer or victor) will be distributed for works withstanding the test of fire. Passages such as 2Timothy 4:7-8, James 1:12, 1Peter 5:1-4, and Revelation 2:10 confirm this truth. The author is passionate about his readers "faring well" at the crowning ceremony.

Note that the readers are never threatened with a loss of salvation. The loss of rewards at the judgment seat of Christ is the issue here along with impending physical death should they disobey. They needed the *"endurance"* (Hebrews 10:36) that springs forth from accepting God's grace for every situation of life (2Corinthians 12:9 applies perfectly

The believer's salvation is secure.

here). Should His grace be accepted, they would walk in God's will and *"receive what was promised"* (Hebrews 10:36)—not only the additional rewards at the judgment seat of Christ, but deliverance from the impending danger of A.D.70.

Verses 37-38 quote Habakkuk 2:3-4, Habakkuk having served as an Old Testament prophet. God had revealed to Habakkuk that certain events would transpire among His people, but he was to *"wait"* in patient endurance (Habakkuk 2:3) and *"faith"* (Habakkuk 2:4) for their fulfillment. Just as God eventually fulfilled what He had prophesied in Habakkuk's day (the destruction of Jerusalem—which occurred at the hands of the Babylonians), these Hebrew Christians were to wait in faith as He fulfilled what He had promised regarding their day (the destruction of Jerusalem—which occurred at the hands of the Romans). Thus, they were to wait on God in the midst of their persecutions, even if He seemed to delay.

The last verse in this chapter confirms that the believer's salvation is secure:

But we are not of those who shrink back to destruction, but of those who have faith to the preserving of the soul. (Hebrews 10:39)

The word *"destruction"* can also be interpreted "perdition," which means more than the loss of physical life. It means utter destruction, complete ruin—which is the final state of the lost. Because believers cannot *"shrink back to"* this type of *"destruction,"* Hebrews 10:39 confirms that New Testament believers are secure once they are placed in Christ (after repenting and believing while depraved). They can certainly disobey and experience God's chastening, but they can't *"shrink back to destruction."* New Testament believers have *"faith to the preserving of the soul"* (v.39). After all, they exercise personal repentance and faith in their lost (depraved) state (Acts 16:31; Acts 26:18; Romans 10:9-10) and receive God's gift of salvation (Ephesians 2:8-9). In conjunction with receiving the gift of salvation (Ephesians 2:8-9), *"each"* is given *"a measure of faith"* to function in the area of his/her unique spiritual gifting (Romans 12:3; 1Peter 4:10). Also, *"faith"* can be *"enlarged"* (2Thessalonians 1:3) as church saints grow in their understanding of the truth. Therefore, believers can disobey but never *"shrink back to destruction"* (Hebrews 10:39). Why? They *"have faith to the preserving of the soul"* (Hebrews 10:39)

In the next chapter we will observe how faith positively affected the lives of some of the godliest individuals who have graced the earth. Isn't the book of Hebrews an amazing letter?

Hebrews 11 Questions

First Day

1. Read Hebrews 11. Don't forget to pray. Considering that the word *"assurance"* can be interpreted "substance," or "the giving of substance to" (v.1), what is *"faith"*? How does Romans 10:17 apply to our present study?

2. How did *"the men of old"* gain God's *"approval"* (v.2)? How were the *"worlds"* created (v.3)? If the word *"worlds"* (v.3) points to the created universe and its order, what does this passage communicate regarding God's power and might? What does the phrase, *"so that what is seen was not made out of things which are visible"* (v.3), communicate to you? If God is omnipotent (powerful) enough to speak the created order into existence, is He capable of meeting your needs through the realm of the unseen? How does this good news encourage you?

3. From Genesis 4:3-5, what did Cain and Abel offer to the Lord? Which offering was accepted? If both Cain and Abel understood that sin offerings were to contain blood (they evidently gained this knowledge from their parents), what does Cain's offering communicate concerning the condition of his heart?

4. Considering the previous input, why was Abel's sacrifice better than Cain's? What did Abel's sacrifice confirm regarding the condition of Abel's heart (Hebrews 11:4)? Was his offering offered in *"faith"* (v.4)? What does the phrase, *"and through faith, though he is dead, he still speaks"* (v.4), communicate to you? Can you continue to speak on earth even after experiencing physical death? If so, how?

5. Enoch is mentioned next (v.5). All we know about him, outside of his lineage, is recorded in Genesis 5:6-24, Hebrews 11:5-6, and Jude 14-15. How is Enoch described in Genesis 5:22 and 24? Are you viewed as a person who walks with God? If so, why? From Jude 14-15, would you say that Enoch was fearful of preaching the truth? How did God honor Enoch's godliness (Hebrews 11:5)? What encouragement could these Hebrew Christians draw from Enoch's life?

Second Day

1. Read Hebrews 11. According to Hebrews 11:6, what is the only avenue through which we can *"please...God"*? How does Hebrews 11:6 relate to Titus 3:5, Romans 3:20, and Ephesians 2:8-9? If we are to *"believe that He is"* (Hebrews 11:6), does this mean that we simply trust that He is out there somewhere, totally detached from us, and going about His merry way? If not, what is the writer communicating?

2. In verse 6 we find *"that He is a rewarder of those who seek Him."* How do Matthew 6:33 and Psalm 37:4 relate to this truth? How has God rewarded you recently?

3. If someone came to you inquiring how to *"seek"* God (v.6), what would you tell that individual?

4.   Noah is mentioned next (v.7). What does Genesis 6:8-9 state about Noah? What phrase in Hebrews 11:7 confirms that it had not yet rained on the earth when God instructed Noah to build the ark? What frame of mind did Noah possess while building the ark (v.7)? How does 2Peter 2:5 tie in with the phrase, *"by which he condemned the world"* (Hebrews 11:7)? How was Noah rewarded for his *"faith"* (v.7)?

5.   What does verse 8 state regarding Abraham's *"faith"*? How does Genesis 12:1-7 tie in with verse 8? Was it before or after Abraham's arrival in Canaan that God promised him the *"land"* (read Genesis 12:7 and 15:7)? How does this timing relate to the phrase, *"and he went out, not knowing where he was going"* (Hebrews 11:8)? When were you last asked by God to do something that you did not yet understand? How did He honor your obedience?

Third Day

1.   Read Hebrews 11. Describe how Abraham *"lived"* while he dwelt in Canaan (v.9). What statements in verse 9 confirm that Abraham viewed Canaan as his temporary home? Where was Abraham's true home (v.10; Galatians 4:26; 11:16; 12:22-24; 13:14; Revelation 3:12; 21:1-22:5)? (New Jerusalem is the eternal dwelling for all the redeemed.) With this in mind, why should Philippians 3:20 and Colossians 3:2 encourage us even in our day?

2.   Note that Sarah is mentioned in verse 11. From Genesis 16:1-16, does it surprise you that her name is listed in Hebrews 11—the faith chapter? What encouragement do you draw from this fact? What is stated about her *"faith"* (Hebrews 11:11)?

3. How is Abraham described in verse 12? How does Genesis 21:1-3 relate to what is stated in Hebrews 11:12? How many descendants were *"born"* to Abraham as a result of his faith (v.12)?

4. The *"All"* in verse 13 refers to Abraham (vv.8-9), Isaac (v.9), and Jacob (v.9)—for they, along with their descendants, were promised the land of Canaan (Abraham—Genesis 15:7; Isaac—Genesis 26:3; Jacob—Genesis 28:13). Did they see these *"promises"* fulfilled in their lifetimes (Hebrews 11:13)? How does the phrase, *"having welcomed them from a distance"* (v.13), confirm that they understood the concept of resurrection? What were they *"seeking"* (vv.14-16)? What would have occurred had they *"been thinking of that country from which they went out"* (v.15)? Why would the writer address these subjects with his readers?

5. How do verses 17-19 confirm that Abraham possessed *"faith"* in God's *"promises"*? How do these same verses verify that Abraham believed in resurrection?

6. How does Genesis 22:9-19 picture what would later occur with Christ?

Fourth Day

1. Read Hebrews 11. The writer draws attention to how *"faith"* in God's promises brings hope in the face of death (vv.20-22). How do these passages confirm that Isaac, Jacob, and Joseph died in *"faith"*? If you desire more input before answering the previous question, read Genesis 25:23, Genesis 27:1-40 (verses that pertain to Isaac), Genesis 48:8-22 (verses that pertain to Jacob or Israel), and Genesis 50:24-25 (verses that pertain to Joseph).

2. How did Moses' parents display *"faith"* after Moses *"was born"* (v.23)? How did Moses display *"faith"* after he had grown up (vv.24-26)?

3.   Why is it important that we consider *"the reproach of Christ greater riches than the treasures"* of this life (v.26)? Do you live life from this perspective? If not, what needs to occur for you to do so? Why was it important for the recipients of this epistle to respond as Moses had responded?

4.   When Moses *"left Egypt,"* he *"endured"* through what means (v.27)? When was the last time you *"endured"* in this manner?

5.   Two events relating to Moses are mentioned in verses 28 and 29. What are they, and how was *"faith"* demonstrated in each case? (You may need to research these events in the Old Testament.) Understanding that it was Moses who received the Law, why was it important for the readers to be reminded that his *"faith,"* not deeds of the Law, was what caused God to declare him righteous?

6.   What event is mentioned in verse 30, and how does it demonstrate Israel's *"faith"*? If this event occurred in the land of Canaan, and the wilderness wanderings began after Israel crossed the Red Sea (v.29), how many events relating to the wilderness wanderings are recorded in this chapter? What does this communicate regarding Israel's lack of faith in the wilderness?

7.   Who is mentioned in verse 31, and how was her *"faith"* demonstrated? In what way was she rewarded (v.31; Joshua 6:21-25)?

Fifth Day

1. Read Hebrews 11. Several Old Testament believers are cited in verses 32-34. In your opinion, and from what you already know about these individuals, which of them demonstrated the greatest amount of faith?

2. Considering the historical setting of this book, why would the writer mention the sufferings experienced by previous believers (vv.35-38)?

3. What does verse 39 communicate regarding the individuals mentioned in this chapter? What kept them from becoming discouraged?

4. According to verses 39 and 40, why did these Old Testament believers *"not receive what was promised"*? When were they *"made perfect"* (v.40)? How does this tie in with the fact that animal sacrifices could not produce a finished work within the worshipper? If you know Jesus, have you been made perfect in your person—in your soul and spirit (Hebrews 10:14)? The *Romans 1-8* study covers this subject in much greater depth.

Sixth Day

1. Read Hebrews 11. Read this week's lesson and record any new insights. It is quite long, but be sure to read every word. You are doing great!

Hebrews 11 Lesson

This chapter mentions a long list of individuals who possessed incredible faith. Hebrews 6:12 alluded to them: *"but imitators of those who through faith and patience inherit the promises."* What an outstanding collection of believers for these Hebrew Christians to consider as they prepared for the challenges ahead.

The writer begins by describing *"faith"* (v.1), *"faith"* that allows a born again believer to know that God's promises are sure. If God promised that past events would transpire in a particular manner, they occurred as specified regardless of the variables involved. Likewise, God's promises regarding future events will be fulfilled in the exact fashion He has prescribed—with man all the while possessing the freedom of choice. (This subject is covered in much greater depth in the *God's Heart* series distributed by this ministry.) For these Hebrews Christians to reach spiritual maturity, they had to appropriate God's promises regarding things to come—confident that He would meet their needs every step of the way.

The writer records:

> *Now faith is the assurance of things hoped for, the conviction of things not seen.* (Hebrews 11:1)

The word *"assurance"* can be interpreted "substance," or "the giving of substance to." The Amplified Bible renders it as *"confirmation."* *"Faith,"* therefore, assures us that the *"things hoped for"* exist. The word *"conviction"* (v.1) can be translated "a certain persuasion." It can also mean "evidence" or "proof." Consequently, faith allows believers to perceive as real what has not yet been revealed to the physical senses. A difference exists, however, between believing in something and allowing that belief to impact our behavior. True faith does at least two things: (1) It proves that the unseen exists (2) It fuels a desire to behave in a manner that coincides with what we believe.

A difference exists between believing in something and allowing that belief to impact our behavior.

Through faith, therefore, we can know that God lives. Faith also assures us that His promises are certain. For years I shunned submitting to Christ for fear of believing in a God Who might not exist. To be forced to commit intellectual suicide, that is, wait until physical death to discover if the object of my faith is real, was not my idea of a fulfilled life. Today, on the other hand, I am completely, one hundred percent convinced that Jesus is the Son of God, alive and well at the right hand of the Father. Why? God's Word, viewed through the eyes of the Holy Spirit (and according to the full counsel—every word, of every phrase, of ever verse, of every chapter, of every book), has confirmed it to be so. After all, *"Faith comes from hearing, and hearing by the word of Christ"* (Romans 10:17).

I have also learned why many believers fail to live abundantly. They have never developed an intimate friendship with Christ through prayerfully meditating on His Word. They have not yet understood that time at His feet (so they can learn to live by His life) is the most necessary ingredient for fulfillment, peace, and rest. If you haven't yet done so, won't you consider making time alone with Christ the priority of your day? You will be amazed at the results.

All believers must realize that the object of their faith saves them, not faith itself. When you sit in a chair, the fact that it supports you does not depend on your faith in the chair, but on the strength of the chair. The same applies to our walk with Christ. Faith in our Savior neither saves nor sustains us. The object of our faith, Christ Himself, does so—Jesus being God (Hebrews 1:8). Thus, God saves—but He requires repentance and faith from the depraved prior to making them new.

How did *"men of old"* gain *"approval"*? They gained it through faith (Hebrews 11:2). God's stamp of *"approval"* has always rested upon those who exhibit faith, even though He has chosen various ways to honor their obedience. This chapter will bear this out, so you should be refreshed as we observe God's faithfulness toward those who have a heart for His heart.

In verse 3 we find:

> *By faith we understand that the worlds were prepared by the word of God, so that what is seen was not made out of things which are visible.* (Hebrews 11:3)

The word *"worlds"* actually means "the created universe and its order"—proving that God created the universe (and its order) through resources that are unseen. Thus, if a material need arises, the remedy may not yet be visible to the natural eye. We must be patient, therefore, for God can provide from His limitless supply—simply by speaking a *"word."* How exciting, this life of faith! To depend on what we see, smell, taste, touch, and hear for fulfillment is mundane at best. The recipients of this epistle needed to wake up and believe that God could miraculously come to their aid. It would be done His way, the supernatural way—not through the wisdom or manipulation of man. Their responsibility was to walk by faith, believing that the God Who created all things could meet their needs as well.

To illustrate that through faith *"the men of old gained approval"* (v.2), the writer begins identifying (and honoring) some outstanding Old Testament believers. These men and women walked by faith, viewing the promises of God as the very foundation of their existence. Interestingly, however, they died before receiving what was promised. Yet, they persevered by viewing them (the promises) as having already been fulfilled. The Hebrew Christians addressed in this epistle needed to take courage from the experiences of their ancestors and persevere—in Christ's strength, of course!

We must link several truths together to properly comprehend Hebrews 11, so enjoy what follows.

Even though Old Testament believers are sometimes referred to as *"righteous"* (Genesis 6:9 and Hebrews 11:4 for instance), it is obvious by now that their sins were not removed (Hebrews 10:12; 9:15) nor were they made righteous until the cross (Hebrews 2:9; Hebrews 11:40; 12:23). Thus, they were <u>declared</u> righteous, not <u>made</u> righteous, prior to Jesus' death. They were saved on credit so to speak (Romans 3:25; Acts 17:30), as was discussed earlier in our study of Hebrews 9. Unquestionably, they were individuals who walked with God. But as will be discovered in Hebrews 11:40 (and later in Hebrews 12:23), they were not <u>made</u> perfect or righteous until Jesus died in A.D. 30. Keep this truth at the forefront of your mind as we continue.

Old Testament believers were not made perfect or righteous until Jesus died in A.D. 30.

Abel is listed first (Hebrews 11:4) and is contrasted to his brother Cain:

> *By faith Abel offered to God a better sacrifice than Cain, through which he obtained the testimony that he was righteous, God testifying about his gifts, and through faith, though he is dead, he still speaks.* (Hebrews 11:4)

Both Cain and Abel were sons of Adam and Eve (Genesis 4:1-2) and the first of their children mentioned in Scripture. The brothers understood well that sin offerings were to contain blood. They probably learned this principle from their parents (Genesis 3:21—slain animals supplied the *"skin"* for Adam and Eve's *"garments"*). Consequently, Cain realized that it was improper to present *"the fruit of the ground"* (Genesis 4:3) as an offering for sin. Bloodless sin offerings were not instituted until later (Leviticus 5:11), with only the poor granted the opportunity to participate in such activities. Cain's offering confirms that self-effort never makes an individual right with God. For God to accept us, we must meet Him on His terms—never ours. Only faith in His Son, exercised while depraved, will suffice. Each blood sacrifice in Old Testament

Scripture pointed to the death of Christ, first mentioned in Genesis 3:15 but carried out in A.D. 30.

Don't misunderstand the writer's message. He is not saying that Abel's sacrifice gave Abel a *"righteous"* standing with God (Hebrews 11:4), for man can never gain salvation through *"righteous" "deeds"* (Titus 3:5). Also, we have spent much time confirming that animal sacrifices were incapable of removing the sin or the Adamic nature of the Old Testament believer. But Abel's offering <u>did</u> confirm his desire to please God—and that prior to this point he had exercised faith (while depraved) in the *"seed"* of Genesis 3:15. Thus, through his act of obedience, *"he obtained the testimony that he was righteous"* (Hebrews 11:4). (Remember: Abel was declared righteous at this time—not made righteous until the cross). Cain's offering, on the other hand, confirmed his lack of faith as well as his desire to walk in rebelliousness.

The latter part of Hebrews 11:4 is extremely thought provoking: *"and through faith, though he is dead, he still speaks."* What is Abel's faithful obedience speaking today? It is speaking at least two things to the New Testament believer: (1) That God imparts righteousness to those who exercise faith in the *"seed"* of Genesis 3:15, who is *"Christ"* (Galatians 3:16)—a personal faith exercised while depraved (2) That a blood sacrifice is required for man's problem with sin. Ponder this next thought as well. One of the greatest blessings associated with an intimate walk with Christ is that our lives speak positively after we are gone. The recipients of this epistle needed to wake up and consider Abel's example, not by placing themselves under the sacrificial system in Jerusalem, but by walking in faith. Only then could they live in victory over their present circumstances and leave a lasting testimony for generations to come. The historical record confirms that this is exactly how they responded, for they responded in faith.

Enoch is mentioned next (Hebrews 11:5). All we know about him, outside of his lineage, is stated in Genesis 5:6-24, Hebrews 11:5-6, and Jude 14-15. One fact is certain: He *"walked with God"* (Genesis 5:22 and 24). What a way to be remembered! In fact, the greatest compliment offered an individual is that he/she walks with the Creator. Enoch also spoke truth without compromise (Jude 14-15), the by-product of intimacy with the Source of truth.

From all indications, Enoch was further along in his spiritual maturity than Abel. He walked so closely with God that God just *"took him up"* (Hebrews 11:5). Consequently, he did *"not see death."* Hence, Enoch's fellowship with Jehovah paid huge dividends. Can New Testament believers reap similar dividends as they develop intimacy with Christ? The writer desired that his readers believe and that they stop contemplating returning to the temple sacrifices and go on to spiritual maturity.

Amidst all the great names of faith mentioned in this chapter, the writer records the following:

> *And without faith it is impossible to please Him, for he who comes to God must believe that He is, and that He is a rewarder of those who seek Him.* (Hebrews 11:6)

Let's consider all that is included in this fascinating statement.

No one can come *"to God"* without *"faith"* (v.6). *"Works"* will never do the job (Titus 3:5; Romans 3:20; Ephesians 2:8-9). Therefore, exercising personal faith while depraved is not a work (Romans 3:27-28; Romans 4:5; Romans 9:32).

To live the life of *"faith"* we begin by believing *"that He is"* (Hebrews 11:6). This belief is more than intellectually acknowledging His existence. We must, in the midst of our depravity, repent (turn from sin) and exercise personal faith (turn to God) before God bestows salvation. Thus, in the recesses of our heats, we *"must believe that He is"* (v.6).

Something else is required before we can walk intimately and passionately with Jehovah. We must believe *"that He is a rewarder of those who seek Him"* (v.6). What great news! Many, however, due to an improper view of His Person, fail to establish a close, meaningful friendship with Him. Why? He is incorrectly perceived as an oppressor Who inflicts pain at the slightest sign of disobedience. Others perceive Him as passive, condoning every act of sin that satisfies man's cravings. Until a proper view of God is firmly established, we will never walk a consistent lifestyle of faith. *"Faith"* only works *"through love"* (Galatians 5:6). Consequently, until we fall in love with Christ, as a result of knowing His heart, we will never walk in the power and authority made available to the redeemed. Yes, a proper view of God does wonders for the believer's faith.

Until a proper view of God is firmly established, we will never walk a consistent lifestyle of faith.

I was speaking with someone recently regarding how unfulfilling and downright boring life would be void of faith. Just think of what would be omitted from our daily experiences. To begin with, all conclusions would be drawn from sensory input alone—a limited view indeed. We could never, in other words, believe that our needs could be met through the realm of the invisible. We would also forfeit the friendship of our consistent, loving, compassionate, and forgiving companion— God Himself. Faith, on the other hand, allows us to live life fully. In fact, faith is an exhilarating privilege—not a mundane trek into nothingness. If we will but trust God, He will never take away anything, or ask us to relinquish anything, that could be used for our good. He has only our best interests in mind because *"He is a rewarder of those who seek Him"* (Hebrews 11:6).

No wonder King David said:

> *When Thou didst say, "Seek My face," my heart said to Thee, "Thy face, O Lord, I shall seek." (Psalm 27:8)*

In Psalm 9:10 he also wrote:

> *And those who know Thy name will put their trust in Thee; For Thou, O Lord, hast not forsaken those who seek Thee. (Psalm 9:10)*

He even recorded in Psalm 14:2:

> *The Lord has looked down from heaven upon the sons of men, To see if there are any who understand, Who seek after God. (Psalm 14:2)*

God desired that David *"seek"* His *"face,"* His heart, His Person, above all else in life—and David knew it. As a result, he was greatly rewarded.

By now you may be asking, "If God rewards those who seek Him (Hebrews 11:6), how does one seek an invisible Creator?" "How" one seeks God is easily reconciled. Yet, finding the time to implement the "how" is the major culprit. Let me explain.

A correct view of God's heart flows from prayerfully studying His precepts (His truths) and allowing them to direct one's life. To seek God's face, therefore, begins with observing His perfect character through His infallible letter to man. This is "how" one seeks His heart. Most believers, however, struggle to find ample time to invest in such an endeavor. For this reason, many church saints bypass the greatest privilege available to the redeemed.

No doubt, to seek God means to prayerfully pursue Who He is (His heart) through His Word. How much time should we spend doing so? Another psalmist wrote:

> *Seek the Lord and His strength; Seek His face continually. (Psalm 105:4)*

Can you imagine the benefits associated with seeking God *"continually"* through prayer and study? *"Continually"* doesn't mean that we lock ourselves in a room, appearing only randomly from our haven of solitude. It does mean, however, to think on the things of God while at work, play, or rest—as much of the day as possible.

We will now examine how God rewarded additional persons of faith. Noah, a man who *"found favor in the eyes of the Lord"* (Genesis 6:8), *"a righteous man"* who was *"blameless in his time"* (Genesis 6:9), is mentioned next (Hebrews 11:7):

By faith Noah, being warned by God about things not yet seen, in reverence prepared an ark for the salvation of his household, by which he condemned the world, and became an heir of the righteousness which is according to faith. (Hebrews 11:7)

Noah was *"warned by God about things not yet seen"* (Hebrews 11:7). He was *"warned,"* in other words, of a *"flood"* that would cover the entire *"earth"* (Genesis 6:13, 17; 7:19, 21-24). One slight hurdle existed. It had never rained! Thus, a flood was a foreign concept to those who heard Noah's message. Can you imagine the awkwardness of attempting to explain what man had not yet witnessed? But Noah obediently fulfilled his calling. He was ridiculed, laughed at, made fun of, and I am sure, considered insane. But Noah was not affected by public opinion. He was a man who *"walked with God"* (Genesis 6:9), and with that sort of man obedience is the key to fulfillment and contentment—not the praise of those to whom he is called to carry the message.

Obedience is the key to fulfillment and contentment.

That *"in reverence"* Noah *"prepared an ark"* is intriguing (Hebrews 11:7)—especially considering that the words, *"in reverence,"* can be interpreted, *"having become reverent."* Only after Noah had become reverent, therefore, did he build the ark—a remarkable thought indeed. Unless a man is first passionate about God's heart, and desires to walk in intimacy with Him, he will give way to the trials associated with his calling. Noah *"walked with God"* (Genesis 6:9). His God was all he needed. God blesses men and women who have learned to live from this perspective, for Noah's entire *"household"* was saved (Hebrews 11:7). Yet, as *"a preacher of righteousness"* (2Peter 2:5), *"he condemned the world"* (Hebrews 11:7). In fact, he *"became an heir of the righteousness which is according to faith"* (v.7). What more could he have desired? What a successful, meaningful, and fulfilled life he experienced as God's man of the hour!

In Hebrews 11:8-22, the writer addresses the faith of the patriarchs. He first mentions Abraham (v.8)—the man chosen by God to begin a new race of people—the father of the Jewish nation:

By faith Abraham, when he was called, obeyed by going out to a place which he was to receive for an inheritance; and he went out, not knowing where he was going. (Hebrews 11:8)

Abraham immediately obeyed God's call. Actually, he obeyed even as God *"called"* him. How do we know he responded in this fashion? The phrase, *"he was called"* (v.8), is a present participle. Consequently, the phrase can be translated: "When he was being called." As God was in the process of encouraging him to leave, he left. What faith! Abraham traveled toward the *"place which he was to receive for an inheritance,"* but *"he went out, not knowing where he was going"* (v.8). (You can read about this segment of Abraham's life in Genesis 12:1-7.) It was only after he arrived in Canaan that God promised him the land (Genesis 12:7; 15:7). Yes, God honored Abraham's faith beyond measure.

While Abraham lived in Canaan, *"the land of promise,"* *"he lived as an alien...dwelling in tents with Isaac and Jacob, fellow heirs of the same promise"*—men to whom God had also promised the land (Hebrews 11:9; Genesis 26:3; Genesis 28:13; Exodus 6:8). Why did Abraham live in this manner, having previously been given the land by Jehovah? He was *"looking for the city which has foundations, whose architect and builder is God"* (Hebrews 11:10). He was *"looking"* to New Jerusalem, heavenly Jerusalem, *"the city"* of God. (Passages such as Galatians 4:26, 11:16, 12:22-24, 13:14, Revelation 3:12, and 21:1-22:5 also provide insight into this fascinating subject.) One detail is undeniable. New Jerusalem is the eternal dwelling of all the redeemed. Thus, Abraham lived in tents as though his earthly stay was temporary. We need to adopt this same perspective. For certain, the Hebrew Christians addressed in this epistle should follow Abraham's example.

Some have misunderstood Abraham's passion for New Jerusalem and concluded that he had no expectations regarding the <u>literal</u> fulfillment of God's original promise concerning the physical land (*"From the river of Egypt as far as the great river, the river Euphrates"*—Genesis 15:18). They erroneously presume that the church, in the "allegorical" sense, is fulfilling this promise. This argument simply will not stand, for the promise regarding this significant piece of real estate is associated with a literal, unconditional covenant, known as the Abrahamic covenant. Either God fulfills this covenant in the literal sense or He will be proven unreliable—and anything but God.

Sarah is mentioned in verse 11:

> *By faith even Sarah herself received ability to conceive, even beyond the proper time of life, since*
> *she considered Him faithful who had promised;* (Hebrews 11:11)

Although Sarah failed to demonstrate the type of faith we might expect, she is still listed among the names of the faithful. Her inclusion should encourage us when faith seems difficult to embrace. Instead of waiting on God's perfect timing, she became impatient and suggested that Abraham have a son through Hagar (Genesis 16:1-2). As a result, Ishmael was born (Genesis 16:3-16). His descendants have been a persistent thorn in Israel's side, and will continue to be until Jesus returns. But Sarah, somewhere within the core of her inner being, *"considered Him faithful who had promised"* (Hebrews 11:11).

By faith Abraham, when he was past the normal age of producing offspring (v.12), had Isaac (Genesis 21:1-3) through his wife Sarah. Isaac then had Jacob (and Esau, of course—Genesis 25:19-26). Jacob had twelve sons, through whom came the entire nation of Israel—the twelve tribes. Naturally, therefore, the writer pens, *"as many descendants as the stars of heaven in number, and innumerable as the sand which is by the seashore"* (Hebrews 11:12)—a quote from Genesis 22:17.

The Promised Land was never possessed and controlled by Abraham, Isaac, or Jacob. Only when Joshua led Israel into Canaan, almost 500 years after Jacob's death, did the nation possess and control a large <u>portion</u> of the real estate originally promised in Genesis 15:18. Joshua 21:43 verifies this statement:

> *So the LORD gave Israel all the land which He had sworn to give to their fathers, and they*
> *possessed it and lived in it.* (Joshua 21:43)

This passage is a prime example of the value of "context." Although Israel *"possessed"* the land originally promised, she did not control all of the land originally promised. How do we know this to be true? Many enemies remained, living in isolated pockets of territory within the land (read Joshua 23:1-13). Due to Israel's sin subsequent to Joshua's death, several of these nations continued to dwell on Israeli soil. Hence, the fulfillment of Genesis 15:18 is yet future—making the events of our day extremely compelling:

> …*"To your descendants I have given this land, from the river of Egypt as far as the great*
> *river, the river Euphrates:* (Genesis 15:18)

The Jews, having been driven out of Canaan by the Romans in AD 70, began returning in large numbers in 1948. Yet, they will not possess (and control) the land in its entirety until the Millennium, the one thousand year reign of Christ. At that time they (the Jews) will possess and control every square inch of what God originally promised (read Ezekiel 20:41-42; 28:25-26; 36:26-28). Guess who will be there to enjoy the festivities? Abraham, Isaac, and Jacob will be there in their resurrected bodies to witness firsthand God's uncompromising faithfulness.

The previous input confirms why the writer followed with, *"All these died in faith, without receiving the promises"* (Hebrews 11:13). The *"all"* here refers to Abraham, Sarah, Isaac, and Jacob. They died before witnessing the <u>fulfillment</u> of the promises, yet they lived *"having seen them and having welcomed them from a distance"* (v.13). This expression of faith means that they understood the concept of resurrection. They realized that should they die before possessing what God had unconditionally guaranteed, they would possess it later in their resurrected state. For this reason

> *They were willing to wait on God's perfect timing.*

they viewed themselves as *"strangers and exiles on the earth"* (v.13). They were willing to wait on God's perfect timing only because of their unwavering trust in His promises. The Hebrews addressed in this epistle needed to note their response! So do we!

The patriarchs could wait patiently because they were *"seeking a country of their own"* (v.14). They were seeking New Jerusalem. Had they failed to do so, they would have returned to the *"country from which they went out"* (v.15)—the land *"from which they"* were called.

By mentioning the patriarchs' steadfastness, the writer is encouraging his readers to refrain from returning to the sacrificial system in Jerusalem, the place *"from which they went out"* (v.15). No doubt, the temporary dwellings (tents) of the patriarchs in no way hindered their pursuit of their *"heavenly"* home (vv.15-16). Due to inhabiting these transitory shelters, none of the trappings of this life could obstruct their view of the things of eternal significance. And so, *"God is not ashamed to be called their God; for He has prepared a city for them"* (v.16)—New Jerusalem.

Knowing that the patriarchs believed in a resurrection adds insight into verses 17-19:

> *By faith Abraham, when he was tested, offered up Isaac; and he who had received the promises was offering up his only begotten son; it was he to whom it was said, "IN ISAAC YOUR DESCENDANTS SHALL BE CALLED." He considered that God is able to raise men even from the dead; from which he also received him back as a type.* (Hebrews 11:17-19)

Abraham was asked to sacrifice Isaac (v.17; Genesis 22:1-8), the son through whom God would multiply his *"descendants"* (v.18; Genesis 21:12). He obeyed, but God intervened before Abraham could thrust his knife through the son of promise (Genesis 22:9-19). God's pledge freed Abraham to respond so faithfully, for He had sworn that the patriarch would have offspring through Isaac. Thus, Abraham had complete confidence that should Isaac's physical life be taken, God would *"raise"* him *"from the dead"* (Hebrews 11:19).

The phrase, *"received him back as a type"* (v.19), can be interpreted "in a parable he obtained" or "figuratively speaking he obtained." Because Abraham had decided that Isaac would die, the boy, in one sense, was raised *"from the dead"* (v.19)—even though he was not actually killed and raised back to natural life. This event, therefore, was a picture of what occurred later between the Heavenly Father and His Son, Jesus Christ. God literally offered Christ, His only Son, Who was literally resurrected (1Corinthians 15:12-19).

Believers are not only capable of living in victory, but dying in victory as well. In Hebrews 11:20-22, the writer gives examples of how *"faith"* brings hope in the face of death. Isaac is mentioned first (v.20). He was the son of Abraham and the father of Jacob and Esau. Even though Isaac possessed character flaws (read Genesis 25:19-27:46), in dying he displayed great faith. Note how he demonstrated it.

God had promised that Isaac and his *"descendants"* would one day possess the Promised Land (Genesis 26:3). Because the patriarchs viewed God's promises as their inheritance, they desired to pass them on to their descendants. God, however, had made an additional promise to Rebekah—that Esau's descendants, the Edomites, would serve Jacob's descendants, the nation of Israel (Genesis 25:23). Although this promise existed, Isaac desired that Esau receive the blessing. Yet, after Jacob stole his brother's birthright and gained (through deception) Isaac's blessing (Genesis 27:1-29), the blessing was irrevocable—belonging to Jacob alone (Genesis 27:30-40). Thus:

By faith Isaac blessed Jacob and Esau, even regarding things to come, (Hebrews 11:20)

Jacob is again mentioned in Hebrews 11:21. His life is addressed in the following Old Testament passages: Genesis 25:26-35:29; 37:1-36; 42:1-43:15; 45:16-49:33. (You can read these verses when time permits.) Although he lacked consistency in his walk with Jehovah, in dying he displayed tremendous faith. In fact, while living in Egypt, he pronounced blessings on Joseph's sons, Ephraim and Manasseh (Genesis 48:8-22)—blessings that would be fulfilled subsequent to his death (Hebrews 11:21). Accordingly, Joseph received *"one portion more than"* each of his *"brothers"* (Genesis 48:22), two instead of one. These territories weren't received by the tribes of Ephraim and Manasseh until Joshua led Israel into Canaan later in the nation's history—verifying that *"faith"* truly *"is the assurance of things hopes for, the conviction of things not seen"* (Hebrews 11:1).

Joseph, mentioned in Hebrews 11:22, lived most of his life in Egypt. He was sold into slavery by his brothers, only to become Pharaoh's right-hand man. When he died, however, he desired that his *"bones"* be returned to Canaan (Genesis 50:24-25). Why? He knew well, through faith, of God's original promise to Jacob—that his people would return to the land (Genesis 46:4). As a result, he could make this request prior to the nation's exodus from Egypt. He relied on God's promises and, through the eyes of faith, perceived the nation as returning to the land.

The writer moves next to events associated with Moses (Hebrews 11:23-29), dealing initially with his parents' *"faith"* (v.23). First, realizing their son's uniqueness, they hid him *"for three months"* (v.23). After all, *"He was a beautiful child"* (v.23), a description of the special role he would play in Israel's future (also read Acts 7:20). Consequently, Moses' parents, through faith, risked their lives to preserve his. They disregarded the king's edict, an edict that required all Jewish boys to be killed at birth (Exodus 1:15, 16, and 22), and hid their son until he was sovereignly retrieved from the Nile by Pharaoh's daughter (Exodus 2:1-10).

Moses' parents' faith became the standard for their son. After having been raised in royalty (Exodus 2:10), he, through *"faith,"* *"refused to be called the son of Pharaoh's daughter"* (Hebrews 11:24). He relinquished his status as a royal prince, in fact, *"to endure ill-treatment with the people of God"* (v.25). Israel is God's chosen *"people,"* not the Egyptians. Why would Moses opt out for the temporary comfort of Egypt when he could receive eternal rewards available to the faithful? He could easily avoid *"the passing pleasures of sin"* (v.25), that is, a life of ease in Egypt, so long as he remained focused on what awaited him through faith. In fact, he considered *"the reproach of Christ greater riches than the treasures of Egypt"* (v.26). Moses, obviously, didn't possess the fuller revelation of Christ that we have received. But he, along with Abraham (John 8:56) and other Old Testament believers (1Peter 1:10-11), realized that a Messiah would come Who would die for the sin of man. In this sense Moses could consider *"the reproach of Christ."* Moses also, like the Messiah, relinquished his royal status to identify himself with an enslaved people. Remember, *"he was looking to the reward"* presented to those who exemplify faithful obedience (v.26). The recipients of this epistle needed to consider Moses' example and stand!

"Faith" allowed Moses to decide wisely and accurately how Egypt's material resources were to be perceived. Such wisdom is a natural by-product of the heart whose passion is God's heart. Physical resources will never sway our thinking, therefore, so long as our focus is Christ. Being only stewards over them, they must never own us.

> *Physical resources will never sway our thinking so long as our focus is Christ.*

Moses departed from Egypt *"without fearing the wrath of the king"*—Pharaoh (v.27). He departed, in fact, due to having been rejected by his own people (Exodus 2:11-14). No doubt, Moses realized that he was Israel's deliverer, for one of the Hebrews who had heard of the previous day's events (Moses had killed an Egyptian who was mistreating a Jew) even said to him, *"Who made you a prince or a judge over us?"* (Exodus 2:14). Yet, it would be another 40 years before God would use Moses to free His people. How did he endure? *"He endured, as seeing Him who is unseen"* (Hebrews 11:27). We too can endure the valleys of life by focusing on Christ. So could the Hebrew Christians addressed in this epistle.

Moses' *"faith"* allowed him to keep *"the Passover"* (v.28). He even had the Hebrews kill the *"Passover"* lamb and sprinkle its blood *"on the two doorposts and on the lintel of"* their homes (Exodus 12:3-13)—an act that prevented their *"first-born"* from being *"destroyed"* (Hebrews 11:28; Exodus 12:27-30). God also honored Moses' faith by allowing *"the sons of Israel"* to pass *"through the Red Sea as though they were passing through dry land"* (v.29; Exodus 14:21-22, 29), the same sea that drowned the *"entire"* Egyptian *"army"* (v.29; Exodus 14:23-28). With this incident, Israel's wilderness wanderings began.

Hebrews 11 doesn't mention it, but Moses received the Law on Mount Sinai soon after Israel crossed the Red Sea (Exodus 19-24). Since Moses is so closely identified with the Law (sometimes called the Mosaic Law), the writer reminded his readers (Hebrews 11:6, 24-29) that Moses was saved by *"faith"*—not by the deeds of the Law. Once again, the writer's goal was to encourage them to lay aside the idea of returning to the sacrificial system in Jerusalem.

Israel's *"faith"* demonstrated in taking Jericho is mentioned next (v.30). (Joshua 6:1-27 records this amazing miracle.) Keep in mind that Jericho was situated in the land of Promise—not in the wilderness. The author of Hebrews skips Israel's wilderness wanderings altogether, for little or no faith was exemplified during that critical season of the nation's history. Faith prevailed, however, as Israel entered Canaan under Joshua.

If we blend in with the world, and few take issue with our lifestyles, somewhere along the way we have compromised.

"Rahab the harlot," a citizen of Jericho, exercised *"faith"* by assisting the Hebrew spies (v.31; Joshua 2:1-21). She had *"heard"* of God's mighty deeds (Joshua 2:9-10) and, as a result, believed on Him (Joshua 2:11). God not only spared her life when Israel destroyed the inhabitants of the city (v.31; Joshua 6:21-25), but allowed King David to be born her descendant (Matthew 1:5-6).

Hebrews 11:32-38 can be summed up as follows: If we walk by *"faith,"* we will suffer for our *"faith."* Jesus said, *"Woe to you when all men speak well of you"* (Luke 6:26). Even Paul wrote that we are *"an aroma"* of *"death"* to those who do not believe (2Corinthians 2:15-16). If we blend in with the world, and few take issue with our lifestyle, somewhere along the way we have compromised. The believers addressed in this epistle were contemplating returning to the Law to avoid persecution. In effect the writer says, "Wake up! You aren't the first Jews to suffer for the faith. You aren't in this alone." He then mentions Gideon, Barak, Samson, Jephthah (all judges), David (a king and a prophet), Samuel (a judge and a prophet), and the prophets, each of whom had their faith tested to the max (Hebrews 11:32).

Through faith, Gideon took 300 men and annihilated hoards of Midianites (Judges 6-7). Barak (through faith) destroyed the army of the Canaanite king, Jabin, as well as Jabin's commander, Sisera (Judges 4). God used Samson mightily to war against the Philistines (Judges 13-16), and Jephthah delivered his people from the threat of the Ammonites (Judges 11). David, the only king listed, was a mighty warrior and leader of Israel (2 Samuel 5:1-25; 8:1-18). Samuel, a godly man, was the last prominent Old Testament judge. He also functioned as a prophet. He anointed Saul, the first king of Israel (1 Samuel 10:1), and David (1 Samuel 16:13), who succeeded Saul. (Samuel's life is addressed in 1 Samuel 1:1-25:1.) The writer also refers to the prophets, all of whom walked by *"faith"* (Hebrews 11:32-33). Although some had character issues, the writer mentions not a single flaw. The reason: In the end, they all allowed *"faith"* to triumph over fear of the enemy.

The men addressed here were delivered from enormous difficulties through God's power. They:

> *...conquered kingdoms, performed acts of righteousness, obtained promises, shut the mouths of lions, quenched the power of fire, escaped the edge of the sword, from weakness were made strong, became mighty in war, put foreign armies to flight.* (Hebrews 11:33-34)

Verses 35-38 confirm that whether dying at the hands of an enemy or experiencing God's supernatural deliverance, *"faith"* is victorious over death. The first phrase of verse 35 is noteworthy *("Women received back their dead by resurrection")* because almost every *"resurrection"* back to <u>natural</u> life recorded in the Scriptures took place on behalf of *"women"* (read 1Kings 17:17-23, 2Kings 4:18-37, Luke 7:11-15, and John 11:1-44). The individuals who were resurrected, of course, experienced a second physical death. (If they were believers, they will one day receive a glorified body.) Those who *"were tortured"* and killed, and not resurrected back to natural life, died hoping for *"a better resurrection"* (Hebrews 11:35). They looked forward to their future *"resurrection,"* a *"better"* one, when they too will receive an immortal body like Christ's.

They looked forward to their future resurrection, when they will receive an immortal body like Christ's.

Those who walked by faith experienced tremendous adversity. Some were mocked and scourged, sometimes even chained and cast into prison (v.36). Others *"were stoned," "sawn in two"* (tradition holds that Isaiah died in this fashion), *"tempted,"* slain *"with the sword,"* forced to walk *"about in sheepskins, in goatskins, being destitute, afflicted, ill-treated"* (v.37). These believers were *"men of whom the world was not worthy"* (v.38). They wandered *"in deserts and mountains and caves and holes in the ground"* (v.38). The writer is giving a clear, direct message to the Hebrew Christians contemplating returning to the sacrificial system: "You have had a cakewalk compared to what some have suffered. Stop feeling sorry for yourselves, exercise your faith, and walk in the authority and power of God's truth!"

Although the individuals honored thus far *"gained approval through their faith,"* they failed to *"receive what was promised"* (v.39). Consequently, they placed their faith, not in the immediate fulfillment of what God had specified, but in its eventual fulfillment according to His perfect timing. The Messiah was the ultimate promise through which God's words would achieve their desired end. For instance, God guaranteed that Abraham, Isaac, and Jacob, along with their descendants, would possess and control *"From the river of Egypt as far as the great river, the river Euphrates"* (Genesis 15:18), the land of Canaan. This full control will not occur until the one thousand year reign of Christ—established in association with His Second Coming. Also, the *"new covenant"* of Jeremiah 31:31-34 does not experience its complete fulfillment until the Jewish remnant exercises faith in Jesus at the end of the Tribulation—prior to His Second Coming. (The church reaps the benefits of the New Covenant now—only partially fulfilling the conditions of the covenant.) The Old Testament believers, therefore, looked forward to the day when God would fulfill His promises through the Messiah.

Because Jesus' First Coming did not occur in the Old Testament believers' lifetimes, their understanding, obviously, was less detailed than ours. Note Peter's words:

> *As to this salvation, the prophets who prophesied of the grace that would come to you made careful search and inquiry, seeking to know what person or time the Spirit of Christ within them was indicating as He predicted the sufferings of Christ and the glories to follow.* (1Peter 1:10-11)

Our advantage as New Testament believers is undeniable. Yet, even though blessed with this fuller revelation, we often lack the faith to live in the power and authority of the believers of old.

Shame on us!! And shame on the Hebrew Christians addressed in this letter. How could they dare choose a life of compromise considering all they understood regarding the Messiah?

The final verse of Hebrews 11, verse 40, carries much weight:

> *because God had provided something better for us, so that apart from us they should not be made perfect.* (Hebrews 11:40)

The writer states that New Testament believers receive *"something better"* than those who lived (and died) prior to Jesus' death. Old Testament believers were <u>not</u> made perfect until the cross, a point the writer expresses by penning, *"that apart from us they should not be made perfect"* (v.40). (This topic will be discussed in more detail when we cover Hebrews 12:23.) We, as New Testament believers on the other hand, were *"made perfect"* (first phrase of Hebrews 10:14 NIV) and *"holy"* (Ephesians 1:4) the moment we accepted Christ. This truth cannot be debated. Thus, *"God had provided something better for us"* (Hebrews 11:40).

We were made perfect and holy the very moment we accepted Christ.

Two more weeks and we will have covered the entire book of Hebrews. You should be extremely pleased with your progress.

Hebrews 12 Questions

First Day

1. Read Hebrews 12. From what we studied in Hebrews 11, what group of people made up the *"cloud of witnesses"* mentioned in verse 1? Why would the readers be encouraged to consider these individuals?

2. What two things were these Hebrew Christians to *"lay aside,"* and why (v.1)? (The word *"encumbrance"* actually means "bulk, weight, burden, or impediment.") What were they to do after laying *"aside"* such things (v.1)? What are you doing to make sure that you stay free of such hindrances?

3. Notice that verse 2 does not say, *"fixing our eyes on* the one running against us," or *"fixing our eyes on* our brothers and sisters in Christ," or even *"fixing our eyes on* the Holy Spirit" (although we are encouraged by fellow believers and the Spirit's guidance). On what were these believers to fix their *"eyes"* (v.2)? How is Jesus described in verse 2, and how does this description encourage you? What does the writer mean when he states that Jesus is *"the author and perfecter of faith"* (v.2)?

4. If happiness is dependent on circumstance, while joy is independent of circumstance, explain how Jesus could walk to *"the cross"* with *"joy"* (v.2)? How can we experience *"joy"* in the midst of difficult circumstances?

Second Day

1. Read Hebrews 12. If the word *"consider"* (v.3) means to "consider attentively," why did the writer desire that his readers *"consider"* Jesus (v.3)? Had they yet lost close friends due to persecution (v.4)? How does this fact confirm that they were not part of the church at Jerusalem, especially considering that Steven (Acts 7:59-60) and James (Acts 12:2) were members of the Jerusalem fellowship prior to being slain?

2.   From verses 5 and 6, what had the readers *"forgotten"*? The word *"discipline"* (verses 5-11) is used both as a noun and a verb, and means "to train a child." In the broad sense it means "educating, training, nurturing, or correcting a child, as when a parent teaches a child." It does not carry with it the idea of wrathful punishment! Try to think of an Old Testament believer who received God's discipline in the form of correction. How did it benefit that individual?

3.   What were the readers not to do when disciplined by the Lord (v.5)? Which of these two diametrically opposed responses do you struggle with the most after having received God's discipline (v.5)? Why is this the case? What does God's discipline confirm to us (v.6)?

Third Day

1.   Read Hebrews 12. Don't forget to pray. Who does God *"discipline"* (vv.7-8)? Who never receives His discipline (v.8)? How will this truth impact your response the next time you experience God's discipline?

2.   How does *"discipline"* affect a child's attitude toward the father who enforces the *"discipline"* (v.9)? How did the discipline you received from your earthly father affect you, and why? No earthly parent knows the exact amount of discipline to administer (v.10). Not so with our heavenly Father (v.10). What encouragement do you draw from what the writer records here?

3.   Why does God discipline His children (v.10)? Is verse 10 speaking about holiness in our behavior or holiness in our person (who we are)? Explain your answer.

4. From the first half of verse 11, what does discipline initially produce within a believer? From the last half of verse 11, what does discipline eventually yield? Is this speaking of righteous behavior or the righteousness of our new man (who we are as New Testament believers)?

Fourth Day

1. Read Hebrews 12. These Hebrew Christians are exhorted to live in a way so as not to stumble fellow believers (vv.12-13). How were they to respond (vv.12-13)? How would this impact the *"lame"* (weaker believer)? When did you last view yourself as setting the pace and establishing a path for those who are following in your footsteps?

2. According to verse 14, what were these believers to *"pursue"*? Is this verse teaching that salvation is based on works? If not, what is it communicating? Does the *"sanctification"* addressed here (sanctification has to do with holiness) relate to these believers' behavior or to their person? What would their observers *"see"* in them as they pursued a holy lifestyle (v.14)?

3. Why were these readers encouraged to refrain from falling *"short of the grace of God"* (v.15)? (Grace can be defined as "the power to do God's will.") Is the writer teaching that they were not to come short of salvation? If not, what is he communicating? The phrase, *"and by it many be defiled"* (v.15), refers to whom: (1) The readers, who were contemplating rejecting God's grace and going back under the Law (2) Those observing their lives?

4. Are verses 16 and 17 teaching that Esau lost his salvation through disobedience? If not, what did he lose? What does the statement, *"for he found no place for repentance, though he sought for it with tears,"* communicate to you? Why would the writer desire that his readers consider these words regarding Esau?

Fifth Day

1.   Read Hebrews 12. Verses 18-24 contrast two mountains. Name them, and name the *"covenant"* (old or new) that each represents. Which *"mountain"* represents *"heavenly Jerusalem"* (New Jerusalem)? Who inhabits *"heavenly Jerusalem"* (vv.22-24)?

2.   From what we know concerning the animal sacrifices, why does Jesus' *"blood"* speak *"better than the blood of Abel"* (v.24)? If Jesus' *"blood"* speaks better than the blood of animal sacrifices, why should these readers have listened to Jesus' words rather than the words of the unbelieving Jews (v.25)? According to verse 25, from where is Jesus *"speaking"* (warning)? From what location did Moses warn Israel (v.25)? How does verse 25 confirm the superiority of the new covenant?

3.   According to verses 26-27, what will one day be removed? What will *"remain"* (v.27)? What type of *"kingdom"* do we *"receive"* as believers (v.28)? How should we respond to this wonderful news (v.28), and why (v.29)? How does verse 29 relate to what would soon befall Jerusalem?

Sixth Day

1.   Read Hebrews 12. Read this week's lesson and record any new insights.

Hebrews 12 Lesson

The writer desires that his readers draw encouragement from the faithful addressed in Hebrews 11, so he records:

> *Therefore, since we have so great a cloud of witnesses surrounding us, let us also lay aside every encumbrance, and the sin which so easily entangles us, and let us run with endurance the race that is set before us,* (Hebrews 12:1)

The believers of old are portrayed as spectators, not literally watching New Testament believers and cheering them on, but witnessing to the church (through their righteous past) regarding the life of faith. By laying aside everything that served as a hindrance, they finished the race with astounding resolve. Thus, the readers were to *"lay aside every encumbrance"* (v.1). The word *"encumbrance"* actually means "bulk, weight, burden, or impediment." They were to *"run"* with ease, as did their forefathers, totally unencumbered by the trappings of the world.

They were also to lay aside *"sin,"* for *"sin"* short circuits faith (v.1). Notice the definite article *"the"* preceding *"sin"*—*"the sin"* (v.1). The writer may be referencing the particular *"sin"* the readers were contemplating, the sin of returning to Judaism. He could, on the other hand, be referencing *"sin"* in general. Either way, sin *"entangles"* the believer.

A spider capturing its food perfectly illustrates how sin entangles a believer. Once an insect (or anything edible) flies into its web, a spider spins additional webbing, totally enveloping its prey—completely inhibiting freedom of movement. The same is true with sin. Its entanglement restricts our spiritual life, preventing us from running *"with endurance the race that is set before us"* (v.1). Through remaining alert, however, we can say "no!" to sin and run in the strength that God supplies. I don't know about you, but I can think of nothing more exciting than winning (through God's strength) the race of faith, a race run against our archenemy, Satan. These Hebrew Christians needed to heed the writer's message, yield to Christ's indwelling presence, and finish *"the race"* with energy to spare.

Along with laying sin aside and considering the faithful of old, these believers were to fix their *"eyes on Jesus"* (v.2):

> *fixing our eyes on Jesus, the author and perfecter of faith, who for the joy set before Him endured the cross, despising the shame, and has sat down at the right hand of the throne of God.* (Hebrews 12:2)

Note that the verse does not say, "fixing our eyes on the one running against us," or "fixing our eyes on our brothers and sisters in Christ," or even "fixing our eyes on the Holy Spirit" (although we are encouraged by fellow believers and the Spirit's guidance). Victory is guaranteed only as we gaze at God's holy Son. This amazing truth reveals that the difficulties encountered in the race are not to be viewed as overwhelming. If it rains, snows, or hails; if the wind is never at our backs; if all sorts of obstacles cross our paths; we must run by looking at Jesus alone—never our circumstances. Have you noticed that a problem is never overcome by focusing on the problem? Problems are overcome through focusing on, and yielding to, Christ Himself. Through considering His pain, along with the positive ramifications of His faithful obedience, we, along with Paul, can classify all hardship as *"momentary, light affliction"* (2Corinthians 4:17).

We are to fix *"our eyes on Jesus"* because He is *"the author and perfecter of faith"* (Hebrews 12:2). The word *"author"* means "the chief leader," for He modeled *"faith"* as no one else. As our "Leader," He *"endured the cross"* with *"joy"* (v.2), knowing that His submission to crucifixion accomplished the Father's will (Matthew 20:28). Notice that the writer pens the phrase, *"the joy set before Him,"* and not, "the happiness set before Him." Happiness is dependent on circumstance. *"Joy,"* on the other hand, is totally independent of circumstance. This difference means that joy is accessible to the believer when happiness has vacated the scene. Christ, therefore, joyfully *"endured the cross, despising the shame"* (Hebrews 12:2).

Undeniably, the Father honored the Son's compliance, for Jesus *"sat down at the right hand of the throne of God"* (v.2). Consequently, Christ's *"faith"* was brought to completion. It was perfected. He obeyed until He could finally say, *"It is finished"* (John 19:30). Thus, He is *"the author"* (leader) *"and perfecter of faith"* (Hebrews 12:2). He is our pioneer and premier example. In fact, as we choose to fix *"our eyes on Jesus"* (Hebrews 12:2), He (being *"God"*—Hebrews 1:8) makes certain that our faith is perfected as well (Philippians 1:6). Through this means, therefore, we will receive the reward for faithful service. This reward is not heaven, for heaven is guaranteed to every New Testament believer. This reward is what we receive at *"the judgment seat of Christ,"* the compensation for deeds done in faith (2Corinthians 5:10; 1Corinthians 3:10-15)—deeds accomplished by Christ as we choose to live by His indwelling presence. No doubt, we should all *"press on toward the goal for the prize of the upward call of God in Christ Jesus"* (Philippians 3:14).

What prevents us from becoming discouraged as we participate in the race of faith? The answer is easily understood but many times difficult to apply:

> *For consider Him who has endured such hostility by sinners against Himself, so that you may not grow weary and lose heart.* (Hebrews 12:3)

We are to *"consider"* Jesus when severely challenged—the word *"consider"* means to "consider attentively," not just passively. As we look at, meditate upon, ponder, and think through the sufferings of Christ, we are motivated to persevere in His strength regardless of the cost. Unquestionably, through focusing on Him we do *"not grow weary and lose heart"* (v.3). Jesus obeyed due to *"the joy set before Him"* (v.2), a *"joy"* fixated on what the Father, the Spirit, and all people of faith would gain through His willingness to die. His *"joy"* was also linked to His future position, that of sitting *"at the right hand of the throne of God"* (v.2). In fact, He ran in such a way that everything He said and did lined up perfectly with God's will (John 5:19; 12:49)—even in the midst of unimaginable pain and suffering. We can respond much the same—in His strength of course.

A friend once related a personal story regarding suffering. Facing enormously difficult circumstances, he called a man who also had endured extreme pain. After describing each of his problems, he expected the man to give council pertaining to each dilemma. Instead, the man offered only a question: "Have you considered Gethsemane lately?" These words so transformed my friend's perception of his state of affairs that he was never the same. For this reason we, along with all who desire to walk victoriously, are to *"consider"* Jesus.

These Hebrew Christians, as a corporate group, had not lost a single person to death through persecution:

> *You have not yet resisted to the point of shedding blood in your striving against sin;* (Hebrews 12:4)

This verse confirms that the readers were not part of the church at Jerusalem, for by this time both Steven (Acts 7:59-60) and James (Acts 12:2) had died. They had *"forgotten"* a critical principle, however. God *"disciplines"* those who are His (Hebrews 12:5-6). Is it not amazing what occurs when we fail to meditate on truth? We forget it (Hebrews 2:1; Proverbs 3:21; 4:21), or at least forget how it is to be applied, and begin to adopt the mindset of the world. It is then that the Lord implements chastening, or discipline, to restore a biblical point of view.

The word *"discipline"* (Hebrews 12:5-11) is used both as a noun and a verb. It means "to train a child." In the broad sense it points to "educating, training, nurturing, or correcting a child." In other words, it is not synonymous with wrathful punishment. Believers will reap consequences in this life for their misdeeds (Colossians 3:25), but these sins never induce God's wrath (Romans 8:1). His wrath is reserved for the unsaved (Revelation 20:11-15)—everyone who refuses to repent and believe while depraved.

God's Word records several examples of believers who received God's discipline. One such example is David. It is not surprising that after being chastened of the Lord, he loved Him more, desired more fervently to walk in holiness, and was used mightily to demonstrate God's grace, mercy, and compassion. Thus, God disciplines to encourage us in the way of righteousness. He never disciplines for the purpose of condemning our person (Romans 8:1).

God uses discipline in a variety of ways, one of which is to teach us about Himself. This heightened understanding of His character, along with the resulting wisdom, positively affects how we respond to the challenges of our day. It also deepens our message. Once discipline has its way, however, *"the peaceful fruit of righteousness"* is displayed in the choices we make as believers (a subject covered later in Hebrews 12:10-11). Again, these Hebrew Christians had forgotten that God chastens children who walk in unrighteousness.

Two improper reactions to God's discipline are recorded in Hebrews 12:5.

> *and you have forgotten the exhortation which is addressed to you as sons,* "MY SON, DO NOT REGARD LIGHTLY THE DISCIPLINE OF THE LORD, NOR FAINT WHEN YOU ARE REPROVED BY HIM;* (Hebrews 12:5)

Would either of these diverse scenarios describe us? When God brings *"discipline,"* do we *"regard"* it *"lightly"* by acting as if it does not exist? Do we go merrily about our way as though God were doing nothing to encourage us to repent (2Corinthians 7:9)? If so, we can expect His discipline to intensify. Or do we respond in a totally polarized fashion by fainting *"when ...reproved by Him"* (Hebrews 12:5)? At the first sign of His correction, do we become defeated and disheartened, totally incapacitated by His compassionate response? If so, we are viewing His discipline improperly. We need to perceive Him as correcting us for our good. We also need to consider the positive aspects of having a Father who cares enough to address our weaknesses. We must never forget that He disciplines us because of His love for us. Yet, most believers who *"faint"* while being corrected have a problem accepting criticism. Why? They possess a poor self-image. Having struggled in this area myself, I realize that the only remedy is to discover who we are in Christ—who God made us into when we exercised personal repentance and faith while depraved. Only then will we begin to view ourselves from God's frame of reference and allow Him (and others) to point out behavioral flaws that prevent us from experiencing His best. (This subject is addressed in more depth in the *Romans 1-8* study distributed by this ministry.)

No doubt, God's discipline confirms His love for us:

> *For those whom the Lord loves He disciplines,* AND HE SCOURGES EVERY SON WHOM HE RECEIVES.*" (Hebrews 12:6)

While disciplining us, God, like all parents who love their children, does so with much anguish. In fact, disciplining a child normally grieves the parent more than the child. It is the same with God!

God's discipline also confirms our sonship: *"And He scourges every son whom He receives"* (v.6). Only God's children receive His discipline. Just as a father is <u>not</u> required to discipline children outside his family, neither is God. Although God loves non-family members (John 3:16; 1Timothy 2:4), they will receive His wrath (Revelation 20:11-15), not His correcting discipline. They will receive His wrath due to rejecting the truth of the gospel, which they were more than capable of accepting in their spiritually unregenerated (depraved) state. After all, should God withhold the freedom to believe from certain individuals, and later condemn them for failing to believe, He would prove Himself not only unloving (and unjust), but contradictory as well! Such a being could never serve as the sovereign ruler of man. (The *God's Heart* series distributed by this ministry addresses this topic in much greater depth.)

The word *"scourges"* (Hebrews 12:6) means "to whip with cords of leather." Yes, God sometimes "whips" his children when they refuse to heed His correction. In fact, His "whippings" can become severe if the disobedience continues. But they are administered in love, with a tear in His eye—not in an attitude of rage.

Hebrews 12:7 confirms that God's discipline validates our Sonship:

> *It is for discipline that you endure; God deals with you as with sons; for what son is there whom his father does not discipline?* (Hebrews 12:7)

What *"father does not discipline"* His own *"son"* (v.7)? Some would ask, "What about those persons who give lip service to knowing Christ but wallow in blatant disobedience. Are they true believers"? The answer is: "If they are not receiving God's discipline, they have never met Jesus." No wonder the writer states,

> *But if you are without discipline, of which all have become partakers, then you are illegitimate children and not sons.* (Hebrews 12:8)

Only God's children experience His discipline.

A critical truth must be grasped here: The properly disciplined child respects his/her parents (v.9):

> *Furthermore, we had earthly fathers to discipline us, and we respected them; shall we not much rather be subject to the Father of spirits, and live?* (Hebrews 12:9)

The converse is true as well: The undisciplined child does not respect his/her parents. Why? A parent's wise discipline confirms the parent's love for the child.

I will never forget a phone call I once received from a despondent mother. Her daughter, whom she loved deeply (and loved enough to discipline), but whose father had abandoned the family, had "temporarily" run away from home. I knew the daughter and had become somewhat of a father figure to her. After receiving permission from the mother, I left a message for the daughter to contact me when she returned home. Upon receiving her call, I said, "The next time you disobey as you did tonight, I am going to drive to your home, turn you over my knee, and spank you like you were my own" (she was a fifteen-year-old teenager at the time). I didn't know how she would respond, but amazingly she replied, "Would you really do that? Would you love me enough to give me a spanking?"

As a result of that experience, Hebrews 12:9 was cemented in my soul for all eternity. Young people need to know their boundaries, for without discipline they cannot reach their full potential. No doubt, my actions gained her respect. In fact, should she see me today, she would thank me for the events of that action-packed evening. (Oh, by the way, this was a very special case. I, by no stretch of the imagination, am suggesting that we implement this type of action in all situations.)

*S*evere consequences result when believers reject God's discipline.

Severe consequences result when believers reject God's discipline. In some cases, in fact, the consequence has been physical death (read 1Corinthians 5:5; 1Corinthians 11:30; 1John 5:16). Only when we are *"subject to the Father"* do we truly *"live"* (Hebrews 12:9). We not only live physically, but *"abundantly"* as well (John 10:10).

Note Hebrews 12:10:

> *For they disciplined us for a short time as seemed best to them, but He disciplines us for our good, that we may share His holiness.* (Hebrews 12:10)

Our earthly father's discipline only lasts *"for a short time"* (v.10), only so long as we are "under his roof." Also, his discipline is based on what he deems "best," whether it is *"best"* or not (v.10). As a result, most fathers would admit that the type and amount of discipline to direct toward a disobedient child is normally difficult to determine. In other words, their discipline is never as accurate and thorough as that of the heavenly Father. Thus, when the Scriptures say, *"He disciplines us for our good"* (v.10), we can rest assured that the discipline administered is precisely what is needed for the situation at hand. Unlike the "temporary" discipline we received from our earthly fathers, the Lord's discipline is administered as needed until we see Him face to face.

God's discipline is always *"for our good"* (v.10)—always! He desires that we walk in a *"holy"* manner (1Peter 1:15-16) since we were made *"holy"* in our souls and spirits the moment we were made new (read Ephesians 1:4; Ephesians 5:27; Colossians 1:22). Stated differently, He longs for our behavior to line up with who He made us into when we were justified. Consequently the statement, *"that we may share His holiness"* (v.10), points to our behavior becoming increasingly holy—not our person. Our person (the new creation—consisting of soul and spirit) was *"perfected"* (and made holy) the moment we accepted Jesus (Hebrews 10:14), never to be improved upon.

Hebrews 12:11 confirms what we have just studied:

> *All discipline for the moment seems not to be joyful, but sorrowful; yet to those who have been trained by it, afterwards it yields the peaceful fruit of righteousness.* (Hebrews 12:11)

The *"discipline"* we receive from the Lord is never *"joyful."* It is always *"sorrowful."* It does, however, yield *"the peaceful fruit of righteousness."* Notice that the writer pens *"fruit of righteousness"* and not "righteousness." It is important that we understand what is communicated here. We—who we are, our person—was made *"the righteousness of God"* the moment we accepted Christ (2Corinthians 5:21). We became as righteous as God is righteous and will remain so forever. But we do not yet behave as righteously as we would like. Thus, verse 11 is pointing to righteous behavior, the *"fruit"* (or result) of having been made righteous in soul and spirit. God's discipline, therefore, teaches us how to act in a way that begins to line up with who He made us into at the point of justification (salvation). This amazing adventure doesn't end here! Through learning to walk (behave) in a way that increasingly emulates what God made us into the moment He made us new, we experience true peace—for this is a *"peaceful fruit"* (v.11).

In verses 12 and 13 of Hebrews 12, these Hebrew Christians are encouraged to live in a way so as not to stumble fellow believers:

> *Therefore, strengthen the hands that are weak and the knees that are feeble, and make straight paths for your feet, so that the limb which is lame may not be put out of joint, but rather be healed.* (Hebrews 12:12-13)

These readers' disobedience had not only negatively impacted their own ability to persevere but the perseverance of the weaker believers as well. They are first encouraged to *"strengthen the hands that are weak and the knees that are feeble"* (v.12). While running a race, drooped hands and wobbly knees are sure signs of fatigue. These believers had become *"weak,"* much like a runner who has begun to tire in a race. Their conduct had caused others to weaken as well. They were also to *"make straight paths for"* their *"feet"* (v.13). All runners realize that *"straight paths"* are the fastest and least tiring. A straight path also allows a follower to track with greater ease. If these Hebrew Christians would but fix their *"eyes on Jesus"* (v.2), they, along with those following in their footsteps, would have strengthened *"hands,"* stable *"knees,"* and a path both *"straight"* and sure (vv.12-13). The weaker brother or sister who was *"lame"* (v.13)—who was considering dropping out of the race due to disappointment in a fellow believer—would also *"be healed"* (v.13). Note: Believers who drop out of the race do not lose their salvation. They do, however, receive fewer rewards at *"the judgment seat of Christ"* (2Corinthians 5:10) due to a compromised lifestyle.

Verse 14 must be handled with care:

> *Pursue peace with all men, and the sanctification without which no one will see the Lord.*
> (Hebrews 12:14)

On the surface, this passage seems to teach that salvation is based on works. Yet, the writer is communicating that as believers *"pursue peace"* with fellow believers—and as their behavior grows in *"sanctification"*—onlookers will *"see the Lord"* in their lives. Thus, *"sanctification"* in this case relates to behavior—not person. (As we learned in Hebrews 10:10, our "person" was completely *"sanctified"* at the point of justification, never to be improved upon). Paul addressed the sanctification associated with our behavior while writing to the church at Galatia:

> *My children, with whom I am again in labor until Christ is formed in you*— (Galatians 4:19)

Paul desired that the Galatians live (behave) in such a way that Christ's life inside them (Galatians 2:20) might manifest itself to others.

Without doubt, the moment the depraved repent of sin and accept Christ as Savior, they are made into the most *"sanctified"* beings imaginable (read Hebrews 10:10, realizing that the word *"sanctified"* is in the perfect tense, pointing to past action, completed action, with a resulting state of being). Hebrews 12:14, however, is not dealing with the believer's person, but with his/her behavior. We must remain alert, therefore, when studying passages that address the term "sanctification." To confuse the sanctification associated with our person with the sanctification associated with our behavior brings nothing but confusion and despair. In fact, it places us under a performance based acceptance with God—a legalistic arrangement that can never produce peace.

As was confirmed earlier in our study, grace can be defined as "the power to do God's will." If we are wise, we will take advantage of the grace that God supplies. When grace is accepted, we walk in victory, regardless of the circumstance (tie this in with Hebrews 4:16). When grace is rejected, defeat is certain. No wonder the writer declares:

> *See to it that no one comes short of the grace of God; that no root of bitterness springing up*
> *causes trouble, and by it many be defiled;* (Hebrews 12:15)

The readers are not being exhorted to perform righteous deeds for the purpose of retaining their salvation. Such an idea is found nowhere in the Scriptures. Rather, they are not to come *"short of"* accepting God's *"grace"* for the trials experienced as a believer. Consequently, when we reject God's grace we come *"short of the grace of God"* (v.15). Actually, when grace is rejected over an extended period of time, we begin to blame God (or someone else) for the consequences generated by our unwise choices. This situation occasionally produces *"bitterness"* (v.15), which negatively impacts not only our own lives, but the lives of fellow saints. In other words, we cause *"many"* to *"be defiled"* (v.15)—cause some who may be observing our lives to grow bitter in the process.

Esau is a prime example of an individual who rejected God's grace while facing difficult circumstances. What was the root cause of his improper behavior? He was more concerned with instant gratification and pleasure than with obeying God. His sin resulted in a loss of both spiritual and physical blessings, for he *"sold his own birthright for a single meal"* (v.16). Whether Esau was or was not a believer is not the issue here, for the writer is basically communicating that Esau's sin caused him to circumvent God's blessings and walk in bitterness. (For more on the subject, read Genesis 25:19-34 and 27:1-41.) Esau made an irreversible decision. The Hebrew Christians addressed here were on the verge of doing the same. If they returned to Judaism, they would subject themselves to the judgment of A.D. 70. They would also receive fewer rewards at *"the judgment seat of Christ"* (2Corinthians 5:10)—where all church saints will be rewarded for deeds done in faith (1Corinthians 3:10-15).

The life of faith yields both physical and spiritual blessings, but the desire for the spiritual must supersede the desire for the physical for true material blessings to come our way (Matthew 6:33). Esau was concerned with the physical aspects of his birthright alone, for he sold it thinking he could somehow gain it back. His preoccupation with the temporal, therefore, resulted in a loss of spiritual sensitivity. Thus, when he lost the birthright, *"he sought for it with tears"* (v.17). No doubt, a huge gulf exists between being saddened over our losses and repenting of the sin which brought them about. For this reason, Esau *"found no place for repentance"* (v.17).

Clearly, verses 16 and 17 are <u>not</u> teaching that Esau was saved and, through disobedience, lost his salvation. The writer is simply saying: "If you Hebrew Christians return to Judaism, you will, as did Esau, miss out on physical and spiritual blessings alike. In the realm of the physical, you will subject yourselves to the judgment of A.D. 70. In the realm of the spiritual, you will receive fewer rewards at the judgment seat of Christ."

In verses 18-24 the writer again contrasts the physical with the spiritual. He compares Mount Sinai, the physical mountain which represents the Law, with *"Mount Zion,"* or *"heavenly Jerusalem,"* New Jerusalem, the spiritual city which represents grace. (New Jerusalem is also alluded to in passages such as Galatians 4:26, Hebrews 11:10, 11:16, 13:14, Revelation 3:12, and 21:1-22:5.)

The writer wants his readers to know that if they return to the Law, terror and fear awaits them. They will also abandon a lifestyle of blessing and reward—but not their salvation. The loss of their salvation is addressed nowhere in the book of Hebrews, for their high priest, Jesus Christ, saves *"forever"* (Hebrews 7:25).

> *T*he loss of salvation is addressed nowhere in the book of Hebrews, for Jesus Christ saves forever.

The recipients of this epistle had *"not come to a mountain that may be touched"* (Hebrews 12:18). *"Heavenly Jerusalem,"* or *"Mount Zion,"* since it is in heaven (v.22), cannot *"be touched."* Mount Sinai, on the other hand, can *"be touched."* It is a physical *"mountain"*—even though the Jews were prohibited from touching it in the one instance of Exodus 19:12, a topic also addressed in Hebrews 12:20. These Hebrew Christians were to seek *"Mount Zion"* (New Jerusalem) and walk by grace. They were to abandon Mount Sinai and the accompanying bondage associated with the Law.

When God descended upon Mount Sinai, *"blazing fire"* enveloped the mountain (Hebrews 12:18; Exodus 19:18). *"Darkness and gloom and whirlwind, and...the blast of a trumpet"* also accompanied this amazing manifestation of God's presence (Hebrews 12:18-19; Exodus 19:16-19; 20:18; Deuteronomy 4:11). The people were so frightened by the overwhelming nature of the moment that they *"begged that no further word should be spoken to them"* (Hebrews 12:19; Exodus 20:18-19). Even Moses was gripped with *"fear and trembling"* (Hebrews 12:21). But *"Mount Zion...the heavenly Jerusalem"* (v.22), the city of grace, is just the opposite. It is *"the city of the living God"* (v.22), which is also inhabited by *"myriads of angels"* (v.22), *"the church"* (v.23), *"the spirits of righteous men made perfect"* (the Old Testament believers—v.23), *"Jesus"* (v.24), and *"the sprinkled blood, which speaks better than the blood of Abel"* (v.24). It is a city that provides peace, joy, and rest for all its inhabitants. Thus, the life of grace (under the *"new covenant"*—v.24) offers blessings that the old covenant of Law simply cannot provide. How could these believers even think of returning to Judaism and the accompanying legalism?

The last phrase of verse 23 is one of the most compelling statements in this entire epistle:

> *to the general assembly and church of the first-born who are enrolled in heaven, and to God, the Judge of all, <u>and to the spirits of righteous men made perfect</u>,* (Hebrews 12:23—emphasis added)

Who are the individuals described as, *"the spirits of righteous men made perfect"*? Apparently, they are the Old Testament believers, believers (including John the Baptist) who died before Jesus' crucifixion. If you have taken the *Romans 1-8* course (distributed by this ministry), you know that our *"old self"* (Adamic nature) was eradicated the moment we (while depraved) chose to repent and believe (Romans 6:6). This same truth applies to all church saints—to all believers who live between Acts 2 and the Rapture of the church. Scripture seems to indicate, however, that the old self (Adamic nature) in an Old Testament believer was not eradicated until the cross (Hebrews 10:10; 11:40; 12:23). Unquestionably, Old Testament believers were not perfected (in their person) until A.D 30. They were declared righteous (perfect) when they, while depraved, believed God's promises and exercises faith in the *"seed"* of Genesis 3:15. They were not made righteous (perfect), on the other hand, until Jesus died. Neither were their sins forgiven until A.D. 30 (Hebrews 9:15; Romans 3:25), for Jesus died for all of mankind's sin *"for all time"* (Hebrews 9:26; Hebrews 10:12; John 3:16; 1John 2:2; etc.). Remember, Old Testament believers' sins were only covered through the Old Testament sacrifices, not removed—Hebrews 10:4, 11. Only the blood of Jesus could accomplish complete forgiveness—the removal of sin.

Also notice what is stated in verse 24:

> *and to Jesus, the mediator of a new covenant, and to the sprinkled blood, which speaks better than the blood of Abel.* (Hebrews 12:24)

In Hebrews 11:4 we learned that Abel's sacrifice for sin was not only accepted by God, but *"still speaks"* today. It has communicated for centuries that blood is the means through which God deals with sin. What did the blood of Abel's offering do for his sin? It only covered sin until Jesus could die on the cross (Hebrews 10:4; 10:26). Thus, Abel's sacrifice only atoned for (covered) sin which Jesus later removed. No wonder the blood of Jesus *"speaks better than the blood of Abel"* (Hebrews 12:24)! Also, Jesus' blood, having been offered in the *"tabernacle"* in heaven (Hebrews 9:11-12, 23-26), speaks from heaven to earth. The *"blood"* of Abel's sacrifice, offered on the earth, speaks on the earth alone.

Jesus' *"blood"* is now speaking (Hebrews 12:24). Therefore, these Hebrew Christians were not to *"refuse"* His message (v.25) since He *"warns from heaven"* (v.25). Moses *"warned"* Israel from *"earth"* (v.25; Exodus 20:22) after the nation requested that he speak with them rather than God (Exodus 20:18-19). Those who heard Moses *"did not escape when they refused him who warned them on earth"* (Hebrews 12:25), for their disobedience begat physical death in the wilderness. Because Jesus' blood ushered in a better covenant, and because He *"warns from heaven"* (v.25), believers who disobey under the new covenant cannot expect to escape God's chastening—chastening which He applies with a tear in His eye rather than a scowl on His face. No doubt, should the readers return to Judaism, they would experience physical death in the destruction of A.D. 70—a consequence that would break God's heart. They would not, however, lose their salvation.

As God's *"voice shook the earth"* when He descended upon Mount Sinai (Hebrews 12:26; Exodus 19:18), His *"voice"* will once again *"shake not only the earth, but also the heaven"* (Hebrews 12:26). Because the phrase, *"Yet once more I will shake not only the earth, but also the heaven,"* is a quote from Haggai 2:6, we can determine when this shaking will occur simply by studying Haggai 2:1-9. It will take place in conjunction with the Tribulation and Second Coming of Christ in preparation for the Millennium. The purpose of this shaking is to remove everything *"which can be shaken,"* so only that *"which cannot be shaken may remain"* (Hebrews 12:27). The fact that Mount Sinai was shaken (Exodus 19:18) shows that the old covenant, the covenant that existed during the dispensation of Law, was temporary. The Law, however, being part of the Word of God, *"abides forever"* (1Peter 1:23-25). No wonder Paul teaches that *"through faith...we establish the Law"* (Romans 3:31) yet live *"under grace"* (Romans 6:14)—for the Law was used of God to show us our need for a Savior. Thus, the Law continues to do its work and do it well, bringing conviction to the lost (Galatians 3:24; 1Timothy 1:8-11).

Because we *"receive a kingdom which cannot be shaken,"* believers everywhere should *"show gratitude...to God"* (Hebrews 12:28). We can do so through *"acceptable service"* performed in an attitude of *"reverence and awe"* (v.28). Considering all that the writer has communicated regarding the cross and the new covenant, why would any believer refuse to serve God in an attitude of devotion, worship, and praise? After all, *"faith"* works most effectively *"through love"* (Galatians 5:6).

*A*ll believers *"receive a kingdom which cannot be shaken."*

Knowing that *"God is a consuming fire"* (Hebrews 12:29) should have also encouraged these Hebrew Christians to forsake Judaism. If they refused to do so, they would die physically when Jerusalem was destroyed by *"fire"* in 70 A.D.

One more week and we will have finished this masterpiece of truth. Aren't you pleased with your growth?

Hebrews 13 Questions

First Day

1. Read Hebrews 13. How does verse 1 confirm that these believers had previously loved *"the brethren"*? How does Hebrews 6:10 verify the same? What does Hebrews 10:25 communicate regarding their present concern for fellow believers?

2. What do 1John 4:11, John 15:17, John 13:34-35, 1John 3:14, and Psalm 133:1 state regarding *"love"*? What do you find most difficult about loving God's people? Are you continuing to love *"the brethren"*?

3. What were these believers *"not"* to *"neglect"* (v.2)? How does this relate to Galatians 6:10? Are you hospitable? If so, how has God blessed your obedience?

4. *"Some"* of these believers, through showing *"hospitality to strangers,"* had *"entertained angels without knowing it"* (v.2)? List at least one instance in Scripture where an angel appeared in the form of a man. Have you *"entertained"* an angel lately? If so, when?

5. With what two classes of people were these readers to identify themselves (v.3)? According to the last phrase of verse 3, why were they to do so? What do the following passages communicate concerning the body of Christ: Romans 12:4-5; 1Corinthians 12:12, 20, 27. Why should we, as did Paul, learn to welcome pain (2Corinthians 12:9-10; 2Corinthians 1:3-7)? Can we conclude from Hebrews 10:32-34 that these believers had suffered sufficiently to identify with those mentioned in Hebrews 13:3?

Second Day

1. Read Hebrews 13. Don't forget to pray. In your own words, what is stated about the marriage relationship in verse 4? Why is the sanctity of marriage so important to the Creator? Marriage is a picture of what?

2. Does the phrase, *"for fornicators and adulterers God will judge"* (v.4), teach that a believer who commits sexual sin loses his/her salvation? If not, what is it communicating? How does 1John 3:9 tie in here? What famous Old Testament king, who had a heart for God, committed adultery and murder? Did his sin cause him to lose his salvation (use Scripture to confirm your answer)? Remember, if one loses his/her salvation, it can never be regained (Hebrews 6:6).

3. Our *"character"* should *"be free from the love of money"* (v.5). Why so? How do 1Timothy 3:3 and 1Timothy 6:10 relate to this subject matter? With what were these believers to be *"content"* (v.5)? In my opinion, the definition of true wealth is found in Philippians 4:11-12. Why would I draw such a conclusion? What is stated in Hebrews 13:5-6 that confirms God's commitment to caring for His people?

4. Who were these readers to *"remember"* (v.7)? What were they to consider while remembering these individuals (v.7)? What were they to *"imitate"* (v.7)? Do you live in such a way that someone might desire to imitate your faith? If not, how can this become a reality?

5. How is Jesus described in verse 8? Has He always been God-man (Philippians 2:7-8)? Has He always been a *"high priest"* (Hebrews 2:17)? What then is verse 8 communicating?

Third Day

1.   Read Hebrews 13. According to verse 9, what were the readers to guard against? How were they *"to be strengthened"* (v.9)? What would fail to strengthen them (v.9; Colossians 2:20-23)? Why would the writer make such statements?

2.   To understand verses 10-12, we must review what we studied earlier in Hebrews 9 regarding the Day of Atonement —which is addressed more specifically in Leviticus 16. What type of animal was sacrificed for the high priest's personal sin? Where was its blood sprinkled? Two goats were brought to the high priest. What determined which goat would die? What occurred with the blood of the sacrificed goat, and whose sin did it cover? What was done with the goat that remained alive?

3.   The Levitical priests were allowed to partake of certain offerings (Leviticus 10:14; Numbers 18:11). Were they permitted to eat the carcasses of the animals *"burned outside the camp"* on the Day of Atonement (Hebrews 13:11)? What privilege did these readers possess, as priests (1Peter 2:9), that was unavailable to the priests who served under the Levitical priesthood (v.10)? Where was Jesus offered (Hebrews 13:12; John 19:17)? What did His blood provide (Hebrews 13:12)?

4.   How does Hebrews 13:13 relate to the historical backdrop of this epistle? What city should these believers have been *"seeking"* (v.14)? Why would the writer desire that they cease seeking earthly Jerusalem?

5.   What were these believers to *"continually offer up...to God"* (v.15)? What does the phrase, *"sacrifice of praise to God"* (v.15), communicate to you? Must we always feel like praising God to praise Him? When was the last time you praised God when you felt like doing just the opposite? What effect did it have on your day?

Fourth Day

1. Read Hebrews 13. What types of *"sacrifices"* were the readers to offer (v.16)? How are their *"leaders"* described in verse 17? How does this relate to James 3:1? If you are a leader in the body of Christ, what does Hebrews 13:17 communicate regarding the importance of your position? Considering the historical background of this epistle, what would occur if the readers disregarded the instruction of their teachers?

2. What does the writer request of his readers in verse 18? We who live on The Hill are humbled by the extent of your support in this area. Of what was the writer *"sure"* (v.18)? Note Paul's words regarding this topic in Acts 23:1, Acts 24:16, 1Timothy 1:5, 1Timothy 1:19 and 2Timothy 1:3? What occurs when your conscience is violated?

3. What did the writer believe their prayers would accomplish (v.19)? What hinders you from possessing this type of confidence in intercessory prayer?

4. In a sense, verses 20-21 serve as a benediction. How is *"God"* described in verse 20? How is Jesus described in verse 20? What type of *"covenant"* is in effect during the church age (v.20)? Does this mean that the New Testament believer is secure in Christ?

Fifth Day

1. Read Hebrews 13. Who equips us for service (vv.20-21)? Through what avenue does *"the God of peace"* do His work *"in"* and *"through"* us (v.21; Galatians 2:20; Colossians 1:27)? How does Philippians 2:13 relate to this subject matter? Who, then, receives the glory from the work done *"in"* and *"through"* our lives?

2.   How does the writer describe this epistle (v. 22)? Why would he classify it as "brief" (v.22)?

3.   Who would possibly accompany the writer in his return visit (v.23)? How does verse 24 confirm that a plurality of leadership existed in this local body of believers? Why would the writer refer to believers as *"saints"* (v.24)? Can we conclude, therefore, that the New Testament believer is a saint who sometimes sins rather than a sinner saved by grace? What does the last phrase of verse 24 communicate to you?

4.   Why would the writer close this epistle with these words: *"Grace be with you all"*? Where would the readers find such *"grace"*? Where will we find ample *"grace"* to finish the race?

Sixth Day

1.   Read Hebrews 13. Read all of this week's lesson and record any new insights. You have done well in finishing the course. God is pleased and will reward your diligence. Keep in touch, and let us know if we can assist you in any way. We would love to hear from you.

Hebrews 13 Lesson

Hebrews 13 should be extremely useful, for it describes specific, practical behavior that can bring glory to Christ. Now that the readers had been reminded of the supremacy of Christ, and the surpassing value of the new covenant, they were to live out this teaching through the power of the Holy Spirit.

These Hebrew Christians were to *"Let love of the brethren continue"* (v.1). The writer's use of the word *"continue"* confirms that they had loved *"the brethren"* previously (Hebrews 6:10). *"Some"* of them, however, had temporarily separated themselves from other believers (Hebrews 10:25). They are encouraged to change their ways (Hebrews 12:1). Since *"God...loved us,"* we should *"love one another"* (1John 4:11). Even Jesus said, *"This I command you, that you love one another"* (John 15:17).

We are to *"love...the brethren"* (Hebrews 13:1) for several reasons. First, it is *"good and...pleasant"*—not only to those who choose to love, but also to God (Psalm 133:1). Second, it confirms to the world that we are Jesus' *"disciples"* (John 13:34-35). Third, it reminds us, and thus adds assurance, that we are God's children (1John 3:14).

Do you find yourself loving *"the brethren"* these days, or are you withdrawing from fellowship due to a less than pleasant experience with God's people? Have you somehow become discouraged and given up on establishing meaningful relationships with fellow believers? If so, God says, *"Let love of the brethren continue"* (v.1). Make a choice and choose to love. You won't be sorry, for God will honor your commitment and bless you abundantly.

Realizing that many Christians had lost their homes, the writer pens the following:

> *Do not neglect to show hospitality to strangers, for by this some have entertained angels without knowing it.* (Hebrews 13:2)

When given opportunity, those who possessed houses were to share them with those in need. This exhortation lines up perfectly with Paul's words to the church at Galatia:

> *So then, while we have opportunity, let us do good to all men, and especially to those who are of the household of the faith.* (Galatians 6:10)

I know in our own situation, some of our greatest blessings (and fondest memories) have come through sharing our living quarters with the homeless. And yes, possibly we have *"entertained angels without knowing it"* (Hebrews 13:2). The Greek word for *"angels"* actually means *"messengers,"* but it is indisputable that God can use literal angels to communicate messages to man. The account of the *"three men"* appearing to Abraham (Genesis 18:1-2) confirms that angels can appear as human beings. One of the men was *"the Lord"* (Genesis 18:1), while the other two were *"angels"* (Genesis 19:1). So yes, we can very well entertain *"angels without knowing it"* (Hebrews 13:2). Be sure to remain alert! One may cross your path this very day!

These readers were to identify themselves with two classes of people (Hebrews 13:3): (1) Those *"in prison"* (2) Those being *"ill-treated."* Why? They were members of the same *"body"* (v.3; Romans 12:4-5; 1Corinthians 12:12, 20, 27). This passage illustrates that when one member hurts the whole *"body"* should hurt. One of the greatest needs in the church today is for believers to relate to the pain of fellow believers. We, obviously, have little ability to minister in areas we have not yet suffered (2Corinthians 1:3-6). Realizing this should allow us to welcome pain, as did Paul (2Corinthians 4:17-18; 12:9-10). Yes, God uses adversity to teach us to identify with those in need—deepening our message and widening His sphere of ministry in and through us each step of the way. These Hebrew Christians had been persecuted for their faith (Hebrews 10:32-34), so they were well equipped to encourage the imprisoned and mistreated.

What a bold statement the writer records in verse 4:

> *Let marriage be held in honor among all, and let the marriage bed be undefiled; for fornicators and adulterers God will judge.* (Hebrews 13:4)

"Marriage" is honorable because it is a picture of our relationship with Jesus. We are now *"betrothed"* to the Son and will one day marry Him (2Corinthians 11:2; Revelation 19:7). In fact, the excellence of the church's relationship with Christ will, at some point in the future, serve to encourage the nation of Israel to repent and return to the Father (Romans 11:11; Hosea 5:15). Therefore, the marriage union is much more than *"two"* becoming *"one"* (Ephesians 5:31). It mirrors God's relationship with His people. Thus, it is to be honored.

These believers were not only to hold *"marriage...in honor,"* but make certain that *"the marriage bed be undefiled"* (Hebrews 13:4). Under the Law, if a *"man"* committed *"adultery with another man's wife,"* both *"the adulterer and the adulteress"* were to *"be put to death"* (Leviticus 20:10). Why does God so detest adultery? Marriage is a picture of the Father's relationship with the Jewish people (and as was stated earlier, Christ's relationship with the church). God married the nation of Israel at Mount Sinai (Exodus 24:1-8; Deuteronomy 5:2-3; Jeremiah 31:32). As a result, when she (Israel) offered sacrifices to other gods, she committed *"adultery"* (Hosea 4:12-13; Ezekiel 16:30-34). Adultery essentially says, "God alone is not enough." Homosexuality is even worse, for it proclaims: "No need exists for God at all." Undeniably, marriage is the union of a man and a woman—never a coming together of two people of the same sex.

We must be certain to interpret the last phrase of Hebrews 13:4—*"for fornicators and adulterers God will judge"*—in its proper context. God's Word teaches that individuals who walk in blatant sin (and have no desire to repent) are lost. In fact, 1John 3:9 states:

> *No one who is born of God practices sin, because His seed abides in him; and he cannot sin, because he is born of God.* (1John 3:9)

Certainly, *"No"* man who knows Jesus *"practices sin"*—that is, lives a lifestyle of habitual, continual sin, enjoying every second of the experience. He can't do so due to being a *"new"* creation (2Corinthians 5:17), a *"new"* creation who hates sin. He will, nevertheless, occasionally sin—but his sin he will no longer enjoy. The phrase, *"and he cannot sin"* (1John 3:9), also verifies that a believer *"cannot"* live in habitual disobedience—the word *"sin"* is in the present tense, pointing to a lifestyle of *"sin."* This phrase, therefore, can be viewed as communicating: "and he cannot live a lifestyle of habitual sin."

If a man continually walks in sin, and senses no need to repent, he cannot be a believer.

If a man continually walks in sexual sin, or any sin for that matter, and senses no need to repent, he cannot be a believer. He will face God's judgment, the *"great white throne"* judgment of Revelation 20:11-15, the judgment directed toward unbelievers. Believers will not face such judgment for *"no condemnation"* awaits them (Romans 8:1). Consequently, the phrase, *"for fornicators and adulterers God will judge"* (Hebrews 13:4), refers to the lost, those who lead a lifestyle of habitual adultery or fornication. The phrase is not addressing believers who might commit such sin during a moment of weakness. King David, who was guilty of adultery and murder, is living proof. The fact that his sin broke his heart (read Psalm 51) confirms that he was a believer. He will not face God's judgment of Revelation 20:11-15. In fact, he will rule as *"prince"* during the Millennium (Ezekiel 34:24; 37:25). God truly is gracious!

All of us can relate to Hebrews 13:5:

Let your character be free from the love of money, being content with what you have; for He
Himself has said, "I WILL NEVER DESERT YOU, NOR WILL I EVER FORSAKE YOU,"
(Hebrews 13:5)

Although every believer's *"character"* should *"be free from the love of money,"* many saints fail to live there. Paul realized the value of this truth as well, for he informed Timothy that church leadership should be *"free from the love of money"* (1Timothy 3:3). He also taught:

For the love of money is a root of all sorts of evil, and some by longing for it have wandered
away from the faith, and pierced themselves with many a pang. (1Timothy 6:10)

Note that *"the love of money"* is the culprit, not money itself. Paul could speak with authority here. He had learned the secret of living in contentment—regardless of the condition of his bank account (Philippians 4:11-12). As a result, he was a wealthy man, since true wealth is *"being content with what you have"* (Hebrews 13:5).

Only through making God the Source of our trust can we be freed *"from the love of money"* (vv.5-6). When we realize that He will *"never desert"* or *"forsake"* us (v.5; Deuteronomy 31:6, 8; Joshua 1:5) and is our *"helper"* (v.6; Psalm 118:6), we are liberated from fearing what *"man"* can *"do to"* us (Hebrews 13:6). The writer urges these Hebrew Christians to stop worrying about the future. Regardless of how much persecution came their way, God would somehow provide. Since He used *"the ravens"* to feed Elijah (1Kings 17:4-6), He could do the same for them—and the same for us today. We could write a book on all the different ways God has provided for this ministry. Yes, the life of faith, though challenging at times, is the most exciting thing going!

The readers are next challenged to:

Remember those who led you, who spoke the word of God to you, and considering the result of
their conduct, imitate their faith. (Hebrews 13:7)

This passage confirms that the elders of their local church, who had taught them *"the word of God,"* had died. Because the elders had finished their course, these readers were to consider *"the result of their conduct"* and *"imitate their faith."* We must, therefore, ask ourselves, "Do I live in such a way that someone might desire to imitate my faith?" If *"faith"* is enhanced through basking in *"the word of Christ"* (Romans 10:17), where should we be investing much of our time?

Even though the recipients of this epistle had been taught sound doctrine (Hebrews 13:7), they needed to be reminded that the Savior, with Whom the doctrine is associated, is unchanging. After all, an inconsistent Jesus would generate an inconsistent doctrine—and an unstable set of beliefs would naturally follow. However:

Jesus Christ is the same yesterday and today, yes and forever. (Hebrews 13:8)

In His divine nature, Jesus is from eternity past through eternity future *"the same."* He has always been *"God"* and will always be *"God"* (Hebrews 1:8). But consider the following. Before He came to earth (at His First Coming) He had not yet taken on humanity. Thus, at His First Coming, He became the one and only God-man (Philippians 2:7-8). In Hebrews 2:17 we also learned:

...He had to be made like His brethren in all things, that He <u>might become</u> a merciful and
faithful high priest in things pertaining to God, to make propitiation for the sins of the people.
(Hebrews 2:17—emphasis added)

This verse in no way contradicts Hebrews 13:8, for becoming a high priest had no effect on

Jesus' nature. How so? His nature remained the same even while inhabiting a physical body. He took on humanity, yet remained God.

The writer next records:

> *Do not be carried away by varied and strange teachings; for it is good for the heart to be strengthened by grace, not by foods, through which those who were thus occupied were not benefited.* (Hebrews 13:9)

Having been properly taught, the readers were not to *"be carried away by varied and strange teachings"* (Hebrews 13:9). Even Paul, in his epistle to the Galatians, encouraged the Galatians to turn away from Law and remain true to *"the gospel of Christ"* (Galatians 1:6-9; 3:1-2, 24). Paul also wrote to the church at Corinth:

> *But food will not commend us to God; we are neither the worse if we do not eat, nor the better if we do eat.* (1Corinthians 8:8)

If the Law cannot save (Romans 3:20), if rules and regulations cannot impart life (Colossians 2:20-23), those addressed in the book of Hebrews were to make a tough choice. They were to abandon Law, as well as *"varied and strange teachings"* (Hebrews 13:9), and walk empowered by God's grace. This instruction was difficult due to having observed Jewish regulations relating to certain *"foods"* (Hebrews 13:9) from childhood. However, because of the unchanging nature of their Savior (Hebrews 13:8), He could be trusted to sustain them even through circumstances resulting from their abandoning Judaism and the Law.

Note how previous lessons bring Hebrews 13:10-12 alive:

> *We have an altar, from which those who serve the tabernacle have no right to eat. For the bodies of those animals whose blood is brought into the holy place by the high priest as an offering for sin, are burned outside the camp. Therefore Jesus also, that He might sanctify the people through His own blood, suffered outside the gate.* (Hebrews 13:10-12)

To comprehend these passages, it is essential that we review the activities associated with the Day of Atonement (Leviticus 16)—addressed earlier in Hebrews 9. The high priest first sacrificed a *"bull"* for his own sins (Leviticus 16:6, 11) and sprinkled a portion of its blood *"on"* and *"in front of the mercy seat"* in the Holy of Holies (v.14). He would then *"cast lots"* for *"two male goats"* taken from the people (vv.5, 7-8). *"The goat on which the lot...fell"* was offered as a *"sin offering...for the people,"* and its *"blood"* was sprinkled in the same manner as that of *"the bull"* (vv.9, 15). The priest would also take *"blood"* from both *"the bull"* and *"the goat"* and *"make atonement for"* the brazen *"altar"* (vv.18-19). Finally, he would *"lay both of his hands on the head of the live goat,"* *"the scapegoat,"* and *"confess all the iniquities of the sons of Israel"* (vv.10, 20-22). The *"goat"* was then sent *"into the wilderness"* (vv.20-22).

The readers needed to realize that they had *"an altar, from which those who serve the tabernacle have no right to eat"* (Hebrews 13:10). From the phrase, *"those who serve the tabernacle,"* we can know that the sacrificial system was functioning at this time (notice the present tense *"serve"*). However, these Hebrew Christians possessed an advantage over the priests who served in Jerusalem. They had *"an altar"* from which *"those"* priests had *"no right to eat"* (v.10). Why? The *"bodies of"* the *"animals"* offered for sin on the Day of Atonement were *"burned outside the camp"* (Hebrews 13:11). Even though the priests were allowed to partake of other types of offerings (Leviticus 10:14; Numbers 18:11), they had no right to eat any of the carcasses of the animals offered on the Day of Atonement. Jesus, therefore, *"that He might sanctify the people through His own blood, suffered outside the gate"* (Hebrews 13:12). No doubt, Jesus died *"that He might sanctify"* those who accept Him as Savior (refer to the lesson associated with Hebrews 10:10 and Hebrews 10:14 for additional input). Hence, it is not surprising that Jesus died *"outside the gate"* (Hebrews 13:12), *"outside"* Jerusalem, confirming that Law must be abandoned to partake of Christ.

Jesus was taken outside the city of Jerusalem and crucified (John 19:17) due to having been rejected by the very people who should have received Him as Messiah. These Hebrew Christians were to *"go out to Him outside the camp, bearing His reproach"* (v.13). In other words, they were to leave Jerusalem and accept the *"reproach"* of the unbelieving Jews. By heeding the instruction of this epistle, along with Christ's words of Luke 21:20-24, not one Jewish believer died in the destruction of A.D. 70. They saw Jerusalem for what it was—a city which would soon be burned (Hebrews 13:14)—and fled. They also sought the Jerusalem *"which is to come,"* New Jerusalem (v.14). We should do the same, joyfully accepting all persecution as part of God's perfect will for our lives (Luke 6:26; 2Timothy 3:12).

The writer makes an astounding statement in Hebrews 13:15, especially considering the circumstances that surrounded his readers. The recipients of this epistle were suffering greatly at the hands of the unbelieving Jews, yet he encourages them to *"praise"* the Lord in the midst of their trials:

> *Through Him then, let us continually offer up a sacrifice of praise to God, that is, the fruit of lips that give thanks to His name.* (Hebrews 13:15)

Basically the writer is saying, "Being of Jewish descent, I realize that you are accustomed to offering animal sacrifices. But now that you are believers in the Messiah, and priests (1Peter 2:9), your sacrifice is to be praise." Ever tried to *"praise"* God when things are extremely hard? It truly is a *"sacrifice."* But *"praise,"* being the fuel for faith, allows us to view our circumstances from God's perspective—as that which is *"good"* (Psalm 119:71) and to His *"glory"* (John 11:4)—and trust Him to see us through.

God is also *"pleased"* with *"sacrifices"* such as *"good"* deeds and *"sharing"* of material resources (Hebrews 13:16). These deeds must be done in Christ's strength, however, trusting His indwelling presence to accomplish the work (Philippians 4:13). They must never be achieved through the power of our flesh.

To walk as God desired, these believers were to *"submit"* to the authority of their *"leaders"* (Hebrews 13:17):

> *Obey your leaders, and submit to them; for they keep watch over your souls, as those who will give an account. Let them do this with joy and not with grief, for this would be unprofitable for you.* (Hebrews 13:17)

In 1Thessalonians 5:12 we find a similar statement:

> *But we request of you, brethren, that you appreciate those who diligently labor among you, and have charge over you in the Lord and give you instruction.* (1Thessalonians 5:12— emphasis added)

Submitting to God-ordained *"authority"* (Romans 13:1) is sometimes challenging, especially when its counsel differs with our desires. In the case of these readers, it was either *"obey"* their godly (and wise) *"leaders"* or die in the destruction of A.D. 70.

All *"leaders"* within the body of Christ must realize that *"they keep watch over"* men's *"souls"* (Hebrews 13:17). What an awesome responsibility! Not only this, but they are to lead *"as those who will give an account"* (v.17). Even James 3:1 states:

> *Let not many of you become teachers, my brethren, knowing that as such we shall incur a stricter judgment.* (James 3:1)

Leaders, be they administrators, pastors, teachers—whatever—will give an account to those whom they instruct. Consequently, if called to lead, we should make certain that what we do and say are according to the full counsel of God's Word. If not, we will rightly incur the *"judgment"* and condemnation of those who have sat under our instruction (James 3:1).

The readers are next encouraged to allow their *"leaders"* to serve *"with joy"* (Hebrews 13:17). They were to do so by going on to spiritual maturity. *"Grief"* many times rests upon *"leaders"* who train disinterested students (v.17). Jeremiah, the weeping prophet, validates this fact in Jeremiah 9:1-3. No doubt, apathy toward God's instruction is extremely *"unprofitable"* (Hebrews 13:17), for His chastening rests upon those who walk in disobedience (Hebrews 12:5-13).

Paul describes the proper student/teacher relationship in 1Thessalonians 5:12 (referenced earlier). May we remember this passage as we interact with those whom God has ordained to mentor His people.

Leaders need the prayers of the saints, for God honors prayer in amazing fashion. It is for this reason that the writer states, *"Pray for us"*:

> *Pray for us, for we are sure that we have a good conscience, desiring to conduct ourselves*
> *honorably in all things.* (Hebrews 13:18)

I would venture to say that nothing gets done outside the realm of prayer's influence. Here at The Hill we have witnessed time and time again the positive impact of the prayers of God's people. Paul reveals his perspective of the subject in passages such as Ephesians 6:18-19, 1Thessalonians 5:25, and 2Thessalonians 3:1. The statement that should boggle our minds, however, is 1Thessalonians 5:17:

> *Pray without ceasing,* (1Thessalonians 5:17)

These three remarkable words were written by a man (Paul) who also stated:

> *for we do not know how to pray as we should* (Romans 8:26)

What passion! What humility! Yes, God transforms the character of those who prayerfully seek His heart.

The writer next confirms that a *"good conscience"* allows the believer to respond *"honorably in all things"* (Hebrews 13:18). Paul has much to say about the subject in Acts 23:1, Acts 24:16, 1Timothy 1:5, 1Timothy 1:19 and 2Timothy 1:3. Note Acts 24:16:

> *I also do my best to maintain always a blameless conscience both before God and before men.*
> (Acts 24:16)

We would do well to implement this mindset, for believers who possess a *"good conscience"* (Hebrews 13:18) are filled to overflowing with God's authority and power. The reverse is true as well, for compromise and deceit continuously lead to ineffective living. Why so? Sin blocks communication between God and His people. The pursuit of an uncompromised conscience, therefore, is non-negotiable! Anything that prevents us from possessing *"a blameless conscience...before God and...men"* (Acts 24:16) must be dealt with, not tomorrow or next week, but now.

The writer sought the prayers of his readers, not due to perceiving himself superior, but that he might *"be restored to"* them *"the sooner"* (v.19). Like Paul (Romans 15:30-31), he believed in the power of corporate prayer.

Verses 20-21, in a sense, serve as a benediction:

Now the God of peace, who brought up from the dead the great Shepherd of the sheep through the blood of the eternal covenant, even Jesus our Lord, equip you in every good thing to do His will, working in us that which is pleasing in His sight, through Jesus Christ, to whom be the glory forever and ever. Amen. (Hebrews 13:20-21)

Note that God is described as *"the God of peace"* (v.20). Why so? He grants *"peace,"* *"the fruit of the Spirit"* (Galatians 5:22), to all who choose to obey.

God also *"brought up from the dead the great Shepherd of the sheep"* (Hebrews 13:20), verifying His limitless omnipotence (power). Because Jesus is *"the great Shepherd of the sheep,"* He never fails to abundantly provide for His flock (read Psalm 23).

Note as well that the *"covenant"* instituted through Christ is *"eternal"* (Hebrews 13:20), confirming our security within God's family. We need not worry about God casting us aside, for we are eternally His and *"heirs"* of all He possesses (Romans 8:17).

Verse 21 validates that God equips (or prepares) us *"to do His will."* The writer is not teaching that God forces His will upon believers, but rather that He equips them *"to do His will"* as they choose to obey. Therefore, if we walk in His will, or decide to reject it, it will be our will, not His, that has determined the response. As a new believer, however, and totally inexperienced in the ways of God, I set out to equip (prepare) myself through Bible study, prayer, and various spiritual disciplines. I view the subject much differently today. Only God, *"working in us what is pleasing in His sight"* (v.21), can *"equip"* us (through granting wisdom, insight, etc.) to choose the excellent over the evil of our day. He equips us (on an ongoing basis) *"through Jesus Christ"* (v.21), Who not only lives in us (Galatians 2:20; Colossians 1:27), but is *"our life"* (Colossians 3:4). What an awesome truth! In fact, this

As a new believer, I set out to equip myself. I view the subject much differently today.

was a revelation of such magnitude that it changed everything about my Christian experience. Thus, when God desires to use me, He not only equips (prepares) me through the truth I have studied in His Word, but performs the task through me as I yield (by means of my own will) to His Son's indwelling presence. (Passages such as Joshua 24:15 and Luke 7:30 verify that man, most definitely, possesses the freedom of choice.)

No wonder Paul wrote:

Not that we are adequate in ourselves to consider anything as coming from ourselves, but our adequacy is from God. (2Corinthians 3:5)

Don't misunderstand. We need the spiritual disciplines of Bible study, prayer, etc. to possess ample knowledge of God and His ways (Psalm 103:7). But He must work through us (once we submit to His will) if anything of eternal significance is to be accomplished. Therefore, our choosing to live by His life allows Him to receive, not some, but all *"the glory"* from the magnificent results— *"to whom be the glory forever and ever. Amen"* (Hebrews 13:21).

Indeed, the book of Hebrews is a *"word of exhortation"* (v.22):

But I urge you, brethren, bear with this word of exhortation, for I have written to you briefly. (Hebrews 13:22)

Hebrews was written to encourage the reader to exchange spiritual apathy for a passionate pursuit of God's best. The writer, therefore, exhorts his readers to *"bear with"* (*"to listen to"*) his words (v.22). I almost chuckle when I observe the last phrase of this passage: *"for I have written to you briefly"* (v.22). My first reading of this epistle caused me to ask, "How could such a lengthy letter be classified as brief?" As I matured, however, I began to understand the author's meaning. The epistle, though containing thousands of words, is short considering the wealth of truth that could have been recorded. I can certainly identify with his struggle, for in writing this course much that could have easily been included was omitted.

"Timothy" had *"been released"* (v.23), evidently from prison, even though the historical details of his imprisonment are unavailable. Timothy, along with the man used of God to record this epistle, would visit these readers should *"Timothy"* come *"soon"* (v.23).

The writer encourages these believers to *"Greet all of your leaders and all the saints"* (v.24). Because this work was written to Hebrew Christians who were considering returning to the sacrificial system in Jerusalem, verse 24 confirms that not everyone in that local assembly had bought in to the idea. Also, the word *"leaders"* allows us know that a plurality of elders existed in this local body—as was the case at Ephesus as well (Acts 20:17). Don't overlook that the writer uses the word *"saints"* (v.24). Without a doubt, a New Testament believer is a saint who sometimes sins and not a lowly sinner saved by grace. Thank you, Jesus!

A New Testament believer is a saint who sometimes sins and not a lowly sinner saved by grace.

The statement, *"Those from Italy greet you"* (v.24), must mean one of two things: (1) The author was in Italy at the time of the writing of this epistle (2) Those helping him in the work were *"from Italy."*

I greatly appreciate how the writer closes this letter. He says, *"Grace be with you all"* (v.25). Once these believers chose to discard Judaism, God's grace empowered them to carry out their decision. In fact, not a single Hebrew Christian died in the A.D. 70 destruction of the temple and city. For more input, review the sections of the **Introduction** titled "Date" and "Historical Background."

As was verified earlier on, *"grace"* (v.25) can be defined as "the power to do God's will." No doubt, sufficient grace was made available to these readers as God had previously vowed (Hebrews 4:16).

By now we should comprehend the importance of pursuing spiritual maturity, for mediocrity never (under any circumstance) yields abundant living. Yes, we are *"forgiven"* for our misdeeds (Ephesians 4:32; Colossians 2:13; 1John 2:12). Neither will we face God's *"condemnation"* (Romans 8:1). Yet, we reap horrific consequence in this life for sins committed as believers (Colossians 3:25).

We must allow nothing, absolutely nothing, to prevent us from approving *"the things that are excellent"* (Philippians 1:10). Life is too short to flounder in the "good." Therefore, may we accept God's *"grace"* for the variables of life, walk in the resulting wisdom, and never look back!

"Grace be with you all" (Hebrews 13:25).

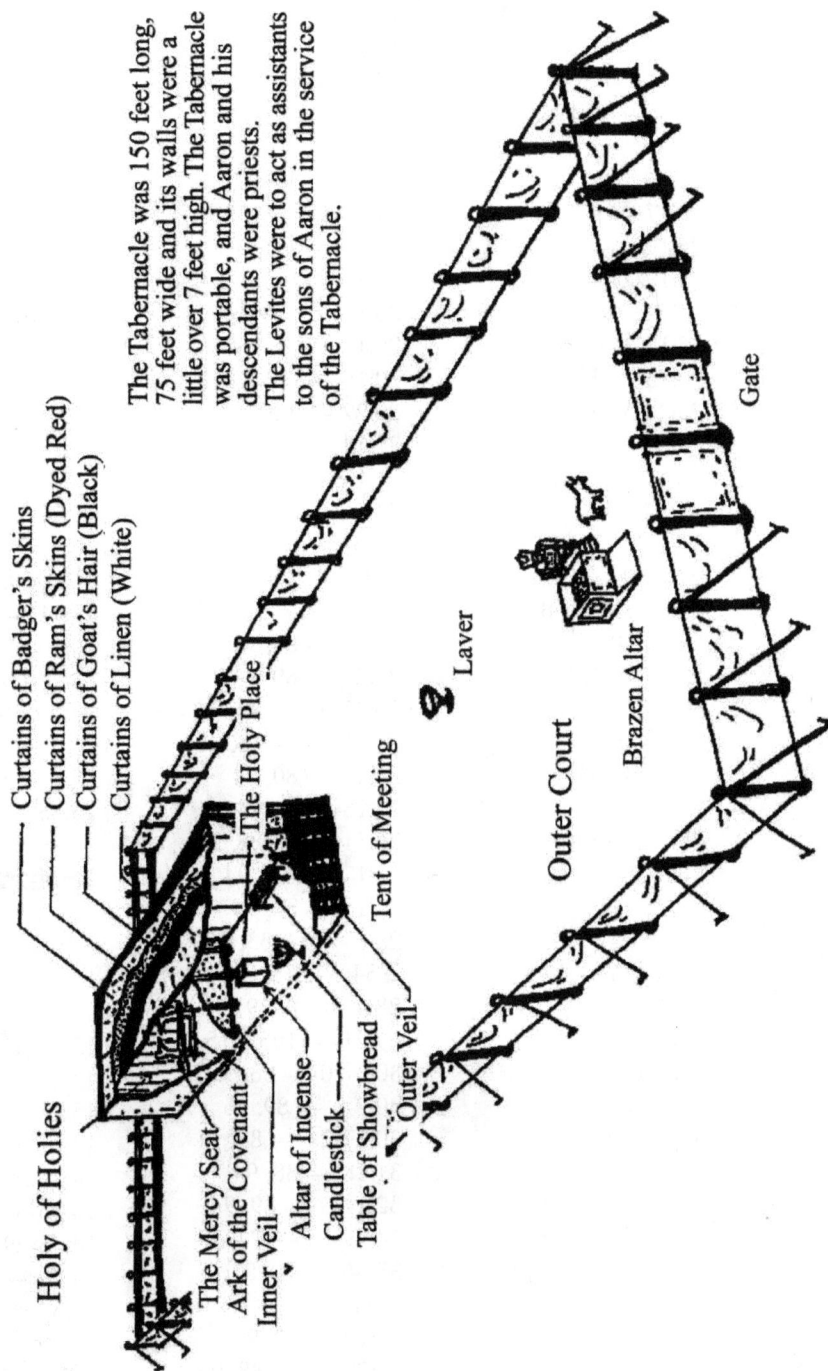

The Tabernacle was 150 feet long, 75 feet wide and its walls were a little over 7 feet high. The Tabernacle was portable, and Aaron and his descendants were priests.
The Levites were to act as assistants to the sons of Aaron in the service of the Tabernacle.

Curtains of Badger's Skins
Curtains of Ram's Skins (Dyed Red)
Curtains of Goat's Hair (Black)
Curtains of Linen (White)

The Holy Place

Holy of Holies

The Mercy Seat
Ark of the Covenant
Inner Veil
Altar of Incense
Candlestick
Table of Showbread
Outer Veil

Tent of Meeting

Laver

Outer Court

Brazen Altar

Gate

The Earthly Tabernacle

18:21 — 71
18:26 — 71
19 — 97, 110
20:1-12 — 29
20:2-13 — 28, 36
20:8 — 36
20:8-12 — 27
20:10 — 36
20:11 — 36
20:11-12 — 24, 33
20:12 — 36, 37
20:13 — 26
20:22-28 — 77
20:24 — 37
20:28-29 — 37
27:23 — 63

Deuteronomy
4:11 — 149
5:2-3 — 158
9:9 — 89, 94
17:2-6 — 107, 118
18:15 — 2, 6
18:18 — 25, 34
27-28 — 80, 84
28:1 — 26, 27
28:7 — 26, 27
31:6 — 159
31:8 — 159
32:35-36 — 107, 119
34:4-5 — 29, 37

Joshua
1:5 — 159
2:1-21 — 136
2:9-10 — 136
2:11 — 136
6:1-27 — 136
6:21-25 — 126, 136
7:24-26 — 11, 16
21:43 — 133
21:44 — 26, 27, 29, 42, 47
22:4 — 26, 27, 29, 42, 47
23:1 — 26, 27, 29
23:1-13 — 42, 47, 133
24:15 — 163
24:33 — 77

Judges
4 — 136
6-7 — 136
11 — 136
13-16 — 136
20:28 — 77

1Samuel
1:1-25:1 — 136
10:1 — 136
16:13 — 136
17:11 — 46
17:26 — 46

2Samuel
5:1-25 — 136
8:1-18 — 136

1Kings
17:4-6 — 159
17:17-23 — 137

2Kings
4:18-37 — 137

1Chronicles
17:11-12 — 70, 74
17:11-14 — 9

Ezra
2:61-63 — 71, 75

Psalms
2:6-8 — 70, 74
8:4-6 — 12, 18
9:10 — 131
14:2 — 131
20:6 — 79, 83
23 — 163
27:8 — 46, 131
37:4 — 123
40:6-8 — 111
44:3 — 79, 83
51 — 158
60:5 — 79, 83
63:8 — 79, 83
72:8 — 74
76:2 — 70, 74
95:7 — 26, 46
95:7-8 — 39

95:7-11 — 27, 35, 36, 46
95:8 — 28, 31, 36
102:25-27 — 5, 10
103:7 — 163
105:4 — 131
110:1 — 113
110:4 — 2, 6, 60, 68, 73, 76
118:6 — 159
118:16 — 79, 83
119:71 — 20, 161
133:1 — 152
138:7 — 79, 83

Proverbs
3:21 — 144
4:21 — 144

Ecclesiastes
4:9-12 — i

Isaiah
1-66 — 6
1:11-15 — 102, 110
30:23-26 — 12, 18
35:1-2 — 12, 18
55:12-13 — 12, 18
65:17-25 — 12, 18

Jeremiah
1-55 — 6
6:20 — 102, 110
7:22-23 — 102, 110
9:1-3 — 162
31:31-33 — 116
31:31-34 — 81, 85, 86, 91, 97, 137
31:32 — 158
31:33 — 86, 97, 114
31:33-34 — 104, 110, 113
31:34 — 97, 114

Ezekiel
1:1 — 6
2:1 — 12, 18

11:17-20 — 86
11:19-20 — 81, 86, 91, 98, 114
16:30-34 — 158
18:4 — 99
20:41-42 — 133
28:14 — 10
28:17-18 — 99
28:18 — 99
28:25-26 — 133
34:24 — 158
36:24-27 — 86
36:26-27 — 81, 86, 91, 98, 114
36:26-28 — 133
37:25 — 158

Daniel
7:1 — 6

Hosea
4:12-13 — 158
5:15 — 86, 158

Joel
2:21-27 — 12, 18
3:18 — 12, 18

Amos
5:22-24 — 102, 110

Obadiah
1 — 6

Micah
6:6-8 — 102, 110

Habakkuk
2:3-4 — 108, 120

Haggai
2:1-9 — 150
2:6 — 150

Zechariah
6:12-13 — 70, 74
12:10 — 86
14:4-11 — 12, 18
14:9 — 74

5:10 — 59, 65, 93,
101, 107, 120,
144, 148, 149
5:17 — 32, 58, 65,
79, 83, 90, 96,
97, 110, 112,
114, 116, 158
5:21 — 20, 51, 55,
147
7:9 — 145
7:9-10 — 116
10:3-5 — 27
11:2 — 158
12:9 — 108, 120
12:9-10 — 152,
157

Galatians
1:6-9 — 160
2:20 — 20, 26, 46,
64, 81, 86, 109,
112, 148, 155,
163
2:21 — 72, 75
3:1-2 — 160
3:7 — 67
3:11 — 72, 75
3:16 — 67, 98,
110, 130
3:19 — 4, 8
3:21 — 72, 75
3:24 — 16, 22, 73,
76, 77, 85, 150,
160
3:29 — 22, 67
4:19 — 148
4:26 — 124, 132,
149
5:1 — 102, 111
5:6 — 131, 151
5:22 — 5, 10, 163
5:22-23 — 18
6:10 — 25, 34,
152, 157
11:16 — 124, 132
12:22-24 — 124,
132
13:14 — 124, 132

Ephesians
1:4 — 23, 32,
112, 116, 138,

147
1:10 — 2, 7, 13, 20
1:13 — 34, 58, 65
2:3 — 115
2:6 — 23, 32, 61,
68, 90, 96, 109,
115
2:8-9 — 52, 55,
62, 77, 118, 120,
123, 130
2:19 — 25, 34
3:5-10 — 9
3:10 — 9
4:22 — 97
4:32 — 27, 109,
164
5:18 — 5, 10
5:20 — 84
5:22-33 — 34
5:27 — 23, 32, 147
5:31 — 158
6:12 — 21
6:17 — 53, 56
6:18-19 — 162

Philippians
1:6 — 34, 104,
113, 144
1:9-10 — 53, 56
1:10 — 164
2:7-8 — 153, 159
2:10-11 — 104,
113
2:13 — 26, 47, 155
3:9 — 72, 75
3:10 — 23, 26, 33,
46, 55
3:14 — 144
3:20 — 23, 32, 124
4:11-12 — 153
4:13 — 161

Colossians
1:13 — 27
1:16 — 2, 7, 9, 13,
20, 24, 25, 33,
46
1:22 — 23, 32, 147
1:23 — 68
1:27 — 13, 20, 64,
81, 86, 155, 163
2:13 — 109, 164

2:14-15 — 104,
113
2:16-17 — 102,
109
2:18 — 8
2:20-23 — 154,
160
3:2 — 23, 32, 119,
124
3:4 — 21, 163
3:9 — 97
3:17 — 84
3:25 — 65, 85,
144, 164

1Thessalonians
4:14-17 — 13, 20
5:12 — 161, 162
5:16 — 26
5:16-18 — 42, 47
5:17 — 162
5:18 — 26
5:23 — 13
5:25 — 162

2Thessalonians
1:3 — 121
2:8-10 — 12
2:8-12 — 18
3:1 — 162

1Timothy
1:1 — 68, 77
1:5 — 155, 162
1:8-11 — 150
1:9-10 — 77, 85
1:11 — 96
1:17 — 70, 74
1:19 — 155, 162
2:4 — 145
2:5 — 85
3:3 — 153, 159
4:14 — 11, 17
6:10 — 153, 159

2Timothy
1:3 — 155, 162
3:12 — 161
3:16 — 42, 46
4:7-8 — 107, 120

Titus
1:2 — 67
3:5 — 52, 55, 58,
62, 65, 77, 123,
130

Hebrews
1 — 1-10
1:1 — 74
1:1-10:25 — 117
1:3 — 20, 24, 33,
43, 48, 103, 112
1:4 — 85
1:8 — 25, 34, 75,
128, 144, 159
2 — 11-22
2:1 — 53, 56, 107,
119, 144
2:3 — ii
2:6 — 46
2:9 — 58, 64, 129
2:14 — 58, 64,
104, 113
2:17 — 77, 78,
100, 153, 159
2:18 — 34, 100
3 — 23-40, 41
3:1 — ii, 27, 66
3:1-6 — 85
3:7 — 42, 46
3:9 — ii
3:17 — ii
3:18-19 — 27
3:19 — 36
4 — 26, 35, 41-49
4:4 — 18, 35
4:7 — 35
4:7-9 — 35
4:8 — 27
4:8-9 — 29
4:9 — 26
4:9-10 — 26, 27
4:9-11 — 27, 111
4:14-15 — 61, 68
4:14-16 — 22, 50,
54, 73, 77
4:15 — 8
4:16 — 68, 90, 96,
105, 108, 115,
148, 164
5 — 50-56
5-10 — ii